Mariners, Marriages and Mansions:
The Bayley Family of Hobart

First published in 2025 by Navarine Publishing
GPO Box 2178, Hobart, Tasmania 7001
www.navarine.net

Copyright © Nicole Mays
Typesetting by Nicole Mays

Printed in Australia by IngramSpark

All rights reserved. No part of this publication may be produced, stored in a retrieval system or transmitted in any form by any means without the prior permission of the copyright owner.

Enquiries should be made to nicmays@gmail.com

ISBN: 9781763725959

A catalogue record for this book is available from the National Library of Australia

Disclaimer
Please note that while the author has intended to provide a definitive and accurate history and profile of Charles, James and Harriet Bayley (previously Bull) and their respective families, some events, names, dates and locations may have been unintentionally and/or incorrectly stated or omitted. Additionally, the author has made inferences as to apparent gaps in their history. Please also note that place names have been used as they were in the times of the Bayley siblings, particularly Van Diemen's Land which was in use up to 1855, and Hobart Town which was in use up to 1880. Further, though correct at the time of publication, some website addresses may have become outdated. The author apologises for any errors or omissions. Steps have also been taken to contact copyright owners of images used in this book. Please email nicmays@gmail.com with any questions.

Aboriginal and Torres Strait Islander people are advised that this book includes images and names of people who have died. The book also contains historical documents, records, newspaper citations, and other publications that may include offensive and derogatory terms which are unacceptable today.

Cover Images
Charles Bayley. Tasmanian Archives (NS1013/1/849).
James Bayley. Tasmanian Archives (NS1013/1/844).
Harriet McGregor (nee Bayley). Tasmanian Archives (PH30/1/7561).
View of 'Lenna'. Tasmanian Archives (NS1013/1/366).

View of 'Runnymede'.
Tasmanian Archives (NS3195/2/1231).
Charles Bayley.
Tasmanian Archives (NS1013/1/849).
James Bayley.
Tasmanian Archives (NS1013/1/844).
Harriet McGregor (nee Bayley).
Tasmanian Archives (PH30/1/7561).

View of 'Lenna'.
Tasmanian Archives (NS1013/1/366).

Contents

Introduction	1
The Whaler of Hobart Town	3
Foundations & Family	19
Arrivals & Departures	27
Births, Deaths & Marriages	37
Shipowners & Shipbuilders	47
Travel & Tasmania	61
Passengers & Properties	71
Whale Oil & Waves	83
Discretion & Deaths	95
Legacies & 'Lenna'	107
Rifts & Romance	123
The Last Surviving Sibling	137
Women's Rights & Generational Patrimony	155
Bayley Family Tree	174
Appendix 1 - The Bayleys of Surrey, Suffolk & Essex	177
Appendix 2 - The Bulls of Burnham-on-Crouch	195
Appendix 3 - Royal Navy Vessels built by Jabez Bayley	204
Appendix 4 - Whaling Voyages of Charles and James Bayley out of Hobart Town	205
Index	207

View of the Port of Hobart from 'Lenna'.
Tasmanian Archives (NS1013/1/340).

Introduction

Over a 10-year period three siblings arrived in Van Diemen's Land (now Tasmania) from England: Charles, Bayley and Harriet Bull. Camouflaging their humble roots they quickly adopted the surname of Bayley, their mother's maiden name and one associated with several prominent shipbuilders from coastal Suffolk and Essex where they had been born and raised. The first to arrive was Charles Bayley (1813-1875) who began work as a mariner in his teens. In 1839, at the age of 26, he was appointed captain of the whaling barque *Wallaby* operating out of the Port of Hobart Town. Charles then spent the next 23 years involved in this industry, helming the vessels *Wallaby, Fortitude* and *Runnymede,* and in the process becoming one of Hobart Town's more wealthy whalers and shipowners. This prosperity transferred to his younger brother Bayley Bull (1823-1894) who arrived in Hobart Town from London in August 1843 as a seaman on board the convict ship *Cressy*. Capitalising on his older brother's resources and reputation, and assuming the name of James Bayley, he also became heavily involved in the whaling industry and maritime trade, countering their inherent risks and dangers to further the family's success.

In 1846 James Bayley returned to London and together with his youngest sister Harriet Bull (1828-1878) arrived back in Hobart Town in January 1847 per the barque *Pacific*. While James resumed his role in the whaling industry, operating as second mate, chief mate and then captain of several vessels, Harriet quickly married Scottish-born shipwright Alexander McGregor who went on to become one of Van Diemen's Lands' respectable and industrious shipbuilders, within a few decades becoming the largest and wealthiest shipowner and merchant in the colony.

Combined, Charles, James and Harriet Bayley (and her husband Alexander McGregor) were tenacious, persevering and calculated risk-takers, building ship and land-based business empires they would never have dreamed possible; Hobart Town at the time offering the opportunity for the foursome to rise well above their rank and succeed in pathways unavailable to them in Great Britain. Despite this affluence they remained unassuming, sagacious and charitable in their approaches to life; enduring the loss of spouses, children and one another; taking on various causes and volunteer opportunities; and helping advance their communities. Their only extravagance appears to have been their penchant to travel back to England and their homes; 'Lenna' at Battery Point and 'Runnymede' at New Town, both stately mansions still in existence.

From the banks of the River Crouch at Burham-on-Crouch to commanding views of the River Derwent from their impressive residences, this is the story of Charles, James and Harriet Bayley: their upbringing, their careers, their spouses and families, their personal losses and grievances, their homes, their good deeds, and their scandals. It is also the story of their legacies and the patrimony that allowed their widows, children and grandchildren to lead privileged yet benevolent lives, championing political, military, social, health and recreational causes and events throughout the greater Hobart area and well beyond, including women's rights and education.

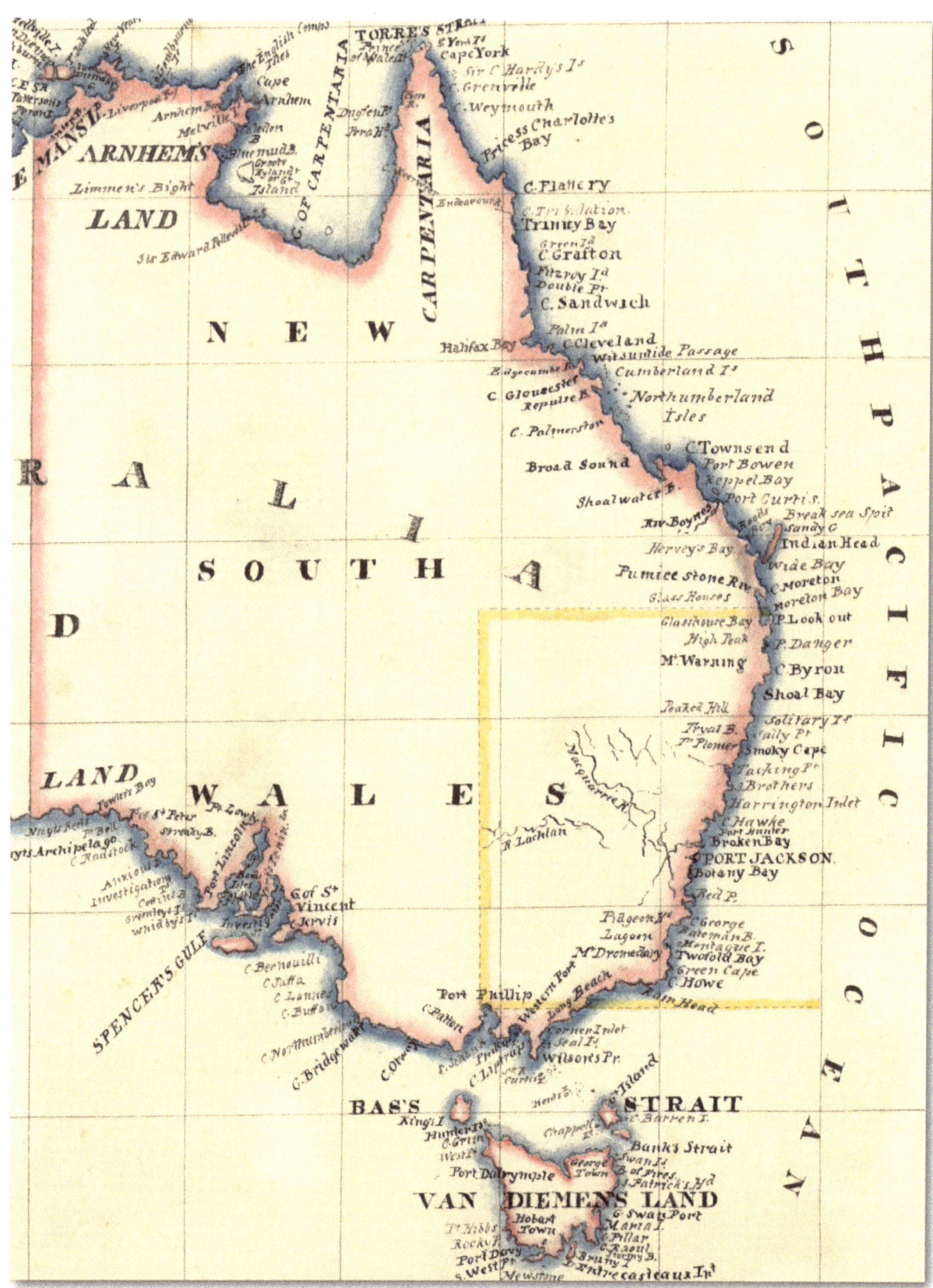

Partial map of Australia, including Van Diemen's Land (c1840).
National Library of Australia (http://nla.gov.au/nla.obj-2044227598).

The Whaler of Hobart Town

The barque *Wallaby* sailed into Hobart Town, Van Diemen's Land, on 19 August 1839 after a four-month voyage. During this period its crew had collected 175 tuns of whale oil and an unknown amount of bone; one tun being the equivalent of eight barrels of oil and a liquid measurement of approximately 951 litres.[1] Sadly the body of its captain, Henry Wishart, was also on board, preserved within a cask of spirits. Following his dramatic death off the coast of Victoria, the *Wallaby*'s chief mate, 26-year-old Charles Bayley, had taken over command of the vessel and immediately set sail for Hobart Town. Charles had previously been known as Charles Bayley Bull, though the reason for him assuming his mother's maiden name remains somewhat of a mystery.

The *Colonial Times* of 20 August 1839 relayed news of the tragedy. 'The whaling ship *Wallaby*, belonging to this port and commanded by Captain Henry Wishart, arrived yesterday from Sealer's Cove, Wilson's Promontory, having fished within a few tons of a full cargo, towards which Mr. Wishart contributed nearly half by killing eleven whales — but with the melancholy intelligence of her Captain being on board a corpse! The particulars of this lamentable event have been related to us by Mr. Bailey [sic], the chief officer, and are nearly as follows: On the 7th inst., a whale was observed at a short distance from the ship: Captain Wishart, giving orders to get the vessel ready to return to Hobart Town, took his boat and crew and followed the whale. He speedily came up and made fast to her when, after dragging the boat for about fifteen minutes, she suddenly stopped and before the boat's way could be checked, it was alongside the fish which by a sudden plunge upset the boat and cast all hands into the sea. Two of the men could not swim: one sank instantly without an effort; the other, Capt. Wishart, observed to be struggling and swimming towards an oar, brought it to the poor fellow, and supporting him thereon conveyed him to the boat. Captain W. then procured a line, the end of which he placed in the hands of the sailor, and by this kind and careful precaution, the man was saved! Captain W., who was an excellent swimmer now made for the land and soon overtook the other three men, who were also good swimmers, but melancholy to relate, when about fifty yards from the shore our poor friend cried out that he was 'gone' — prayed earnestly for Mercy and for Grace — and almost instantly disappeared! The boats, as soon after as possible, put off and the body was found near the spot where he sank, at about a depth of 14 feet. The Chief Officer, who has sailed with Captain Wishart for many years, placed his body in a tight-made case filled with spirits and delivered him yesterday to his mourning relatives, who have the melancholy pleasure of being able to give him [a] Christian burial in consecrated ground with the additional pleasing reflection that besides being universally respected, his last act in life was one of extraordinary fortitude and Christian benevolence.'

---
[1] *Colonial Times*, 9 April, 20 August 1839.

The article continued, '*His body has been submitted to medical inspection and it has been discovered to have two wounds made by a shark, one about the middle of the right thigh and the other rather above the calf of the left leg, which had evidently been inflected during life, and which he, no doubt, received while making for land and which occasioned his death*'.[1] Another newspaper article, with specific reference to Charles Bayley, reported that '*the Chief Mate, (who regarded his Commander as a brother)*' was the one to ensure a '*diligent search*' was made for the captain's body such that it could be '*conveyed to town … to his distressed and mourning relatives.*'[2]

Whaling was a dangerous means of employment at the best of times, let alone bleeding to death by way of a shark bite. As stated in the *Colonial Times* article, Charles Bayley had sailed with Henry Wishart for several years and obviously regarded him very highly. However, since the 284-ton barque *Wallaby* had only been launched in mid-1838, built on speculation by convicts at the Port Arthur Penal Settlement, they had clearly first crossed paths on board another vessel.[3] Originally named *Fanny*, the *Wallaby* had been purchased by George Watson, an enterprising shipowner and merchant of Hobart Town, at a government auction in October 1838 for the sum of £3,500.[4] Intended for the intercolonial trade in which it was initially placed, the *Wallaby*'s maiden voyage was to Port Phillip Bay via George Town in December 1838, with Captain H. B. Hurburgh at the helm, carrying a cargo of sundries and one passenger.[5] Two months later, while docked in Melbourne, it was taken over by Captain Wishart, returning to Hobart Town where the *Wallaby* was loaded with 1,000 sheep for Port Phillip Bay.[6]

Previously, from mid-1836, Henry Wishart had been at the helm of the 246-ton intercolonial trading barque *Lady of the Lake,* primarily carrying whale oil and bone to Hobart Town from a shore-based whaling station at Twofold Bay on the New South Wales south coast.[7] Subsequently fitted out for deep-sea whaling, on 15 April 1838 the vessel had left Hobart Town for the south seas in search of the lucrative species; whale oil then being an extremely valuable commodity with various uses including as fuel for lamps and candles and as a lubricant for machinery.[8] It was also highly sought after for soap making and textile production. It is assumed that Charles Bayley was employed on board the *Lady of the Lake* at this time, though no records have yet been found confirming this premise. It is additionally very likely that Charles Bayley had been working out of the Port of Hobart Town for several years and had also visited it multiple times during the mid-1820s as a teenager. Though information is rather sparse, he was near certainly the seaman of the same name that first arrived in Van Diemen's Land on board the ship *Lang* on 17 December 1825.[9] This particular trading vessel then sailed to Sydney a few weeks later, returning to Hobart Town in April 1826 before making its way back to London.[10]

Charles Bayley appears to have returned to Australian waters sometime in the early-to-mid 1830s in the role of mate. The hierarchy of merchant mariner ranks during this period, i.e., ordinary seaman to able seaman to third mate to second mate followed by chief mate (or officer) and finally captain, is indicative of the general progression and promotion of competent, skilled

---

[1] *Colonial Times*, 20 August 1839.
[2] *The Tasmanian*, 23 August 1839.
[3] *Colonial Times*, 31 July 1838.
[4] *Colonial Times*, 7 August, 9, 16 October 1838; *The Tasmanian*, 17 August 1838.
[5] *The True Colonist Van Diemen's Land Political Despatch, and Agricultural and Commercial …* , 7 December 1838.
[6] *The Hobart Town Courier*, 23 February 1839.
[7] *The Hobart Town Courier*, 5 August 1836; *Launceston Advertiser*, 2 November 1837; *The Tasmanian*, 10 November 1837.
[8] *The Hobart Town Courier*, 27 April 1838.
[9] *The Hobart Town Gazette*, 24 December 1825.
[10] Tasmanian Archives (CSO63/1/1 p190, CSO63/1/1 p209).

By the Ship Lang 357 Ton
Mr. ? Bennu Master & John Lusk Com[mander]
bound for London

Robert Lusk	Commander
Bu[?] Donaldson	1st Mate
Geo. Chapman	2 do
John Buckworth	Surgeon
Thomas Miller	Boatswain
Charles Bent	Carpenter
? Fitz	Cook
Geo. Estell	Steward
J. McHurin	Seaman
? Panton	do
Thos. Bowles	do
? Sadler	do
? Ward	do
? Quinn	do
John Johnson	do
Joseph Lawrence	do
David Cockburn	Cooper
Charles Purry	Steward's Mate
William Wiggins	Seaman
Hugh McMillan	do

Partial manifest of the ship Lang from Hobart Town to London, April 1826.
Tasmanian Archives (CSO63/1/1 p209).

and experienced men during the 1830s and for many decades beyond. Combined with mishaps, accidents and medical emergencies at sea, there were also impromptu opportunities for promotion.

With regards to the movements of the *Wallaby* in particular, in March 1839, following several stints between Hobart Town and Victoria, it was fitted out for a whaling voyage.[1] With Captain Wishart now firmly at the helm and Charles Bayley serving as chief mate, the barque sailed out of Hobart Town for the whale fishery on 6 April 1839.[2] It initially travelled to Portland Bay off the Victorian coast where on 30 May the *Wallaby* was noted to have 65 tuns of oil on board.[3] The vessel and its crew then continued their productive voyage off the southern coast of mainland Australia without mishap until that fateful day on 7 August when Henry Wishart and another crew member lost their lives following the overturning of their whaleboat.[4]

With the *Wallaby*'s arrival back in Hobart Town on 19 August 1839, the funeral for Captain Wishart took place two days later, attended by 150 mourners, indicative of his respect and standing within the Hobart Town community.[5] The late captain's vessel and most of his crew then discharged their cargo, took on stores and readied for another voyage. With Charles Bayley appointed captain, on 4 September the *Wallaby* sailed out of the River Derwent.[6]

After a nearly eight-week stint at sea, hunting for black whales in the sheltered coastal waters off the southern end of Van Diemen's Land, the *Wallaby* returned to Hobart Town on 28 October with another cargo of oil and bone.[7] Though shorter in duration and thereby less lucrative, it was the first of many experiences Charles Bayley would have at the helm of a commercial whaling vessel and the first time he personally realised the monetary incentive that could be gained from obtaining and securing this risky though prized cargo. As captain, his pay was decidedly more than that of a chief mate, and the highest amongst the complement of crew. Uniquely, it was a share of the profits as opposed to a conventional salary and thereby paid out upon the vessel's return to its home port and the discharge of its cargo. While the largest share of the net profit, referred to as a 'lay', went to the shipowner and agent, in the realm of 70 per cent combined, as captain Charles Bayley would have received around eight per cent from the spoils.[8] In contrast, the pay structure would have generally resulted in the chief mate receiving five per cent, all the way down the ranks to the ordinary seaman who received 0.5 per cent. An inexperienced crewman, called a green hand or a cabin boy, would expect to receive a 0.4 per cent share of the profits.[9] Employment contracts called 'articles' were signed in the days prior to the start of a particular voyage, with seamen often receiving an advance on their pay (with interest factored in) which was then deducted from their lay at the completion of the voyage. Also deducted from their final pay were items purchased from the ship's store during the voyage, including clothing, boots, soap and medicine; generally supplied at higher than market prices.

Life on board a commercial whaler was not surprisingly without personal and financial risk. The work was gruelling and isolating and the weather conditions often extreme. There was also the inherent danger involved in procuring whales and bringing them on board, as well as the monotony of work on board the ship. Supplies and provisions often ran low or were completely

---

[1] *Colonial Times*, 12 March 1839.
[2] *Colonial Times*, 9 April 1839.
[3] *The Tasmanian*, 14 June 1839.
[4] *The Cornwall Chronicle*, 6 July 1839; *Colonial Times*, 20 August 1839.
[5] *The Tasmanian*, 23 August 1839.
[6] *The Hobart Town Courier*, 6 September 1839.
[7] *Colonial Times*, 29 October 1839.
[8] E. Hohman (1926). *Wages, Risk, and Profits in the Whaling Industry*.
[9] E. Hohman (1926). *Wages, Risk, and Profits in the Whaling Industry*.

depleted such that by the end of a voyage rations were meagre. Enduring freezing temperatures, winds and storms were symbolic of the job, as was ill-treatment and bullying amongst crew and between ranks, let alone sickness sweeping through crew members living and working in such small and confined spaces. Ships were heavily reliant on its captain to not only oversee the voyage but also manage personnel issues and maintain a good and productive working environment. It was a job not for the faint hearted and often lower-ranking crew members deserted ship, willing to forgo their share of the lay for the sanctity and safety of land. All told, the risks were immense: from accidental and incidental threats to personal health and safety and equipment, to vessel strandings and wrecks, to market fluctuations and the possibility of the voyage resulting in a net loss due to low prices for whale oil and bone following the ship's return to port after many months away. A respected and fair captain was just one facet of a successful voyage.

Most whaling vessels operating out of the Port of Hobart Town in the 1830s and 1840s were around 200 to 300 tons in size, had between 15 to 35 crew members on board and were outfitted with a number of whaleboats, generally about 25 to 33 feet in length.[10] Manned by a crew comprising a steerer and four men at the oars, multiple whaleboats were often deployed upon the sighting of a whale with many hours (sometimes days) then spent chasing the prey. The method of assault was by harpoon attached to a long line, intended to pierce the whale's blubber. Once the harpoon had been lodged into the animal, a menacing, desperate and time consuming ordeal then took place with the boat's crew following the whale and continuing to harass it over many miles in an attempt to get close enough to plunge lances into the whale's vital organs, until death occurred by exhaustion, shock and drowning. The carcass, weighing from five to 50 tons, was then towed alongside until it could be hauled on board the awaiting ship where a tryworks had been erected on deck by those crew members that remained on board. The animal was next systematically cut into strips with long lengths of the blubber pieces boiled in the trypots to render down the oil. Once cooled, the oil was transferred to barrels of 40 gallons and stored on board in the holds. Meanwhile, the whale bone was extracted, boiled, cooled and placed into casks and also stored on board. It was an intricate and physical process that would take days to complete, leaving the ship's crew exhausted, particularly if another whale had been procured during the interim.

Sperm whales were considered the most sought after species in Australian waters at the time, yielding an average of nine tuns of oil per animal, while southern right or black whales were smaller and thus not as profitable, though still procured in high numbers.[11] Given large pods of whales were present off the coast of Van Diemen's Land in the early decades of colonisation, bay whaling associated with shore-based whaling stations had been established several decades prior, and many foreign vessels had used Hobart Town as a refitting and supply base. However, deep-sea whaling vessels operating out of the Port of Hobart Town under the ownership of enterprising and speculative locals had only commenced in earnest in the 1830s. It was thus considered an emerging industry when Charles Bayley became involved.

The price per tun of whale oil and ton of bone was calculated from the market value at the time the cargo was discharged from the vessel, regardless of whether the shipowner retained it for future sale. As stated, the calculation of each crew member's lay in the days immediately following a vessel's return to port was a complicated process, with deductions for advances and items procured on board taken into account, as well as small monetary incentives paid to those

---

[10] H. O'May (1978). *Wooden Hookers of Hobart Town and Whalers out of Van Diemen's Land*.
[11] H. O'May (1978). *Wooden Hookers of Hobart Town and Whalers out of Van Diemen's Land*.

Harpooning a Sperm Whale. Oil painting by Andrew T Fleury (1933).
Maritime Museum of Tasmania (P_1983-005).

crew members who sighted a whale or went over and beyond their scope of work to fasten a whale or aid another crew member. In November 1838 *The Hobart Town Courier* quoted the price of whale bone at £100 per ton, with oil from sperm whales generating £75 per tun, while oil from black whales was priced much lower at £18 per tun.[1] A year later, market prices had risen by an average of £5 to £10 per ton/tun across the three commodities. Whale bone was in high demand at the time, especially in Britain, sought for its use in corsets and other undergarments, including hooped skirts and collars, as well as for more practical applications such as utensil and brush handles, sieves and nets, and components of machinery and tools.

With particular regards to the *Wallaby*'s first complete voyage with Charles Bayley as captain, the vessel returned to Hobart Town in late October 1839. Unfortunately the quantity of whale oil and bone stored on board is not known.[2] However, if we assume a conservative estimate of 50 tuns of sperm oil then a 'back of the envelope' calculation would reveal a potential share in the voyage for Charles of around £300, an increase of just over £100 compared to what he would have received as the vessel's chief mate.[3] Significantly, this amount was equivalent to the annual salary of a high ranking official employed by the Government of Van Diemen's Land at the time, with around £30 the yearly wage of a labourer.[4]

---

[1] *The Hobart Town Courier*, 2 November 1838.
[2] Tasmanian Archives (MB2/39/1/4/ p321).
[3] H. O'May (1978). *Wooden Hookers of Hobart Town and Whalers out of Van Diemen's Land*.
[4] *The Austral-Asiatic Review, Tasmanian and Australian Advertiser*, 6 August 1839.

Cashed up, with hundreds and hundreds of pounds in his pocket, there were obviously many opportunities and diversions for Charles Bayley to spend money in the thriving Port of Hobart Town where pubs, bars and brothels were common establishments of the waterfront neighbourhoods, most catering for rogue and wayward sailors in need of food, accommodation and company. There were also illegal gambling dens and other vices, pastimes often favoured by the lower-ranking crew members. However, Charles Bayley was now a captain and very quickly gaining the respect of his industry and the Hobart Town community with which he was beginning to call home.

Nonetheless, there was little time for too much shenanigans. The *Wallaby* was readied for another voyage. On 12 December 1839, after six weeks in port, the vessel made its way down the River Derwent en route to Port Phillip Bay.[5] Reaching its destination on Christmas Day, its cargo of 130 sheep, nine bullocks, seven horses and 21 passengers were disembarked from the *Wallaby* before it left Melbourne, this time headed for Launceston.[6] While not as lucrative as a whaling voyage, short stints in intercolonial trade were obviously less risky and physically challenging, and also required less crew. For Charles Bayley, by now getting more comfortable being in command of his own vessel, they were likely a welcome reprieve from all that had transpired in the months prior.

The *Wallaby* reached Launceston on 4 January 1840 in ballast.[7] A week later it left the River Tamar headed back to Port Phillip Bay with 1,400 sheep on board.[8] The vessel was in Launceston again on 20 January and then on 8 February, both times loading passengers and livestock intended for Port Phillip Bay.[9] With Charles Bayley remaining at the helm, it was not until 5 March that the *Wallaby* once more docked in Hobart Town, arriving in the Derwent with seven bullocks and four passengers on board.[10]

With some money solidly in his pocket and his job secure, Charles Bayley was now able to consider his future. Both professionally and personally there were big changes heading his way. The first came on 26 March 1840 when he married Eliza Randolph (nee Inglis).[11] The ceremony, performed according to the rites and ceremonies of the Church of Scotland, took place at 31 Brisbane Street, Hobart Town, likely the location of an independent chapel, in the presence of Eliza's father James as well as Samuel Douglas, possibly a friend of the groom. Charles Bayley gave his age as 25, i.e., three years younger than his actual age.

Marriage certificate of Charles Bayley and Eliza Randolph (nee Inglis), 26 March 1840.
Tasmanian Archives (RGD37/1/2 no. 839).

---

[5] *Tasmanian Weekly Dispatch*, 13 December 1839.
[6] *Port Phillip Gazette*, 28 December 1839.
[7] *The Hobart Town Courier and Van Diemen's Land Gazette*, 10 January 1840.
[8] *Launceston Advertiser*, 16 January 1840.
[9] *The Hobart Town Courier and Van Diemen's Land Gazette*, 31 January 1840; *The Cornwall Chronicle*, 8 February 1840.
[10] *The Advertiser*, 10 March 1840.
[11] Tasmanian Archives (RGD37/1/2 no. 839).

Though only 23 years old at the time of their marriage, Charles' new bride Eliza had lived an interesting life up until this point. Just over three years earlier, on 21 December 1836, she had married William Randolph, master of the barque *Scotia*, at the Trinity Church in Hobart Town, in all likelihood without the consent of her parents despite Eliza being considered a minor.[1] Given the 340-ton vessel had only arrived in Van Diemen's Land from London on 6 November, it was a courtship of just six weeks.[2] However, the *Scotia* was a vessel very familiar to Eliza. It was the same craft that she, her parents and younger brother William had all sailed aboard from Leith, Scotland, to Hobart Town as steerage passengers some three years prior.[3] It was during this four-month voyage that Eliza and William Randolph no doubt first established their relationship. While Eliza was only 15 years of age at the time, 24-year-old William, a fellow Scotsman, was unquestionably employed on board as one of the ship's officers.[4] Whether the pair made plans to meet again is not known, though William remained employed on board the *Scotia*, within a few short years becoming its master.

The Inglis family had left their home in Edinburgh, Scotland, in search of a better life.[5] The rapidly growing city was suffering from the effects of industrialisation with large influxes of people making employment and housing difficult to secure. Eliza's father James, an upholsterer by trade, was fortunate that he had been eligible to receive an advance of £20 from the British Government.[6] This token was only given to a limited number of enterprising men, helping to offset the costs of enabling them and their families to emigrate to Australia.

Eliza and her family arrived in Hobart Town at a time of sustained growth. From a rudimentary convict outpost established by Great Britain in 1804, the settlement had grown into a bustling port town. The family moved into a home close to Hobart Town's wharf area, becoming entrenched in the associated maritime community.

Immediately upon her marriage to William Randolph, however, Eliza made the decision not to remain in Van Diemen's Land with her family, at least for the short term. Two days after the ceremony, Eliza and William Randolph boarded the *Scotia* once more, this time heading to Sydney. After a passage of 12 days, the pair arrived in Port Jackson on 4 January 1837.[7] They likely spent the next few weeks enjoying time together in a new colony. However, their next destination was still uncertain with William advertising the *Scotia* available for freight or charter.[8]

Eventually the craft was refitted and readied for another voyage. With William Randolph at the helm, the *Scotia* departed Sydney in ballast on 13 February 1837 en route to Batavia.[9] Now known as Jakarta (Indonesia), Batavia at the time was the capital of the Dutch East Indies and a major trading hub for South-East Asia.

Having been married for less than two months, it was at this point in time that the couple made the decision to separate, though they had likely made plans for William to return to the colonies at a later date where they would be reunited. Instead of remaining on board the *Scotia*, Eliza then sailed to Van Diemen's Land as a passenger on board the brig *Stirlingshire*.[10] Departing Sydney

---

[1] Tasmanian Archives (RGD36/1/3/ no 3325).
[2] *Colonial Times*, 8 November 1836.
[3] Tasmanian Archives (GO3/1/1 p741).
[4] Britain, Merchant Seamen, 1835-1857 for William Randolph.
[5] Bull family tree on ancestry.com.au compiled by the author.
[6] Tasmanian Archives (GO3/1/1 p741).
[7] Tasmanian Archives (MB2/43/1); *The Sydney Herald*, 5 January 1837.
[8] *The Sydney Herald*, 30 January 1837.
[9] *Sydney General Trade List*, 18 February 1837.
[10] *The Sydney Gazette and New South Wales Advertiser*, 23 February 1837.

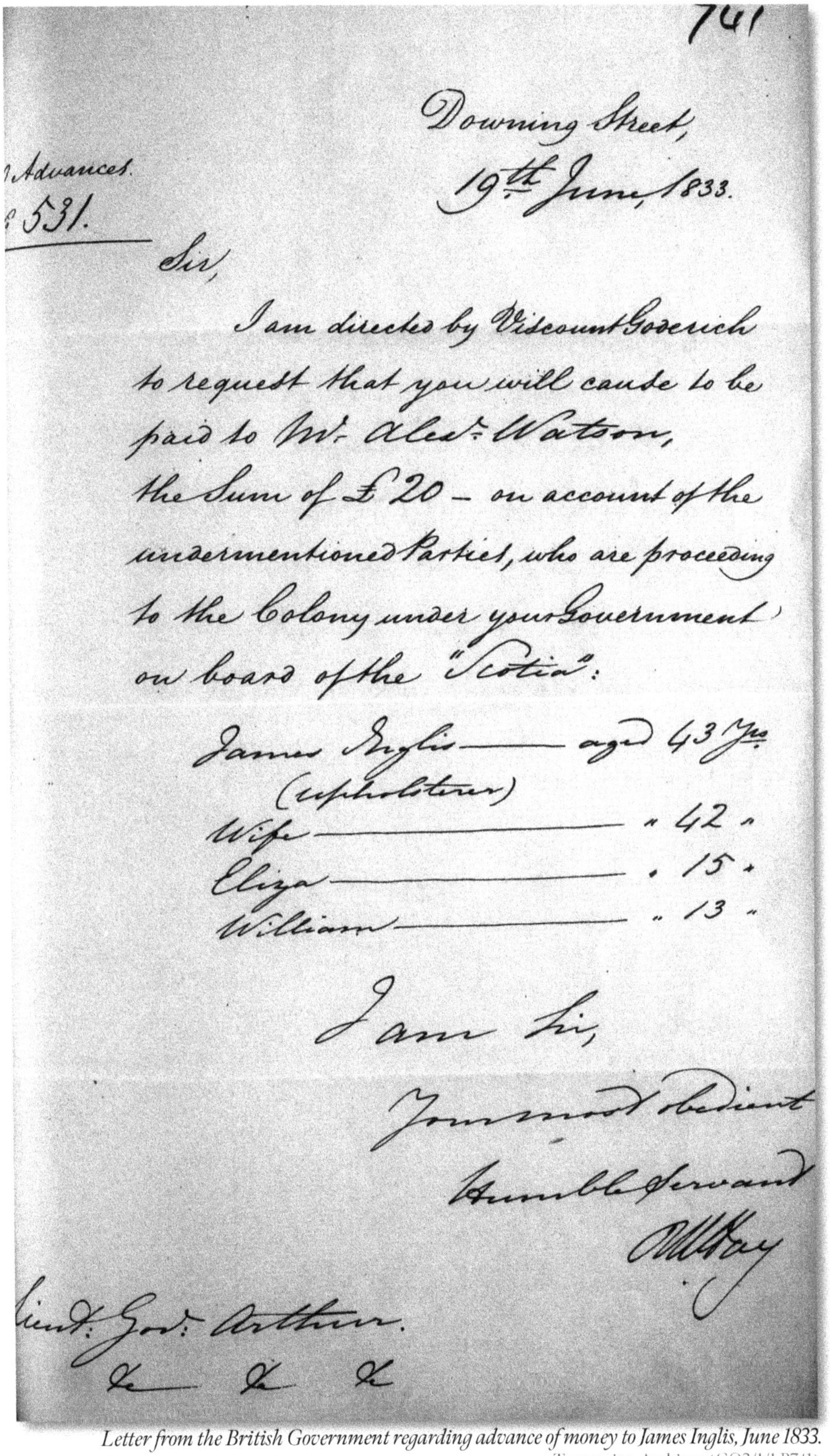

n Advances.
531.

Downing Street,
19th June, 1833.

Sir,

I am directed by Viscount Goderich to request that you will cause to be paid to Mr. Alexr. Watson, the Sum of £20 — on account of the undermentioned Parties, who are proceeding to the Colony under your Government on board of the "Scotia":

James Inglis ——————— aged 43 Yrs.
(upholsterer)
Wife ———————————— " 42 "
Eliza ———————————— " 15 "
William ——————————— " 13 "

I am Sir,
Your most obedient
Humble Servant
R.W. Hay

Lieut. Govr. Arthur.
&c &c &c

Letter from the British Government regarding advance of money to James Inglis, June 1833.
Tasmanian Archives (GO3/1/1 P741).

on 23 February, she arrived back in Hobart Town on 4 March.[1] It had been a whirlwind four months for the teenager. Not only had she been reunited with her first love, but she had married and sailed with him to Sydney.

Eliza waited for news of her husband and his probable return to Van Diemen's Land. Sadly, one came without the other. After departing Sydney and sailing up the north-east coast of Australia, the *Scotia* moored in Batavia on 24 April 1837.[2] It then remained in port for just over a month, loading cargo for Cowes on the Isle of Wight.[3] On 19 July the vessel fell in with another craft while sailing off the south-east coast of Africa where it was reported that the *Scotia*'s crew were '*sickly*'.[4] It had also lost its foretop mast and main topgallant mast, as well as tore most of its sails during a gale on 12 July.[5] The *Scotia* then limped towards the island of St Helena where it took on a new master owing to the death of William Randolph. The vessel left this location on 28 August, arriving in Cowes on 30 October.[6]

Eliza was 19 years of age and a widow. It would be another three years before she married Charles Bayley.

———

Just 12 days after their marriage Charles Bayley said farewell to his new bride Eliza. The *Wallaby* once again slipped out of the River Derwent on another whaling voyage.[7] Eliza no doubt remained in the care of her family at their home. Though she had sailed with her first husband to Sydney, a whaling vessel was an entirely different craft compared to that of a commercial vessel operating in intercolonial trade. The *Wallaby* made its way to South Australian waters, noted to be hunting off Encounter Bay in late May.[8] A month later the vessel had on board 40 tuns of black whale oil and 10 tuns of the higher-priced sperm whale oil.[9] It had notably caught seven whales, averaging nine tons each.[10] The *Wallaby* arrived back in Hobart Town on 23 October after six months spent at sea.[11] However, for reasons not known, its master was now a Captain Giriclan, indicating that Charles Bayley was perhaps ill or had departed the vessel prior to its arrival.

The *Wallaby* remained in port for two months, allowing its crew to get a reprieve from the monotony of shipboard life, spend the Christmas period on firm ground, as well as compete at the 1840 Hobart Town Regatta in a race for six-oared whaleboats.[12] By 11 December 1840 the vessel was noted as once more fitting out for a whaling voyage.[13]

Just after midnight on 31 December the *Wallaby* departed Hobart Town in search of more whales, again with Charles Bayley at the helm.[14] It was to be a long and arduous voyage taking the vessel on an entirely different route than which it had previously experienced. Instead of heading towards South Australian waters, the *Wallaby* made its way north-east, into the vast Pacific Ocean, going so far as searching for whales in the seas as far north as the equator.

---

[1] *The Colonist*, 2 March 1837; *Colonial Times*, 7 March 1837.
[2] *Lloyd's List*, 28 August 1837.
[3] *Public Ledger and Daily Advertiser*, 20 September, 31 October 1837.
[4] *Morning Herald*, 6 October 1837.
[5] *Liverpool Mercantile Gazette and Meyers's Weekly Advertiser*, 9 October 1837.
[6] *Morning Herald*, 31 October 1837.
[7] *Colonial Times*, 7 April 1840.
[8] *Launceston Advertiser*, 28 May 1840.
[9] *The Cornwall Chronicle*, 27 June 1840.
[10] *Tasmanian Weekly Dispatch*, 14 August 1840.
[11] *Colonial Times*, 27 October 1840.
[12] *The Courier*, 27 November 1840.
[13] *The Hobart Town Advertiser*, 11 December 1840.
[14] *The Hobart Town Advertiser*, 8 January 1841.

On 21 April 1841 the *Wallaby* was reported to be at Lord Howe Island with 250 barrels of sperm whale oil on board, equivalent to around 31 tuns.[15] This snippet of information was published in the Hobart Town press on 18 June and is the first update provided of the vessel since it had left Van Diemen's Land nearly six months prior, indicating a lengthy period where family and friends had been without contact with those on board. It is likely, however, that Charles Bayley managed to send letters to his wife Eliza via passing ships, though this process was often unreliable with the transfer of letters between vessels entirely dependent on each ship's particular route, its interactions with other vessels, the graciousness of its officers to ensure the letters were handed over to another vessel or to a post office once in port, and the frequency of a ship's arrival in port. Often family members received no news until the vessel arrived back in its home port.

There were no additional updates with regards to the *Wallaby* published in the Van Diemen's Land papers for the remainder of the year 1841. One can only hope that the crew's letters were able to make it home to their loved ones. Thankfully, the vessel's log remains in existence, significantly part of the Australian National Maritime Museum's collection, and we are able to retrace its voyage, as well as glean important additional information.[16] For example, the crew that left Hobart Town on board the vessel, in addition to Charles Bayley, comprised a chief mate, second mate, third mate, surgeon, a carpenter, several coopers and various able seamen, totalling a complement of 26 men. Indicative of the times, its surgeon, a Mr Scott, was listed as only 19 years of age. There were obviously very few men from the medical profession willing to risk their lives on board a whaling ship and likely minister to a rowdy and onerous bunch of men. It was thus with both naivety and gumption that Mr Scott signed up for the voyage.

The *Wallaby*'s log reveals that the vessel first sighted whales two weeks after departing Hobart Town while sailing in Bass Strait. Several boats were lowered though returned without success. Five days later, on 19 January off the coast of Victoria, more whales were encountered with all four of the ship's boats lowered. Charles Bayley and his chief mate, a Mr Young, fastened on to two black whales which were manoeuvered on board, cut up and the oil extracted. As part of the *Wallaby*'s log, its author, likely one of the ship's mates, kept a running tally in the left hand column as to which crew member had successfully fastened on to a whale, often denoting his master's achievements with a drawing of a whale tail with 'Cap' inscribed in it.

On 29 January 1841 Charles Bayley fastened on to another whale. It was only the start of what would ultimately be a fortunate though very long voyage in terms of whale sightings, slaughterings and oil production.

It was not always smooth sailing, however. The *Wallaby* and its crew encountered gales, lost equipment, had whaleboats damaged, endured illness and injury, and malfunctioning chronometers, pumps and sails. The crew laboured heavily at times in extreme conditions and endured monotonous manual tasks and repetitive rations for most of the voyage. Moreover, whales were often sighted and boats lowered only to return to the *Wallaby* without reward despite the effort. There were also disagreements to manage and personality differences heightened by shipboard life, of which Charles Bayley was charged with alleviating. All told, it was gruelling and dangerous work suited to the most robust and stoic of men who could handle both the physical and psychological demands of the conditions. It appears to have suited Charles Bayley well.

---

[15] *Tasmanian Weekly Dispatch*, 18 June 1841.
[16] *A Log Book Containing the Proceeding on Board the Wallaby from the Port of Hobarton on a Whaling Voyage Commanded by Charles Bailey*. Australian National Maritime Museum.

Extract from the Log of the Wallaby's Whaling Voyage (1840-42).
Australian National Maritime Museum.

After 110 days at sea the *Wallaby* reached Lord Howe Island on 20 April 1841. It was likely a fortuitous time for the vessel to reach land as animosity amongst the crew was starting to disrupt the ship. On 9 April the ship's log noted that, '*Richard Wagstaff & R. Wilkinson positively refused doing any more duty whilst on board. Jno. Williams - Jas. Taylor, & Jas. Beaton also refused doing any duty - saying that as Wagstaff & Wilkinson had knocked off that they would do the same.*' Tempers were likely quite frayed by the time the *Wallaby* sighted land, though Charles Bayley had stepped in to alleviate the friction amongst his crew and sort out the problems.

With the *Wallaby* securely moored close to Lord Howe Island, two boats were lowered and landed. Charles Bayley then set about obtaining stores with half a ton of potatoes, five pigs, 25 pumpkins, 25 melons, one bag of onions and a boat load of wood shipped on board during the next two days. The vessel departed Lord Howe Island on 23 April with Richard Wagstaff still refusing to attend to his duties.

On 15 May 1841, while cruising the waters south of Lord Howe Island, the *Wallaby* had one of its more successful days. With all four boats lowered following the sighting of several whales, Charles Bayley managed to fasten on to three whales and the second mate to one. The accumulation of whale oil and bone on board sporadically increased as the months passed, with the vessel now making its way north into the Coral Sea.

Despite their share of the ship's lay to be paid out on their return to Hobart Town, rebellious crew members continued to be an issue for Charles Bayley. In late July 1841 the *Wallaby* returned to Lord Howe Island where boatloads of men were sent ashore to cut and load wood needed not only for the vessel's stove and heating but also for its tryworks. Crew members also went ashore to hunt pigs which had been introduced to the island by whalers in the 1820s to create a self-sustaining source of food for visiting ships. While they managed to procure a few animals for the vessel, two crew members deserted the ship: Richard Wilkinson and Thomas Burton. With only a handful of residents living on the island at the time, primarily engaged in supplying visiting ships with provisions, there would have been little opportunity for the two men to find employment such that their plan would have been to wait for the arrival of another vessel to which they could work their passage. Knowing their predicament and the need for the two hands to remain on board, Charles Bayley searched the island for them over a period of several days, to no avail.

With the *Wallaby*'s crew now numbering 24, including its captain Charles Bayley, the vessel resumed its voyage, once more heading north into the Coral Sea. Rennell Island was sighted on 21 August, part of the Solomon Islands group. Two days later several boats were lowered to collect water and source more wood. Resuming its voyage around the Solomon Islands, Charles Bayley steered well clear of San Christobal Island; there being neither anchorage nor water available. Instead, an additional few weeks were spent in the vicinity of the larger islands, including Santa Isabel Island, securing additional wood and water, where unfortunately two more crew members absconded: George Down and Edward Jones. Four days later, on 9 September, another three men deserted the *Wallaby*: James Cracknell, James Butler and Robert Sanderson, followed shortly thereafter by Richard Wagstaff.

Persevering, Charles Bayley engaged the remaining crew members with various jobs. By mid-September all six deserters had returned to the *Wallaby*, as well as two Indigenous men from the Solomon Islands enabling the ship to again complete its complement. It once more sailed north in search of whales which, though sighted, were not able to be captured. Making it to the equator, which was crossed on 16 October 1841, upon nearing Micronesia Charles Bayley turned the *Wallaby* around, heading back into southern waters where whale sightings appeared more frequent and were hunted with marked success. After many weeks spent in the vicinity of the island now known as Nauru, including trading with the Indigenous people for coconuts, pigs, chickens and brooms, ultimately the tropical seas had not been as fruitful as expected, several crew members were by now sick, and it was nearing a year since the vessel had departed Hobart Town. It was time to try a new location and climate.

On 20 December 1841 the *Wallaby* began its migration further south, a few days later returning to the Solomon Islands where more wood and water were procured. Continuing on its journey, the vessel then sailed south-east towards Vanuatu, reaching the island of Tanna late in January 1842 where wood was collected despite axes being stolen by members of the local population. Crew absconding continued to be an issue, however, with both Robert Grey and Thomas Williams absenting themselves from the *Wallaby* by stealing a boat and making their way to the island. The ship's mate noted in the vessel's log for 9 February that, '*with the assistance of the Natives brought off Robt. Grey & Tho. Williams, who both refused to do their duty. 4 P.M. Got under weigh*'.

On 6 March 1842 the *Wallaby* encountered the whaler *Highlander* of Hobart Town. This particular vessel had only been two months out at sea and had secured 80 casks of sperm whale oil from Bass Strait. Since it was the first craft from his home port that Charles Bayley had encountered to date, it was likely an interaction where much local news was relayed, in addition to information on whale sightings that might prove more opportunistic. Another serendipitous meeting took place on 18 April when Charles Bayley lowered a boat and went on board the *Prince of Orange* of Leith, Scotland, that had departed Sydney six weeks prior and was en route to Batavia.

As the *Wallaby* continued to make its way south from the Coral Sea into the Tasman Sea, more whales were successfully captured. The vessel then reached the northern tip of New Zealand's South Island in mid-May 1842 whereupon James Butler, Richard Wagstaff and Thomas Brown again absconded. More wood, pigs and potatoes were also procured and transferred on board, though during this process William Barret, another crew member, absconded. A few days later Robert Grey took off while the *Wallaby* was moored in Cloudy Bay undertaking repairs. With a rudimentary fishing camp located nearby, the vessel's chief mate, Mr Young, and another of the crew were invited on shore by the camp's overseer Robert Fife. Unfortunately the invitation proved to be a ruse and while both men were returning to the *Wallaby*, their boat was overtaken and they were forced back to shore. The two men were then physically assaulted, their boat stripped of its gear and the pair held prisoner, though Mr Young managed to escape into the nearby woods. A few hours later Robert Fife and 16 of his men made their way on board the *Wallaby* to inquire about a man who had absconded from their camp, Fife plainly stating that he intended to keep the two *Wallaby* crew members as '*payment*' for the man. Unfortunately the log does not relay in detail what transpired next, though a few days passed before Mr Young and the other crewman made it back on board and the *Wallaby*'s boat was returned, sans several items.

On 21 May 1842 the *Wallaby* set sail for Port Nicholson, i.e., Wellington, arriving the following day. Given the size of the town, numbering in the realm of 5,000 people, it was an opportunity for more crew members to be signed up to work on board, replacing those that had absconded and James Beaton who was discharged, as well as for the ship's stores to be replenished. Of note, the vessel took on board beef, sugar, paint, white lead, canvas, twine, iron, tools, rivets and nails, several sails, four sheep and 25 pounds of mutton. The Wellington Customs House also declared that the *Wallaby* had 900 barrels of sperm whale oil on board of which at least one tun, i.e., eight barrels, was unloaded and deposited with an agent for subsequent sale.[1] Seven casks of rum were additionally declared, though this carefully managed product undoubtedly remained on board as part of the crew's provisions.

The *Wallaby* stayed in Wellington for just over a week before setting sail for the Chatham Islands and its nearby whaling grounds, a distance of 500 miles to the east of New Zealand.[2] It arrived back in Wellington on 28 July after nearly two months spent at sea.[3] Another 11 tuns of whale oil was by now stowed in the vessel's holds while several sharks had also been captured. The crew offloaded eight tuns and 49 gallons of oil at the port for subsequent sale by an agent. Stores were again in much need of replenishment, the *Wallaby*'s log noting that they had run out of meat. Received on board were 12 barrels of beef, one chest of tea, four bags of sugar, 58 gallons of gin and four pigs. However, given the shore-based opportunities available in Wellington, a town very much catering to visiting ships, several crewmen once more absconded, including its third mate, much to Charles Bayley's chagrin.

On 2 August 1842, with the *Wallaby* being readied for another departure, Charles Bayley went ashore in search of his wayward men. Upon finding his third mate and instructing him to

---
[1] *New Zealand Gazette and Wellington Spectator,* 4 June 1842.
[2] *New Zealand Gazette and Wellington Spectator,* 1 June 1842.
[3] *New Zealand Gazette and Wellington Spectator,* 30 July 1842.

return on board immediately, Charles was punched in the face, the impact knocking him down. A police constable was then sequestered with the third mate charged with assault for which a magistrate found him guilty and sentenced him to two months' imprisonment.[4] The *Wallaby* left Wellington without him; Edward Robinson being promoted to third mate in his place. Also not on board were William Riley and Robert Startup. Both men had been charged with refusing to return to the vessel and sentenced to 30 days' hard labour working on the roads.

After sailing from Wellington on 4 August and heading north along the New Zealand coastline, the *Wallaby* encountered more whales, successfully fastening on to several of them. At least nine tuns of oil and 27 bundles of bone were added to the vessel's holds over the next few weeks, though three hundredweight of bone was exchanged for 722 pounds of pork on 23 August.

The *Wallaby* continued hunting for whales in the Tasman Sea for the entire month of September with limited success. In early October it slowly began making its way back to Van Diemen's Land, by now with one passenger on board, Johnny Knox, who had embarked while the vessel visited Mana Island off the south-west coast of New Zealand's Northern Island.[5]

On 2 November the *Wallaby* finally arrived back in Hobart Town having been away for a substantial 672 days. It was undoubtedly a very welcome homecoming for Charles Bayley and those members of his crew that were based out of the port, by this point in the voyage comprising a complement of 31 men. Charles in particular was looking forward to seeing his bride Eliza once more, having spent only 80 of the 952 days since their wedding in one another's company. For a young couple just starting their married life, the forced separation for such a lengthy period would have been emotionally draining. It also meant that they had to delay having children.

Was the isolating, demanding, dangerous and physically and emotionally exhausting work as a whaling captain worth the separation from his wife, as well as Charles Bayley's family back in Burnham-on-Crouch, Essex, on the other side of the world? If personal benefit was his goal, then in the case of this specific voyage of the *Wallaby*, it appears to have been so. Though despite its longevity, it was perhaps not as financially lucrative as the first voyage Charles Bayley had made at the helm of the *Wallaby*. Still, not only did Charles return in good health, so too did his crew and the vessel itself. There was also the matter of the vessel's cargo and his share of the lay. The *Wallaby*'s manifest reveals the details. The vessel returned to Hobart Town with 80 tuns of sperm whale oil, 50 tuns of black whale oil and an undisclosed amount of whale bone in its holds.[6] Together these three commodities were valued at over £4,200 of which Charles would have received at least an eight per cent share of the net profit.[7] However, there was likely more money sent his way as this figure does not include any share of the profit he would have received from the whale oil that was discharged in New Zealand, believed to be around 10 tuns, nor does it include the bonuses he would have received from the eight out of a total of 19 whales that he personally killed.

With several hundreds of additional pounds now in his purse, this voyage also marked the second whaling voyage Charles Bayley had made as captain of the *Wallaby*. His management of the vessel and its crew, even in the most trying of times, his steadfastness and resourcefulness did not go unnoticed. Charles Bayley's favourable standing within Hobart Town's maritime community was definitely on the rise.

---

[4] *New Zealand Gazette and Wellington Spectator*, 4 June 1842.
[5] Tasmanian Archives (MB2/39/1/6 Image 198).
[6] Tasmanian Archives (MB2/39/1/6 Image 198).
[7] R. Richards (2014). *Captain Charles Bayley: Whaling Master 1813-1875*.

Extract from the Log of the Wallaby's Whaling Voyage (1840-42).
Australian National Maritime Museum.

Foundations & Family

Charles Bayley's innate pursuit of financial security at the risk of his own safety and a prolonged separation from his wife undeniably came from his upbringing in Essex, England, whereby his family worked hard though lived with limited means. Charles had also witnessed the success generated by determination and resolve that saw his uncle William Bayley (Jr[2]) become a respectable and wealthy shipbuilder and shipowner in nearby Ipswich, rising to ranks well above his station. Emulating this upward projection, Charles was certainly laying the foundation to building his own empire, with the goal of providing safety and fiscal dependability to his family. Though far from the banks of the River Crouch in Burnham-on-Crouch where his father Charles Bull operated as an oyster dredger and part-time boat builder, Hobart Town was a maritime community growing in population and notoriety; its resources buoyed by the burgeoning commodities of wheat, wool and whales. Given the colony's initiation as a convict settlement only four decades prior, with this offending class still being exploited for their labour, there was much to gain by those that had come 'free' to Van Diemen's Land and were willing to work with grit and calculated risk-taking to expand their own personal brand and worth.

While the weeks after Charles Bayley's return to Hobart Town in early November 1842, following nearly two years at sea, were spent back in the company of his wife Eliza and the comforts of her family's home, he did not remain idle for long. With a sense of optimism Charles Bayley made plans for their future. Importantly, on 5 January 1843 he purchased an allotment of land in Kelly Street, Battery Point, likely with plans to build a small four-room cottage on it. The property, comprising just under ¼ of an acre, was purchased from Thomas Brown and William Knight and had originally formed part of a four-acre parcel owned by Captain James Kelly, the legendary mariner, explorer and harbourmaster.[1] The purchase price was £110. Its location was significant.

For many thousands of years the traditional owners and custodians of Nipaluna (Hobart Town), the Mouheneener band of the South East Nation of Tasmanian Aborigines had utilised the land now known as Battery Point, including its headlands and shoreline. Following European settlement in 1804, the Reverend Robert Knopwood had first moved into the area, on 1 January 1806 receiving a land grant of 30 acres upon which he built his home, 'Cottage Green', on the site's north-west corner, spending £1,000 on its construction as well as other improvements.[2] His grant bordered the burial ground (St David's Park) and extended to the water's edge along Sullivans Cove, with an allowance made for later construction of a roadway. Reverend Knopwood's property

---

[1] Tasmanian Archives (AG193/1/37/71/1, Historic Deed 02/5871).
[2] W. H. Hudspeth (1945). *Note on Cottage Green.*

also encompassed much of present-day Salamanca, though a small portion of land located at the southern point of the harbour had been cordoned off by the Crown for use as a battery.

Owing to financial difficulties, however, in March 1816 Reverend Knopwood was forced to sell 25 acres of his 30-acre parcel to Captain William Townsend Jones, including 'Cottage Green', its buildings, gardens and fruit trees, for the hefty sum of £2,000. The transaction was on the proviso that £1,000 be paid up front and the other £1,000 a year later.[1] While Reverend Knopwood remained living at 'Cottage Green' as a stipulation of the agreement, Captain Jones took immediate possession of the remaining five acres as part of a separate transaction.[2]

Though the Mulgrave Battery, located on what was previously coined 'Knopwoods Point' by Hobart Town's European settlers, was officially opened in honour of the Earl of Mulgrave in July 1818 with works then under construction, including a guard house and home for a signalman, the build-out of Battery Point as a whole was generally quite slow.[3] The bulk of the locale remained largely undisturbed with its landowners placing no urgency on developing or subdividing their properties, including William Sorell, the colony's newly-arrived Lieutenant-Governor who was granted a 90-acre parcel adjacent to Reverend Knopwood's land in 1818.[4]

It was not until May 1820 that the still-vacant five-acre allotment Captain Jones had purchased from Reverend Knopwood four years prior, situated between the latter's property and the Mulgrave Battery, was advertised for sale as part of Jones' deceased estate.[5] The undeveloped parcel was then purchased by Captain Robert Carns who remained another itinerant landowner considering he was sailing ships between London, Australia and India at the time.[6]

Nevertheless, by March 1821 Reverend Knopwood's financial woes were nearing a precipice and he was bordering on insolvency. The administrators of Captain Jones' estate were also unable to meet the final payment of £1,000 owed to him for 'Cottage Green' and its 25-acre allotment.[7] Reverend Knopwood thus appears to have avoided immediately having to vacate the property. However, in October 1823 the inevitable occurred with the local press advertising it for sale by auction.[8]

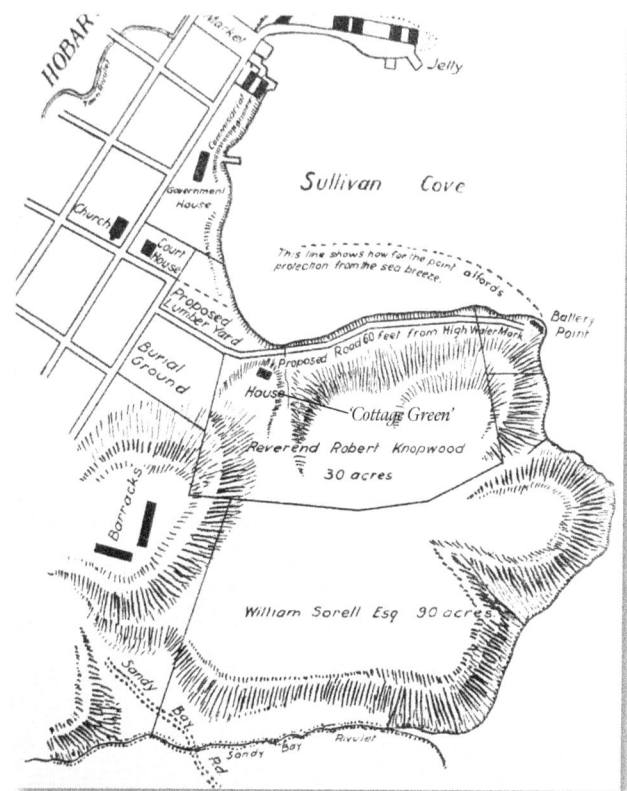

Map of Battery Point showing land grants awarded to Rev Robert Knopwood and Lieutenant-Governor William Sorell (c1826).
A. Rowntree (1968). *Battery Point Today and Yesterday.*

---
[1] *The Sydney Gazette and New South Wales Advertiser*, 7 April 1821.
[2] *The Sydney Gazette and New South Wales Advertiser*, 7 April 1821.
[3] *The Van Diemen's Land Gazette and General Advertiser*, 18 June 1814; *The Hobart Town Gazette and Southern Reporter*, 1 August 1818.
[4] adb.anu.edu.au/biography/sorell-william-2680; A. Rowntree (1968). *Battery Point Today and Yesterday*.
[5] *The Hobart Town Gazette and Southern Reporter*, 20 May 1820.
[6] *Hobart Town Gazette and Van Diemen's Land Advertiser*, 5 May 1821; 1 February 1823, 12 August 1825.
[7] *Hobart Town Gazette and Van Diemen's Land Advertiser*, 17 March 1821.
[8] *Hobart Town Gazette and Van Diemen's Land Advertiser*, 11 October 1823.

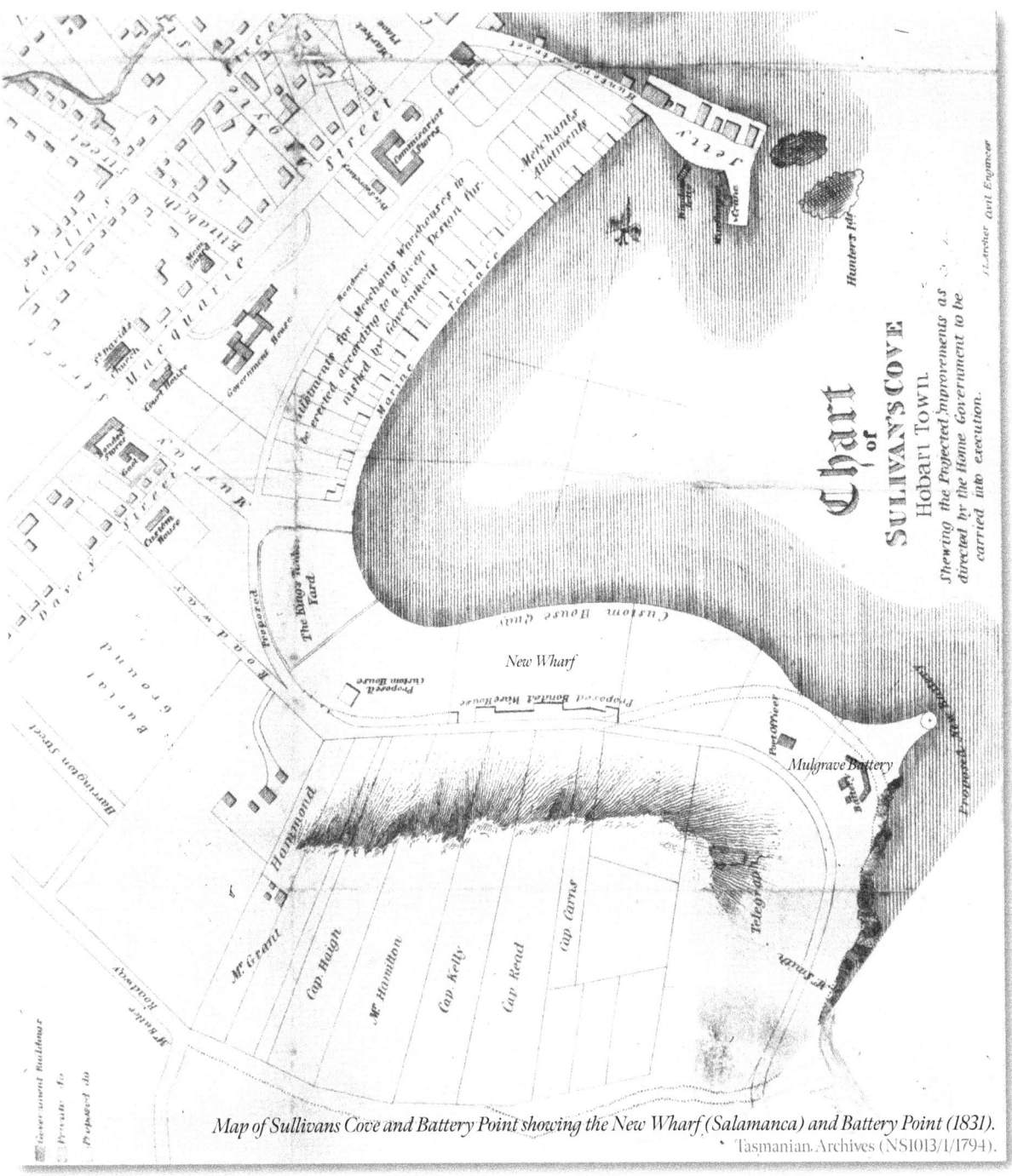

Map of Sullivans Cove and Battery Point showing the New Wharf (Salamanca) and Battery Point (1831).
Tasmanian Archives (NS1013/1/1794).

Failing to sell, the land was subsequently re-surveyed and subdivided. In March 1824 an advertisement in the press stated that up to 20 allotments, part of the 'Cottage Green' property, were for sale on behalf of J. T. Collicott, auctioneer.[9] The purchasers were predominately enterprising and speculative merchants and mariners, namely James Grant, Captain Andrew Haig, a Mr Hamilton, Captain James Kelly and G. F. Reid.

---

[9] *Hobart Town Gazette and Van Diemen's Land Advertiser*, 5 March 1824.

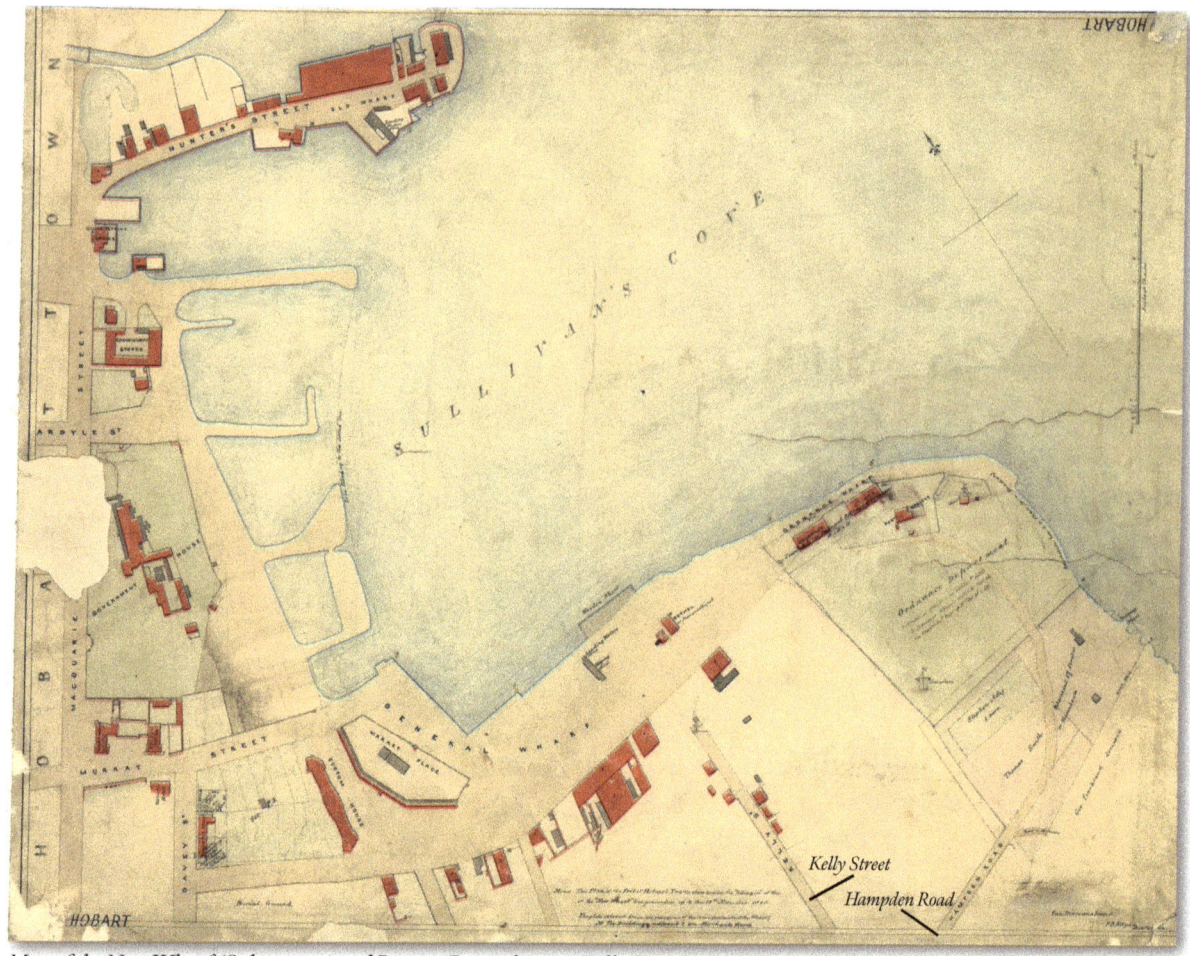

Map of the New Wharf (Salamanca) and Battery Point, showing Kelly Street (c1840s).
Tasmanian Archives (AF394/1/171).

It was the start of a period of immense development and subsequent subdivision of Battery Point into smaller and smaller allotments, mainly at the hands of commercial and mercantile interests, primarily those associated with trade and shipping. This boon was in part due to a survey of the harbour undertaken in mid-1825 which revealed a good depth of water along the eastern side of Sullivans Cove, as well as the sheltered south side of the Mulgrave Battery.[1] The survey inspired the proprietors of nearby properties to offer to the government a portion of their land for construction of a road 60 feet in width.[2] The road was to travel along the front of 'Cottage Green' to the Mulgrave Battery and was deemed of valuable use should the government propose to construct a public wharf in the vicinity, as well as for ships sheltering in the basin by the Mulgrave Battery. Expanded to travel from Davey Street, across 'Cottage Green' to the Battery, the road was well underway in June 1826 with convict gangs noted to be employed on the project.[3] Several months later, a road from the Mulgrave Battery to Browns River, a small settlement located on the edge of the River Derwent some 10 miles to the south, was also under construction.[4]

---

[1] *The Hobart Town Gazette,* 10 September 1825.
[2] *The Hobart Town Gazette,* 15 October 1825.
[3] *The Hobart Town Gazette,* 11 February, 24 June 1826.
[4] *The Hobart Town Gazette,* 19 August 1826.

With all of this development came further subdivision of Reverend Knopwood and Lieutenant-Governor Sorell's original parcels of land. As stated, part of the former's property was divided into allotments suitable for building mercantile stores in association with the New Wharf. With the proposed construction of this shipping precinct, parcels of land located in close proximity suddenly increased ten times in value in 1832.[5]

In the succeeding years more allotments at Battery Point were advertised for sale with further segmentation occurring amongst the original and subsequent property owners such that within a few decades all that remained were small residential building sites. More roads were constructed, parsing through the developing suburb, connecting Battery Point to Hobart Town and the New Wharf area, as well as to Sandy Bay and beyond. Construction of a pier forming the New Wharf, extending from Sullivans Cove to the Mulgrave Battery had also commenced in July 1830.[6] This ambitious project further enhanced Battery Point's appeal to merchants and shipowners. The wharf was first noted to be in use in April 1831.[7]

It was in this context some 13 years later that Charles Bayley purchased his small allotment in Kelly Street, by which point in time comprised only a few cottages. With its views of the port, the river and its close proximity to the New Wharf, he was not only able to see the arrivals and departures of vessels to and from Hobart Town, but be within a few minutes' walk of the action. Situated on the south side of Kelly Street, the property backed onto land then owned by Charles McLachlan.[8] At the time of purchase, it was also bordered by properties owned by David Hogg to the north and Thomas Lucas to the south.

Map showing location of Charles Bayley's Kelly Street property.
Google Earth (2025).

The deed of sale related to David Hogg's property reveals that the south-west corner of his parcel was located exactly 252 feet from the intersection of Kelly Street and Hampden Road. From this information and the stated boundary sizes, we can thereby deduce that Charles Bayley purchased land that encompassed current-day numbers 44 and 46 Kelly Street, as well as the car park of the Prince of Wales Hotel, with David Hogg the owner of land that is now known as 42 Kelly Street.[9] While David Hogg's house, a four-room Georgian cottage completed in 1843, i.e., a year after he purchased the allotment, is still in existence and referred to as 'Kelly Cottage', the original allotment owned by Charles Bayley has since been subdivided with two adjoining houses built on it in the 1920s. However, it is likely that Charles built a similarly-sized modest cottage on the site.

While Charles Bayley organised for the construction of his Kelly Street home, he was also deciding on his professional future. The whaling barque *Wallaby*, which he had helmed

---

[5] *The Colonist and Van Diemen's Land Commercial and Agricultural Advertiser*, 7 December 1832.
[6] *The Hobart Town Courier*, 3 July 1830.
[7] *The Hobart Town Courier*, 9 April 1831.
[8] Tasmanian Archives (AG193/1/37/71/1, AF819/1/135, AF394/1/114).
[9] Tasmanian Archives (Historic Deed 02/5537).

for several voyages since the death of Captain Wishart in August 1839, had been advertised for sale almost immediately upon its return to Hobart Town in November 1842.[1] The vessel's owners, George Watson and Alfred Garrett, were eager to dispose of the craft after its lengthy voyage to the equator and southern whaling grounds. Instead, Charles Bayley was entrusted with the helm of the 255-ton barque *Fortitude*, at the time owned by Askin Morrison, one of Van Diemen's Lands' more prominent merchants, landowners and graziers.[2] Previously involved in the international passenger and cargo trade sailing between Hobart Town and London, the vessel had been built near Sunderland, England, in 1832. It was only the second time it would be utilised for a whaling voyage, having undertaken an expedition to the whaling grounds during the 1842 season under the charge of William Young.[3]

Following just over two months spent ashore, on 13 January 1843 Charles Bayley once more said goodbye to his wife Eliza and her family and sailed the *Fortitude* out of the River Derwent, again headed to the whaling grounds, this time venturing further south into the Tasman Sea, encroaching into sub-Antarctic waters.[4] The vessel was fitted out for an 18-month stint such that Charles expected another lengthy period away from his family.[5] However, a month after departing Hobart Town the vessel was reported to be off Van Diemen's Lands' South-West Cape having already captured three sperm whales and three black whales.[6] After a further five months at sea the *Fortitude* had amassed 180 barrels of sperm whale oil in its holds, equivalent to nearly 23 tuns.[7] The vessel arrived back in Hobart Town on 15 October, ten months earlier than anticipated, with a total of 200 barrels of sperm whale oil on board and a staggering 1,700 barrels of black whale oil, as well as seven tons of whale bone.[8]

It was a fortuitous time to be involved in ship whaling as opposed to bay whaling which, due to overfishing and the movement of the species away from the coast, was experiencing a significant reduction in output. This demise, combined with an increase in global demand, had resulted in the price per tun at the time for sperm whale oil being £80 while the price of black whale oil had nearly doubled to £37 per tun.[9] A scarcity of whale bone had also dramatically increased the price of this commodity to £240 per ton. In consequence, the sale of the *Fortitude*'s oil and bone following its short eight-month voyage would have generated a substantial sum in excess of £11,000.[10] However, given its owner Askin Morrison had fitted the ship out for an 18-month voyage, the net profit was only half this amount, i.e., in the vicinity £5,500.[11]

Despite barely eight months at sea, Charles Bayley returned to Hobart Town with not only his vessel and its 28 crew members free from significant damage or injury, but also contemplating that his share of the lay would be quite bountiful. And it was. Assuming Charles' share was eight per cent of the net profits, then his payment was around £440, i.e., the highest amount he had earned to date from a whaling voyage. There was more rejoicing too when Charles was met by his brother Bayley Bull upon the *Fortitude*'s return to Hobart Town. It had been many years since the pair had last seen one another, and their reunion would have been something quite special.

[1] *The Hobart Town Courier*, 18 November 1842.
[2] R. Parsons (1992). *Australian Shipowners and Their Fleets: Book Thirteen [Hobart to 1859 M-Z]*.
[3] *Colonial Times*, 1 November 1842.
[4] *The Hobart Town Advertiser*, 17 January 1843.
[5] *The Austral-Asiatic Review, Tasmanian and Australian Advertiser*, 10 November 1843.
[6] *Colonial Times*, 28 February 1843.
[7] *The Hobart Town Advertiser*, 5 May 1843.
[8] *Colonial Times*, 17 October 1843; Tasmanian Archives (MB2/39/1/7 p259); R. Richards (2014). *Captain Charles Bayley: Whaling Master 1813-1875*.
[9] *Colonial Times*, 11 April 1843.
[10] *Launceston Examiner*, 21 October 1843.
[11] *The Austral-Asiatic Review, Tasmanian and Australian Advertiser*, 10 November 1843.

Family formed an important part of Charles Bayley's identity and he would have pined for his parents and siblings back in England, despite the fact that he had most certainly settled in to the Hobart Town community and begun building his own lineage and foundations. During his sabbatical in Hobart Town in late 1842 it appears that Charles had sent letters back to England, encouraging his siblings to immigrate to Van Diemen's Land. He undoubtedly also told them of the money he was making as the captain of a whaling barque, perhaps downplaying the dangers of the occupation, and the struggle he felt in not being able to share his successes with his family in Burnham-on-Crouch, as well as introduce them to his wife Eliza. While all of his elder sisters were either married or widowed by early 1843, when the letters would have arrived in England after a four-month passage, his encouraging endorsements invoked his youngest and only surviving brother Bayley Bull to take action. With his experience as a mariner involved in the coastal trade out of Essex and Suffolk, there were plenty of opportunities for 19-year-old Bayley to work his way to Australia. He soon found a position on board the convict ship *Cressy*, signing on as one of 50 crew members in London just as the vessel was being readied for departure.

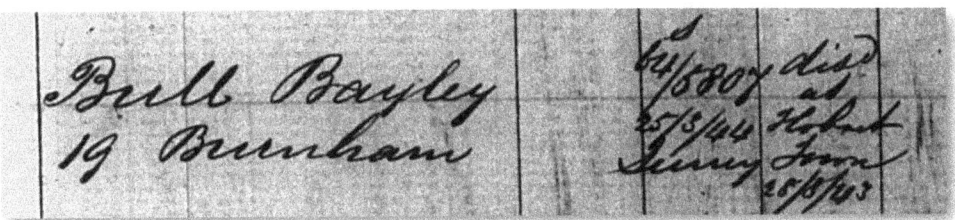

Bayley Bull's listing in the Register of Merchant Seamen, 1843.
Note the year '44 is an error and should be '43.
Britain, Merchant Seamen, 1835-1857.

On 25 March 1843 Bayley Bull departed Deptford on the River Thames on board the *Cressy*, farewelling his parents Charles and Mary Bull and his younger sister Harriet (then aged 15), all living in Burnham-on-Crouch, as well as his three elder sisters Mary, Emmaretta and Keturah, who were living with their respective families on the outskirts of London.[12] Also on board were 50 members of the 99th Regiment, tasked with acting as convict guards for the duration of the voyage, as well as several officers and their families.[13] While the crew and contingent representing the Regiment had all boarded the vessel at Deptford, 295 male convicts embarked after the *Cressy* reached Portsmouth on 30 March.[14] The vessel was then expected to sail for Hobart Town five days later but soon found itself delayed.[15] It was not until nearly a month following, on 30 April 1843, that the *Cressy* finally set sail for Van Diemen's Land, the time spent awaiting the arrival of an important guest, the colony's newly-appointed Lieutenant-Governor, Sir John Eardley-Wilmot, along with his son John (Jr).[16]

The *Cressy* arrived in Hobart Town on 20 August 1843 after a 112 day voyage.[17] It then spent several weeks unloading its passengers, convicts and stores, before loading cargo for Sydney. The vessel sailed out of the River Derwent on 6 September without Bayley Bull on board.[18]

---
[12] *Lloyd's List*, 27 March 1843.
[13] *Maidstone Journal and Kentish Advertiser*, 21 March 1843; *West Kent Guardian*, 25 March 1843
[14] *Lloyd's List*, 31 March 1843; *London Evening Standard*, 1 April 1843; *Sun*, 3 April 1843.
[15] *London Evening Standard*, 6 April 1843.
[16] Tasmanian Archives (MB2/39/1/7 p205).
[17] *Colonial Times*, 22 August 1843.
[18] *The Austral-Asiatic Review, Tasmanian and Australian Advertiser*, 8 September 1843.

As stated, nearly two months after the arrival of the *Cressy* in Hobart Town, Charles Bayley sailed the *Fortitude* back up the River Derwent, arriving on 15 October 1843 with a large cargo of whale oil and bone. With his brother Bayley (from this point forward known as James Bayley) now in Van Diemen's Land, there was little time for sight-seeing nor to spend the money Charles had earned from the *Fortitude*'s most recent voyage, not that he appears to have been extravagant with money. As the vessel had arrived back in Hobart Town much earlier than anticipated, and with 10 months of provisions still on board, it was soon readied for another voyage to the whaling grounds, leaving port on 10 November 1843.[1]

It had been a quick turnaround of only 26 days for the vessel and its crew before it was time to head back to sea. Significantly for Charles Bayley, however, his brother James was now employed on board as one of the crew (an able seaman), intending to use the opportunity to gain valuable experience with the goal of quickly moving up the profession's hierarchy. Moreover, during the short time spent in port, Charles had also managed to get his wife pregnant, though it is extremely doubtful that he knew of this fact before he set sail out of the River Derwent.

The *Fortitude* initially cruised the waters off Van Diemen's Lands' west coast before making its way to the southern tip of New Zealand, incorporating Stewart Island. It then returned to Hobart Town on 15 April 1844 with 300 barrels of sperm whale oil on board, 400 barrels of black whale oil, 2 tons of bone and 50 pounds of ambergris.[2] All told, Charles Bayley's share of the lay was around £350.

Coinciding with his arrival back in port, Charles' wife Eliza was now six months pregnant and their cottage in Kelly Street very likely complete. There was much for Charles Bayley to be thankful for.

---

[1] *The Courier*, 10 November 1843; *The Austral-Asiatic Review, Tasmanian and Australian Advertiser*, 19 April 1844.
[2] Bayley Bull record in Britain, Merchant Seamen, 1835-1857.

Arrivals & Departures

Charles Bayley's wife Eliza gave birth to the couple's first child on 13 July 1844 at their Kelly Street home, a daughter named Jane Mary. Her birth was registered just over a month later by Eliza's father James Inglis. Unfortunately, Charles Bayley was not in port to welcome the new addition to his family. He had departed Hobart Town on board the *Fortitude* for the south seas whaling grounds on 8 May 1844, again with his brother James employed on board, by now as a boat steerer.[3] Having only arrived back in port on 15 April, it was another quick turnaround for Charles, the vessel and its crew.

Birth registration of Charles and Eliza Bayley's daughter Jane Mary, 13 July 1844.
Tasmanian Archives (RGD33/1/2 no. 407).

The *Fortitude* once more travelled to the coastal waters off the South Island of New Zealand, by July noted to be in Akaroa with a catch of nine whales, though it had lost one of its anchors.[4] Remaining in west coast waters, by early August it was noted to have 80 tuns of black whale oil on board.[5] A few weeks later, the vessel was reported to be at Port Cooper (now Lyttelton).[6] After six months at sea the *Fortitude* had amassed 750 barrels of black whale oil in its holds; the search for the more lucrative sperm whale proving not as successful.[7]

After nine months away the *Fortitude* arrived back in Hobart Town on 22 February 1845 with 130 tuns of black whale oil, 20 tuns of sperm whale oil and six tons of whale bone.[8] By this point in time Charles Bayley's infant daughter Jane Mary was seven months of age. He had missed the bulk of her infancy in pursuit of a living to provide for his family. The lay he received, however, proved beneficial, his eight per cent equating to a share of around £400.

In contrast to his previous furloughs, whereby Charles Bayley spent limited amounts of time in Hobart Town with his family, he did not embark on another whaling voyage to the south seas until 2 May, meaning that he spent a solid 2½ months with his wife and daughter.[9] Clearing the River Derwent as winter neared, the *Fortitude* once more sailed for New Zealand's South Island in

---

[3] *The True Colonist Van Diemen's Land Political Despatch, and Agricultural and Commercial ...* , 10 May 1844; Tasmanian Archives (MB2/26/1/139 p776).
[4] *New Zealand Gazette and Wellington Spectator*, 7 August 1844.
[5] *The Cornwall Chronicle*, 28 September 1844.
[6] *Colonial Times*, 12 October 1844.
[7] *The Courier*, 15 October 1844.
[8] *Colonial Times*, 25 February 1845; *The Courier*, 1 March 1845.
[9] *Hobart Town Advertiser*, 6 May 1845.

search of whales. It was a dangerous occupation but one that had obviously treated Charles Bayley well to date. Still, how long could he continue to risk his life, his crew and his vessel chasing these massive animals that were becoming scarcer and scarcer, leading the search to take place in colder and more treacherous waters off the southern coasts of New Zealand and Van Diemen's Land. He persevered.

After nearly three months at sea the *Fortitude* was noted to have 33 tuns of black whale oil on board and seven tuns of sperm whale oil, all taken in New Zealand waters.[1] Two months later the vessel was reported at Jervis Bay on the New South Wales coast with 480 barrels of black whale oil on board and 60 barrels of sperm whale oil.[2] Again absent from home during the Christmas and New Year period, it was not until 15 March 1846 that the *Fortitude* sailed up the River Derwent.[3] After 10 months at sea, its cargo comprised 60 tuns of sperm whale oil, 60 tuns of black whale oil and two tons of whale bone.[4] Charles Bayley used his share of the lay wisely, becoming a quarter-owner of the *Fortitude*, the vessel he had commanded since January 1843.[5] This investment not only secured his interest in the barque but also his share of the owner's lay from future voyages.

Crew of the Fortitude that departed Hobart Town on 17 April 1846. Tasmanian Archives (CUS36/1/222).

On 20 April 1846, just over a month later, the *Fortitude* once more departed Hobart Town en route to the whaling grounds.[6] While Charles Bayley remained at the helm of the vessel, not on board was his younger brother James who had left Hobart Town to sail back to London with the goal of gaining his mate's certificate; the process of obtaining one now becoming more formalised and rigorous than in previous decades. James likely sailed as a crew member on one of several merchant vessels leaving Van Diemen's Land for London in April 1846, including the *North Briton* which sailed for London on 1 April with an 'R. Bailey' listed as able seaman, possibly a data entry error with regards to his name.[7]

[1] *Colonial Times*, 2 September 1845.
[2] *Launceston Examiner*, 1 November 1845.
[3] *Colonial Times*, 17 March 1846.
[4] *The Hobart Town Advertiser*, 20 March 1846.
[5] R. Richards (2014). *Captain Charles Bayley: Whaling Master 1813-1875*.
[6] *Colonial Times*, 21 April 1846.
[7] Tasmanian Archives (CUS36/1/397).

After a voyage of around four months James Bayley would have arrived back in England in late August or early September 1846. He then very likely made his way to Burnham-on-Crouch, reuniting with his family.

With his previous merchant seaman papers voided due to his name change, James Bayley then applied for a new registration ticket, receiving it in London on 5 October 1846. Three days later he cleared out of the River Thames as second mate on board the barque *Pacific* under the command of Captain Robert Gardiner, once more headed for Hobart Town. Of note, Charles and James Bayley's youngest sister Harriet was also on board.

Harriet Bull, now assuming the surname of Bayley, was 18 years old when the barque *Pacific* anchored in Hobart Town on 13 January 1847.[8] She had journeyed on board the vessel

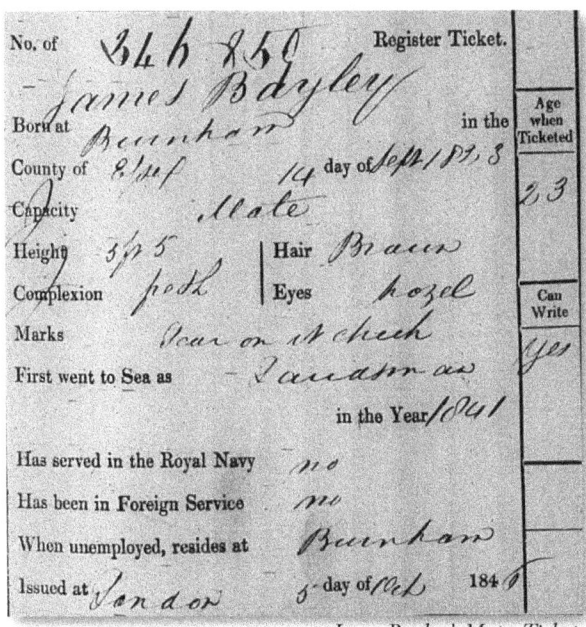

James Bayley's Mates Ticket.
Britain, Merchant Seamen, 1835-1857.

as a passenger while her older brother James had worked his way as one of 30 members of the crew. It was likely that James had helped pay the fare for the voyage, encouraging her to make the 10,000-mile journey with the promise of a better life buoyed by his and Charles' new-found success. Despite its hazards the whaling industry had been more than kind to Charles in particular, and he had accumulated a great deal of wealth since he first became captain of the *Wallaby* in 1839. He had also laid down roots in Hobart Town, owning property, including a part-share in the vessel he sailed, as well as marrying and welcoming a daughter. James was looking to emulate this success.

With the inkling of a better life, Harriet had obviously thrashed over the decision. As the last child born to Charles and Mary Bull, both of whom were entering their twilight years, her father by now approaching his mid-60s, Harriet no doubt felt the strain of guilt at leaving them in Burnham-on-Crouch. However, her father remained active, employed in the local oyster industry, and her parents were comfortable, living in a house in Silver Lane within the town centre and close to the river.[9] Both of Harriet's elder sisters, Mary and Emmaretta, were still living in England at the time such that they would have been able to provide some support or care to their parents. Mary's marriage to Stephen Park, more specifically, appears to have ended by the late 1840s such that she seems to have moved back to Essex to be in close proximity to her parents.[10] There is also the likelihood that Charles and James Bayley, despite the distance, would have been providing some financial support to their parents if not by this time then in the future.

With both of his younger siblings about to join him permanently in Hobart Town, Charles Bayley had remained resolute in his pursuit of whales. As stated, the *Fortitude* had left Hobart Town on 20 April 1846 and immediately sailed north along Van Diemen's Lands' east coast. At Spring Bay the vessel had encountered, and its crew subsequently captured, a sperm whale

---

[8] Tasmanian Archives (MB2/39/1/9 p93).
[9] 1851 England, Wales & Scotland Census for Charles and Mary Rogers Bull.
[10] 1851 England, Wales & Scotland Census for Stephen Park.

Arrival manifest for the barque Pacific showing Harriet Bayley (ex Bull) as the passenger 'Miss Baily', 13 January 1847.
Tasmanian Archives (CUS36/1/222).

yielding seven tuns of oil; an unexpected though bountiful prize hoping to be a harbinger for the start of a fortuitous voyage.[1] By early July the *Fortitude* was noted to be in the Banks Peninsula region of New Zealand's South Island with 700 barrels of black whale oil on board, equivalent to 87 tuns.[2] The vessel returned to Hobart Town on 17 October, after six months at sea, with 134 tuns of black whale oil, eight tuns of sperm whale oil and five tons of whale bone.[3] Despite the shorter duration, the voyage had been well worth the effort, the cargo worth around £6,000, with Charles Bayley's share of the lay and as a part-owner estimated to be well over £500.[4]

For once in port during the latter months of the year, Charles Bayley joined the committee tasked with organising the Tasmanian Anniversary Regatta, to be held on 1 December 1846.[5] By now considered the highlight of the colony's social and sporting calendar, the regatta had first been held in 1838, notably with Lieutenant-Governor Sir John Franklin as patron. Since that time the event had grown into a full-day holiday with most of Hobart Town's population of 15,000 people attending to enjoy the whaleboat and sailing races, place shore-side bets, partake in the sideshow alley and other entertainments, and consume food and beverages offered for sale by local hoteliers. For the crews of whaling vessels at the time in port, the draw of participating in the whaleboat races was insurmountable with prizes, authorised and unauthorised gambling prominent and, of course, bragging rights. Crews regularly practised in the weeks leading up to the races, hoping to improve

---

[1] *Colonial Times*, 28 April 1846.
[2] *Colonial Times*, 25 September 1846.
[3] *The Hobart Town Advertiser*, 20 October 1846.
[4] R. Richards (2014). *Captain Charles Bayley: Whaling Master 1813-1875*.
[5] *Colonial Times*, 20 October 1846; *The Courier*, 21 October 1846.

fitness, team work and tactics, as well as become familiar with the sporadic and testy conditions of the River Derwent. Unfortunately for Charles Bayley and the crew of his vessel *Fortitude*, they were not in town to participate in the event. After only 20 days in port, they once again departed Hobart Town, sailing for the whaling grounds on 5 November.[6]

It is obviously not known what Charles' wife Eliza thought of the long stretches of time her husband spent at sea. While the money he was generating would have been more than welcome, it came with significant downsides. Charles had missed the bulk of their daughter's childhood to date (Jane Mary was by now 28 months of age). It also meant that the couple had only minimal opportunity to expand their family.

Family, however, was extremely important to Charles Bayley and he would have been disappointed to have forgone spending the Christmas and New Year period with his wife and daughter, as well as with Eliza's parents James and Jean Inglis. Charles also would have been dismayed to have missed the arrival of the barque *Pacific* on 13 January 1847, carrying his brother James and sister Harriet to Hobart Town.[7]

Having not been born when Charles Bayley first went to sea in the local Suffolk and Essex coastal trades, and subsequently sailed for Van Diemen's Land a few years later, Harriet Bayley would have spent very little time with her eldest brother; the 15-year age gap and distance resulting in a personal relationship barrier for them, with the only communication pathway available being long-distance letters. In contrast, James Bayley was much closer to Harriet in age, being five years her senior, and the pair had grown up together in Burnham-on-Crouch as the last two siblings born to Charles and Mary Bull. It was thus likely with reserved apprehension that Harriet disembarked from Hobart Town expecting to be reunited with the brother whom she barely knew and possibly did not remember, as well as meet his wife Eliza and daughter Jane Mary. Harriet would not have known that Charles was away at sea again and not expected back for many months. Their reunion would have to wait. Still, she likely found solace in the company of her sister-in-law and niece, enjoying female company and the enthusiasm and wonderment of a toddler.

Harriet Bayley no doubt moved in with Eliza and Jane Mary at their home in Kelly Street, perched on the hill above the New Wharf precinct. The weeks immediately following her arrival were likely spent experiencing the summer months of Hobart Town and becoming familiar with its sights, sounds and routines, as well as being introduced to various friends and associates of her two brothers and sister-in-law. In contrast, James Bayley remained employed as second mate on board the 360-ton barque *Pacific*, which was owned by Charles Seal, a local merchant and shipowner.[8] After unloading the stores and cargo it had brought from England, the vessel was fitted out as a whaler. The *Pacific* left Hobart Town for the south seas whaling grounds on 25 February 1847.[9]

In the weeks prior, however, news began trickling into Hobart Town with regards to a dreadful accident that had occurred on board the *Fortitude* on 5 December 1846 while it was sailing off the Southern Island of New Zealand.[10] The information relayed in the press, and also undoubtedly received via private mail, would have been of grave concern to all of Charles Bayley's family and friends; the dangers of whaling no less evident than in the details provided.

---

[6] *Colonial Times*, 10 November 1846.
[7] *Colonial Times*, 15 January 1847.
[8] *The Hobart Town Advertiser*, 15 January 1847; Tasmanian Archives (MB2/26/1/139 p776).
[9] *Colonial Times*, 2 March 1847.
[10] R. Richards (2014). *Captain Charles Bayley: Whaling Master 1813-1875*.

View of the Port of Hobart Town (1841).
Lithograph by Auguste Etienne Francois Mayer and Guiaud Le Breton.
National Library of Australia (nla.obj-135887131).

On 9 February 1847 *The Hobart Town Advertiser* reported the news. 'By the arrival of the *Young Eagle*, Captain Lathropp, we have been put in possession of the particulars of a melancholy accident that occurred a short time since at the whaling grounds. Two boats, belonging to the *Fortitude*, were fast to a whale, and Captain Bayly [sic], with his boat, was close at hand. It being near dark, he gave directions to the two boats to tow the whale to the ship, saying he would return at once. He then hoisted a sail in his boat and started for the ship. On the return of the two boats to the vessel, it was found that Captain Bayly [sic] had not returned on board, and they became very much alarmed, and hove-to during the night. At daylight next morning a boat was discovered bottom upwards and some body clinging to her, about two miles to wind ward of the vessel. A boat was instantly sent to the relief and it was discovered to be Captain Bayly [sic]. The boat was capsize shortly after hoisting the sail and all the crew got on the bottom of the boat. Capt. Bayly [sic] fortunately got his finger in the plug hole of the boat, and its swelling prevented him drawing it out, and when he became too much exhausted to hold on any longer his finger kept him until taken off the next morning. The rest of the crew, we regret to state, were all washed off the boat and drowned. Captain Bayly [sic] was taken off senseless and his hands and legs were much lacerated, but he is in a fair way of recovering.'[1]

The five crew members that sadly drowned during this incident were James Angus, John Stacey, George Rogers, Henry Marriett and Ahiou, the latter a Solomon Islander who had first

---

[1] *The Hobart Town Advertiser*, 9 February 1847.

shipped on board the *Wallaby* with Charles Bayley at the helm in September 1841.[2] Ironically all five men could swim, it was Charles who could not.

According to the vessel's logbook entry for 7 December 1846, i.e., two days after the tragedy, Charles Bayley remained in a *'very bad'* state such that the crew sailed the *Fortitude* to Port William on Stewart Island off the bottom of New Zealand's South Island, the closest town they could likely procure medical assistance, as well as take on more crew members.[3] Fortunately en route they came in company with the American whaler *Factor* which had a doctor on board that was able to minister to Charles.[4] As the days passed he slowly recovered and within a few weeks was back in the boats chasing whales.

The *Fortitude*'s run of bad luck did not end there, however. Remaining in New Zealand's far south waters, a crewman by the name of James Campbell died in March 1847. Later that month five members of the crew were struck by lightning, with the logbook noting that a few of the men were *'very bad for several hours'*.[5] Given all that had occurred, the *Fortitude* and its crew then limped their way back to Hobart Town, reaching the River Derwent on 1 July 1847 with only 12 tuns of sperm whale oil in its holds.[6] The voyage's logbook ended with the epitaph, '*So ends a bad voyage, and put the ship in the hospital*'.[7]

The barque Fortitude.
Maritime Museum of Tasmania (PGSL149).

---
[2] R. Richards (2014). *Captain Charles Bayley: Whaling Master 1813-1875.*
[3] R. Richards (2014). *Captain Charles Bayley: Whaling Master 1813-1875.*
[4] R. Richards (2014). *Captain Charles Bayley: Whaling Master 1813-1875.*
[5] R. Richards (2014). *Captain Charles Bayley: Whaling Master 1813-1875.*
[6] *Colonial Times*, 2 July 1847.
[7] R. Richards (2014). *Captain Charles Bayley: Whaling Master 1813-1875.*

It was thus no doubt with absolute relief that Charles Bayley disembarked from the *Fortitude* at Hobart Town on 1 July 1847. It had not been the voyage he expected; he had lost six men, nearly lost his own life, and the cargo on board, worth little more than £1,000, would not have generated enough funds to make the journey a profit. He would have to swallow the loss, the first time this hard luck had befallen him in over a decade spent whaling.

There were more surprises in store. While Charles Bayley would have been stunned to find out that his youngest sister Harriet had arrived in Van Diemen's Land just under six months prior with their brother James, and that James had subsequently departed on board the *Pacific* for the whaling grounds, he would have perhaps been equally startled to have missed Harriet's wedding to Alexander McGregor (discussed in more detail in the next chapter), which had only taken place a week prior. Then there was the sight of his wife Eliza holding a three-month-old baby, perhaps a rather awkward experience since, if Charles was able to calculate correctly, he would have been away on a previous voyage when the child was conceived.

Regardless of progeny, the birth of Eliza Bayley (Jr) at the couple's Kelly Street home was registered on 26 May 1846, a month after her birth on 27 April. Once again Eliza's father James Inglis was the informant. Social norms would have dictated that Charles Bayley acknowledge the child as his, which he duly did.

Birth registration of Charles and Eliza Bayley's daughter Eliza, 27 April 1847.
Tasmanian Archives (RGD33/1/3 no. 7).

Marriage registration of Alexander McGregor and Harriet Bayley, 24 June 1847.
Tasmanian Archives (RGD37/1/6 no. 1003).

Births, Deaths & Marriages

*I*t cannot be mere coincidence that Hobart Town's *Colonial Times* of 22 June 1847 reported that the *Fortitude* had '*put into one of the bays down the river*' and two days later Harriet Bayley married Alexander McGregor. Instead of waiting for her eldest brother to arrive back in port, a matter of only a few more days, the couple were married by licence (as opposed to banns) at Charles and Eliza Bayley's Kelly Street home. Witnesses were James Inglis, Eliza Bayley's father, and John Gibson McGregor, Alexander's youngest brother.[1]

Did Harriet and Alexander assume that Charles Bayley would not approve of their union; was the wedding pre-planned and the loved-up couple intent on not delaying the ceremony any further; was Harriet eager to escape the Kelly Street house where her brother and sister-in-law lived, possibly because of the new baby; or was Harriet looking to withdraw herself from her brother's guardianship, seeking respite in an alternative situation as a married woman. The answer to any of these questions is of course not known. There are no private letters nor journals that survive from this period to suggest a motive, nor would there have been any evidence or a paper trail remaining in existence to explain the situation. This was the start of Victorian-era England and any family scandals would have been quietly and discretly masked. Of course, a fiction writer might surmise that the baby born in late April 1847 and registered to Charles and Eliza Bayley was actually Harriet's, that she had left England three months pregnant in October 1846 and that her sister-in-law Eliza had covered up the deed to make the baby legitimate knowing full well that Charles was away at the time of possible conception, though would claim it as his own.

Regardless of the backstory, 19-year-old Harriet Bayley married Alexander McGregor on 24 June 1847. A 26-year-old shipwright from a working-class family, Alexander had been born in the textile manufacturing town of Paisley, Scotland, in 1821, the eldest child of James and Janet McGregor (nee Smith).[2] He had arrived in Hobart Town on 28 February 1831 per the 293-ton ship *Drummore* from Leith as a steerage passenger with his parents, younger brother James and younger sisters Jean and Agnes.[3] Another brother, John Gibson McGregor, had been born at sea after the vessel departed Scotland and was baptised at the Cape of Good Hope in November 1830.[4]

A carpenter by trade, James McGregor had initially established his family in Collins Street, Hobart Town, where on 25 January 1834 his six-year-old daughter Agnes sadly passed away.[5] A

---

[1] Tasmanian Archives (RGD37/1/6 no. 1003).
[2] Select Counties, Scotland, Church of Scotland, Marriages, 1615-1854 for James McGregor and Janet Smith.
[3] Tasmanian Archives (CUS30/1/1 p36); *Colonial Times*, 1 March 1831.
[4] South Africa, Birth and Baptism Records, 1700s-1900s for John Gibson McGregor.
[5] Tasmanian Archives (RGD34/1/1 no. 3622); *The True Colonist Van Diemen's Land Political Despatch, and Agricultural and Commercial ...* , 20 December 1836.

daughter named Elizabeth was born to James and Janet McGregor a year later, and a son named Thomas Joseph had been born a few years prior, though their births appear not to have been registered since it was not a legal requirement until 1837.[1] However, the McGregor family suffered another tragedy on 27 December 1836 when its patriarch and provider James drowned in the River Derwent while crossing to Kangaroo Point on board a ferry. The mishap was the result of a blast of hot wind, referred to in the press as a tornado, that though brief caused a great deal of destruction in Hobart Town, including destroying several chimneys and roofs, downing trees, as well as destroying the verandah of the military hospital. With regards to the drowning in particular, the press reported the following details. *'We are sorry to have to record the loss of one of the ferry boats going to Kangaroo Point, with Mr. John Macdonald and four other persons on board. The boat was seen a few moments before the squall came on, but she did not appear when it cleared away. One of the thwarts, an oar, and a board with the name of the boat on, and the hats of some of the persons on board, are the only traces of their fate that have yet been discovered. The sufferers are Mr. John Macdonald of the Golden Fleece Inn, whose wife has thus become a widow the second time from the same cause – her first husband Mr. A. Buchanan having been drowned crossing this ferry; Mr. McGregor, a carpenter, who has left a large family of helpless children; and two boatmen; besides a gentleman who is supposed to have been in the boat, but this is uncertain; nor can we discover the name of the gentleman supposed to have been aboard.'*[2]

With his father's death, 15-year-old Alexander McGregor was forced to help support his family, thankfully already undertaking an apprenticeship at a Battery Point shipyard owned by John Watson.[3] It was to be a pivotal experience for him, and his youngest brother John in years to come, guiding their professional careers for the next several decades.

First established at Battery Point in 1839 along the Napoleon Street corridor on land originally part of Lieutenant-Governor William Sorell's 90-acre property, and bordering the River Derwent, John Watson's shipyard by the mid-1840s had grown into a large operation not only undertaking repair, refit and overhaul work of commercial vessels involved in the whaling industry as well as intercolonial and international trades, but also building several schooners and barques for enterprising local merchants to ply these trades. By the time of his marriage to Harriet Bayley in June 1847, Alexander McGregor had completed his apprenticeship and gained several promotions. The shipyard was also in the process of building two vessels: the 144-ton barque *Fair Tasmanian* and the 95-ton schooner *Circassian;* the former intended for the Port Albert to New Zealand cattle trade, while the latter was for the Port Phillip Bay trade.

Following their marriage Harriet undoubtedly moved in with Alexander, his mother Janet, and his three brothers and youngest sister (his eldest sister Jean was married by this time) who still remained in Collins Street, possibly living in a cottage rented from William Champion as detailed in the 1842 Census for Hobart Town.[4] As stated, Harriet's brother Charles Bayley returned from his disastrous whaling voyage a week after the couple's marriage. He would have thus been somewhat shocked to not only discover his sister had immigrated to Van Diemen's Land from England during his absence, but that she had also married. However, given Alexander McGregor's family background, professional experience and respectability, he would have been considered a suitable match for Harriet with or without Charles' approval.

---

[1] Tasmanian Archives (RGD37/1/16 no. 373, RDG3/1/1 p47, RGD33/1/6 no. 385).
[2] *The True Colonist Van Diemen's Land Political Despatch, and Agricultural and Commercial ...* , 30 December 1836.
[3] *The Mercury,* 18 March 1887.
[4] Tasmanian Archives (CEN1/1/13).

As also stated, there was additionally the matter of Charles and Eliza Bayley's new baby daughter Eliza (Jr), by now approaching three months of age. And of course there was the perilous state of Charles himself. He had barely survived his most recent voyage and had lost many men through drownings and sickness. There was a great deal to process.

Moreover, financial issues came to bear when the cargo of the *Fortitude* was priced. Having only been able to procure 12 tuns of sperm whale oil, the voyage would have generated a loss in the realm of £600, with Charles Bayley and his co-owner Askin Morrison required to cover the debt in order to pay off the crew and other creditors.[5]

Unusually, Charles Bayley and the crew of the *Fortitude* spent the next four months in port. It was the longest stint that Charles had spent at home during his career so far. Had this sabbatical been at his request, needing to adjust to new family circumstances, or was it due to the disastrous voyage and near-death experience they had all endured during the last voyage? Crew may have also been hard to source; another voyage so quickly after the last that had resulted in a paltry lay for the men not being a great inducement or endorsement for further trips.

Regardless of the reason, by early November 1847 Charles was readying the *Fortitude* for another voyage, though still found time to volunteer on the committee for the upcoming Hobart Town Anniversary Regatta.[6] He was also making plans. On 17 November he purchased more land at Battery Point, this time a small parcel of 26 perches, i.e., around one-sixth of an acre, located on South Street but strategically backing on to his existing property in Kelly Street.[7] Paying £58 for the allotment, the transaction was likely handled with utmost urgency as later that day Charles sailed from Hobart Town as captain of the *Fortitude*, once more headed for the south seas in search of whales.[8] Ironically his brother James had only arrived back in town a few days prior. On 12 November 1847 the *Pacific* had returned to Hobart Town after a nine-month voyage.[9] Its cargo comprised 65 tuns of sperm whale oil, 34 tuns of black whale oil and 1½ tons of bone.[10] The vessel remained in port for less than a month, sailing out of the River Derwent on 6 December 1847 on another whaling voyage with James

Map showing location of Charles Bayley's Kelly and South Street properties.
Google Earth (2025).

---

[5] R. Richards (2014). *Captain Charles Bayley: Whaling Master 1813-1875*.
[6] *The Britannia and Trades' Advocate*, 11 November 1847.
[7] Tasmanian Archives (AG193/1/60/433).
[8] *The Courier*, 20 November 1847.
[9] *The Hobart Town Advertiser*, 16 November 1847.
[10] Tasmanian Archives (CUS30/1/1 p36).

Bayley again on board.[1] Echoing his brother's work ethic and steady bravado, James was certainly on his way to building his own financial portfolio.

With all of the comings and goings, Harriet was likely relieved her new husband Alexander McGregor remained on firm ground, working at a shipyard only a 15-minute walk from their home. With the departure of her two brothers, however, there was still much going on. A period of bereavement would have been initiated following the death of baby Eliza Bayley from dysentery on 26 December 1847, just one day shy of turning eight months old.

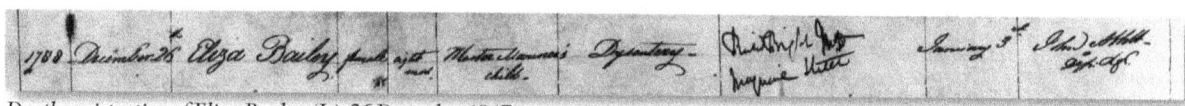

Death registration of Eliza Bayley (Jr), 26 December 1847.
Tasmanian Archives (RGD35/1/2 no. 1788).

Dysentery, i.e., inflammation of the bowel or intestine resulting in diarrhoea and dehydration in young children and babies, often leading to death, was primarily caused through the consumption of food or water that had been contaminated with bacteria or parasites. It was one of several leading causes of infant mortality in Van Diemen's Land at the time, due to lack of adequate clean water supplies and sewerage infrastructure; others being fevers and convulsions likely brought on by teething, as well as scarlet fever and typhoid.

It is not known how soon Charles Bayley would have received the news of his baby daughter's death. Though he had departed Hobart Town in mid-November 1847, the *Fortitude* had not immediately sailed for the southern waters of New Zealand. Instead, Charles had navigated his vessel north along Van Diemen's Lands' east coast into Bass Strait hopeful that the warmer summer temperatures would be a draw for the whales. Seeing some success, on 4 January 1848 the *Fortitude* was noted to be in Spring Bay with 10 tuns of whale oil on board.[2] It then returned to the fiordland region of New Zealand in search of sperm whales.[3] By late June 1848, however, after seven months at sea, the *Fortitude* arrived back in Spring Bay on Van Diemen's Lands' east coast where it took on wood and water before sailing to Bass Strait and the whaling grounds off Kangaroo Island.[4] It was an additional six months before the vessel returned to Hobart Town, via Recherche Bay, its arrival in port on 28 December marking the end of another long voyage that saw Charles Bayley and his crew at sea for over 13 months.[5] Despite its length, thankfully this voyage had been relatively benign in terms of major incidents and accidents. It was also lucrative. The *Fortitude* arrived back in Hobart Town with 60 tuns of sperm whale oil on board and one tun of black whale oil, valued at around £5,200, realising a handsome profit for Charles in terms of both his lay and owner's share.[6]

The years 1849 and 1850 were rather uneventful for both the Bayley and McGregor families in terms of personal news. There are no births, deaths or marriages to report, nor are there any real estate transactions. In terms of professional accomplishments, however, there are several. First, after a month in port the *Fortitude* departed Hobart Town for the south seas whaling grounds on 30 January 1849. Not on board was Charles Bayley who had relinquished the helm of the vessel

---

[1] *Colonial Times*, 7 December 1847.
[2] *The Hobart Town Advertiser*, 18 January 1848.
[3] R. Richards (2014). *Captain Charles Bayley: Whaling Master 1813-1875*.
[4] *The Hobart Town Courier*, 30 June 1848; R. Richards (2014). *Captain Charles Bayley: Whaling Master 1813-1875*.
[5] *The Hobart Town Advertiser*, 21 November 1848; *Colonial Times*, 29 December 1848.
[6] *Colonial Times*, 29 December 1848; R. Richards (2014). *Captain Charles Bayley: Whaling Master 1813-1875*.

Barque Runnymede.
Tasmanian Archives (PH30/1/997).

to Robert Sanderson after seven consecutive voyages.[7] Instead, Charles remained in Hobart Town overseeing the final touches to his new vessel, of which he owned a quarter share.

On 20 March 1849 the *Colonial Times* published the details of the auspicious launch event. 'SHIP LAUNCH — *To-morrow afternoon, between 3 and 4 o'clock, a vessel of 320 tons will be launched from the yard of Mr. John Watson, Battery Point, belonging to Askin Morrison, Esq., New Wharf, and Captain Bailey [sic], of the ship Fortitude.*' Three days later came the outcome. 'SHIP LAUNCH — *On Wednesday afternoon, the Runnymede, a new barque, was launched from the ship-building yard of Mr. Watson, at Battery Point; she is the property of A. Morrison, Esq., and Captain Bailey [sic]. Upon leaving the stocks to her future element, she was christened by Mrs. Bailey [sic], who was surrounded (the weather being very fine) by a great number of ladies. Mr. Watson, with his usual liberality, regaled his friends in a capacious tent, which was elegantly fitted up for the occasion.*'[8]

Given the *Runnymede* was built at John Watson's yard, one can assume that Charles' brother-in-law Alexander McGregor played a large role in securing the contract and also building the vessel. A family affair enjoining both its male and female members, the launch event would have been one filled with pride and a talisman of just how far both the Bayley and McGregor families had come since their collective emigrations to Hobart Town. The local maritime industry was certainly proving favourable for the men stemming from these various branches, whether they be mariners, whalers, shipowners or shipbuilders. Hard work, resilience and dogged determination in particular had seen Charles Bayley transition from the helm of the *Wallaby* to that of the *Fortitude*, in a few short years becoming a part-owner of this vessel as well as the *Runnymede*. Just where would the future lead him, his family and his relatives?

[7] *The Courier*, 31 January 1849.
[8] *Colonial Times*, 23 March 1849.

Built specifically for the whaling industry and likely at a cost of approximately £4,000, the *Runnymede* took several more weeks to complete and then be fitted out. After leaving John Watson's shipyard in early May, it departed Hobart Town on its maiden voyage around a month later with Charles Bayley at the helm.[1] Also on board was his brother James, by now promoted to chief mate.[2] Remarkably, it was the longest period Charles had spent on land since arriving in Van Diemen's Land over a decade prior. During the interim, however, there had been several problems to sort out. There would be more while he was away, including an attempted mutiny on board the *Fortitude* in which he still retained a quarter share. The altercation had taken place in late September 1849 while the vessel was lying off Fortescue Bay on Van Diemen's Lands' Tasman Peninsula and involved 10 of the crew threatening the lives of Captain Robert Sanderson and several of the *Fortitude*'s officers.[3] Managing to retain control of his vessel with the help of local police, Captain Sanderson was able to sail the vessel back to Hobart Town whereby the members of its disruptive crew were handed over to authorities, charged with insubordination and mutinous conduct.[4] In the ensuing court case, the men defended their conduct stating that they had been badly treated on board the vessel, including physically assaulted. However, since the vessel had left Hobart Town several days prior, there were no witnesses left to confirm their side of the story. The men were thus sentenced to 60 days of hard labour.[5]

For Charles Bayley and Askin Morrison, as owners of the *Fortitude*, the entire incident would have been a drain in terms of time, money and resources. The vessel's directive to return to Hobart Town had meant that its voyage plans had changed. Further, though it was not out seeking whales, it was still using up stores and other supplies, resulting in the loss of hundreds and hundreds of pounds. There was also the need to find and contract new crew members to furnish the rest of the voyage, as well as embed a better system of hierarchy on board, specifically one that all crew members would adhere to without the need for abuse or rebellion.

After a chaotic voyage of just over 12 months, the *Fortitude* returned to Hobart Town in early February 1850 with only 27 tuns of sperm oil on board, likely generating just enough income to break even or make a small profit.[6] Less than three weeks later the barque left port on another whaling voyage, once more with Robert Sanderson at the helm; Askin Morrison (no doubt also acting on Charles Bayley's behalf) keen to limit the vessel's time in port and maximise its capacity to generate additional revenue.[7]

On 6 March 1850 the *Runnymede* returned to Hobart Town from its maiden voyage to the south seas. After nine months, the vessel had accumulated 70 tuns of sperm whale oil.[8] Though Charles Bayley now had two vessels with which he could generate income, the price of sperm and black whale oil, as well as whale bone, had remained relatively steady over the years, if not decreased slightly, with sperm whale oil obtaining around £80 per tun, black whale oil £25 per tun and whale bone £140 per ton.[9] The *Runnymede*'s maiden voyage alone therefore produced a potential profit of around £500 for Charles Bayley personally.[10]

---

[1] *The Courier*, 9 May 1849.
[2] Tasmanian Archives (MB2/26/1/139 p776).
[3] *Colonial Times*, 28 September 1849.
[4] *Hobart Guardian, or, True Friend of Tasmania*, 29 September 1849; *The Courier*, 3 October 1849.
[5] *Hobart Guardian, or, True Friend of Tasmania*, 6 October 1849.
[6] *Colonial Times*, 8 February 1850.
[7] *Colonial Times*, 26 February 1850.
[8] *Colonial Times*, 8 March 1850.
[9] *Colonial Times*, 16 February, 5 June 1849.
[10] R. Richards (2014). *Captain Charles Bayley: Whaling Master 1813-1875*.

After six weeks in port the *Runnymede* once more cleared out for the southern whaling grounds on 17 April 1850.[11] After a brief stint hunting in waters off New Zealand, Charles Bayley sailed the vessel to Kangaroo Island where it was noted in late June with four tuns of sperm whale oil on board.[12] It later sailed to the Chatham Islands region off New Zealand's west coast.[13] After a total of 14 months at sea, the *Runnymede* returned to Hobart Town on 15 June 1851.[14] Its cargo comprised 60 tuns of sperm whale oil, 50 tuns of black whale oil and 1½ tons of whalebone, with a combined value of £5,400.[15] Meanwhile the *Fortitude* had also sailed back into port, after nine months at sea, carrying 12 tuns of black whale oil, 22 tuns of sperm whale oil and 3 hundredweight of bone, worth approximately £1,800, and then cleared the River Derwent on 16 January 1851 en route to the whaling grounds, this time in the northern hemisphere.[16] This directive may have been because of a fluctuating local market for the product; need for the commodity becoming somewhat saturated with more than 20 commercial whaling vessels by now operating out of the Port of Hobart Town alone.[17] The price of sperm whale oil had also reduced even further, to £65 per tun, while black whale oil was being sold for £25 per tun and whale bone was valued at £150 per ton.[18]

The early 1850s were generally quiet though industrious years for both the Bayley and McGregor families. While Eliza Bayley had endured the death of her father James in September 1850 at the age of 64 from '*decay of nature*' and would lose her mother Jane in November 1854, also at the age of 64 from '*debility*', whom her husband Charles had both supported in old age, he continued the hard slog on board the *Runnymede,* the wealth he was generating ensuring that Eliza and their daughter Jane Mary were well cared for.[19] James Bayley was also mostly away at sea during this period, from July 1851 promoted to master of the 230-ton whaling barque *Flying Childers* which had recently been purchased by Askin Morrison.[20] The vessel had been built at John Watson's Battery Point shipyard at a cost of £4,000 and launched in late 1846.[21]

As for Alexander and Harriet McGregor, they also remained quietly resourceful with Alexander continuing to work for John Watson whom by now operated three shipyards: two at Battery Point and one at Middleton in the D'Entrecasteaux Channel. The couple had also moved into a home in Hampden Road, Battery Point, in close proximity to not only Alexander's place of work but also Charles and Eliza Bayley's home.[22] Alexander McGregor was increasingly becoming involved in local politics, showing his support for various candidates in City of Hobart municipal elections.[23]

Reunions when both of the Bayley brothers were in port, however, had been limited up until this period. Nonetheless, their presence together in Hobart Town did coincide in June and July 1851 with Charles and James appearing to formulate a plan to sail their respective vessels in company with one another during their next voyage. With James at the helm of the *Flying Childers*, he sailed his barque down the River Derwent on 19 July followed two days later by Charles on

---

[11] *The Britannia and Trades' Advocate*, 18 April 1850.
[12] *Launceston Examiner*, 10 July 1850.
[13] *The Hobart Town Advertiser*, 7 March 1851.
[14] *Colonial Times*, 17 June 1851.
[15] *Colonial Times*, 17 June 1851.
[16] *The Courier*, 7 December 1850; *Hobarton Guardian, or, True Friend of Tasmania*, 18 January 1851; *The Hobart Town Advertiser*, 18 February 1851.
[17] *The Hobart Town Advertiser*, 18 February 1851.
[18] *The Hobart Town Advertiser*, 18 February 1851.
[19] Tasmanian Archives (RGD35/1/3 no. 290, RGD35/1/4 no. 1555, SC195/1/36 Inquest 3437).
[20] *The Hobart Town Advertiser*, 25 April 1851; *The Tasmanian Colonist*, 21 July 1851.
[21] *Colonial Times*, 15, 18 December 1846.
[22] *Colonial Times*, 2 September 1851.
[23] *Colonial Times*, 7 October 1851.

Barque Flying Childers.
State Library of South Australia (PRG 1373/40/1).

board the *Runnymede*.[1] The vessels sailed towards the southern seas off mainland Australia, as well as the remote waters to the south and east of Kangaroo Island.[2]

The *Flying Childers*, under the management of James Bayley, returned to Hobart Town on 25 November 1851 after a four-month stint at sea during which time it had accumulated 42 tuns of sperm whale oil, valued at £2,700; crew insubordination being one of the primary reasons for its early homecoming.[3] Just under a month later, on 20 December, the *Runnymede* also returned to Hobart Town managing to accumulate 62 tuns of sperm whale oil during its five-month cruise, valued at £4,100.[4] A week later, the *Flying Childers* with James Bayley at the helm left port on another whaling voyage, this time sailing to New Zealand waters.[5]

Charles Bayley spent most of the month of January 1852 at home with his family. Several members of his crew also enjoyed the land-based reprieve, successfully winning the five-oared whaleboat race at the Hobart Town Regatta.[6] After a month in port, however, the *Runnymede* sailed out of the River Derwent on 18 January 1852 in search of whales. On board were 36 crew members, including chief mate James McGregor, brother of Alexander McGregor, and several passengers, most notably Charles' wife Eliza.[7] No doubt wanting to spend more time together, embarking on a long, isolating and potentially dangerous whaling voyage was an interesting choice

---

[1] *The Courier*, 23 July 1851.
[2] *The Tasmanian Colonist*, 7 August 1851; *The Courier*, 25 October 1851.
[3] *The Courier*, 26 November 1851; *The Hobart Town Advertiser*, 28 November 1851.
[4] *The Hobart Town Advertiser*, 23 December 1851.
[5] *The Hobart Town Advertiser*, 30 December 1851.
[6] *The Courier*, 7 January 1851.
[7] *The Hobart Town Advertiser*, 20 January 1852; Tasmanian Archives (CUS36/1/458 p1).

for the wife of a master mariner to make. Not willing to risk their entire family, the couple's eight-year-old daughter Jane Mary had remained in port, in all likelihood staying with Harriet McGregor and her husband Alexander.

On 28 February 1852 the barque *Fortitude* returned to Hobart Town after a long voyage of 13 months encompassing the Bering Strait, separating Russia and present-day Alaska.[8] It had been an unusual decision for Charles Bayley and his co-owner Askin Morrison to send the vessel so far into the northern hemisphere, some 8,000 miles from home, particularly since the presence of large numbers of bowhead whales in this locality, a species that is found exclusively in Arctic and Subarctic waters, had only recently been identified. While the crew of the *Fortitude* failed to procure any of these animals, its voyage was still somewhat successful; the craft's cargo comprising 35 tuns of black whale oil, 28 tuns of sperm whale oil and three tons of whale bone, having a combined value of just over £3,000.[9]

Whales, however, were becoming more and more difficult to source and secure, their worldwide populations by now under threat by the large numbers of whalers in search of them over several decades. The industry was also very slowly being superseded by the increasing availability of petroleum which could be used to fuel oil lamps and street lights, up until this point in time two of

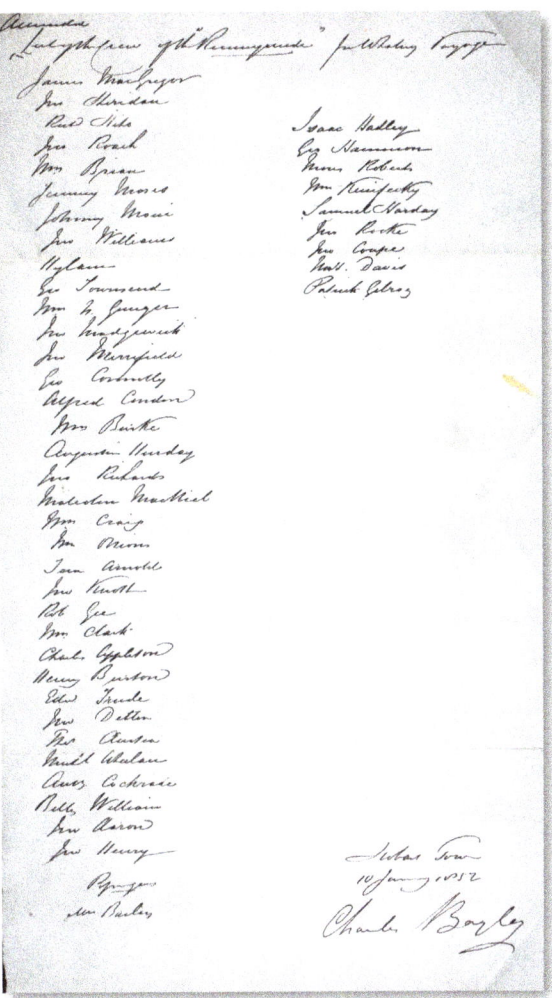

Runnymede manifest, 18 January 1852.
Tasmanian Archives (CUS36/1/458 p1).

the major uses of whale oil. The first petroleum refinery had been established in the United States in 1850, producing kerosene from crude oil. Many more refineries would come on line in the years that immediately followed. Meanwhile oil shale deposits had been found in New South Wales in the 1850s leading to the establishment of a new industry as extraction of the product took place.

Crew to furnish commercial whaling vessels were additionally becoming harder to find; the continued willingness of labouring mariners of lower ranks and pay schedules to spend months at sea in often dangerous working conditions becoming less than ideal, particularly when new avenues of employment were becoming established, including industrialised factories and mechanical trades. There was another diversion in play too, particularly for Australia's sea-going workforce: gold mining. The prized metal had first been found in California in 1848 leading to a worldwide influx of goldseekers to this area, including hundreds and hundreds of men (and sometimes their families) from Van Diemen's Land. Dozens of commercial vessels are reported to have sailed

---

[8] *Colonial Times*, 2 March 1852.
[9] *Colonial Times*, 2 March 1852; *The Hobart Town Advertiser*, 2 March 1852.

from Hobart Town to San Fransisco coinciding with the gold rush, carrying on board passengers hopeful of striking it rich in the goldfields, while speculative merchants had also loaded vessels filled with supplies needed to build temporary towns and infrastructure to accommodate the large influx of new arrivals. However, often the vessels were forced to remain in San Fransisco harbour, many of the crew deserting their ship in lieu of the return voyage to also try their luck in the fields. The owners of commercial whaling ships were heavily impacted by this burgeoning threat to their employees, including shipowners Charles Bayley and his partner Askin Morrison. Perhaps more worrying was the discovery of gold in Victoria in 1851, obviously a location with more of a draw for those eager to join the search from Hobart Town. There were many vessels also trading between the two locations at the time, with most arriving in Geelong, the closest port to the goldfields then being established in Ballarat and Bendigo. It is therefore of no surprise that speculative investors also made the trip, whether to see the goldfields themselves or to gain first-hand knowledge of the significant growth and development then going on throughout this colony.

Another industry being impacted in Hobart Town by a mass exodus of its workforce to the goldfields of Victoria was the local shipbuilding industry, including the yards situated at Battery Point. Having been employed at John Watson's shipyard since he was a teenager serving his apprenticeship, this period was likely a tumultuous one for Alexander McGregor with a general sense of not knowing how secure his professional future was. Not alleviating this sense of doubt was the fact that Alexander's long-time employer John Watson was facing bankruptcy, having to sell various personal, property and shipyard-related assets to thwart off the inevitable.[1]

---

[1] *Colonial Times*, 1 April, 27 June 1851.

Shipowners & Shipbuilders

Charles Bayley sailed the barque *Runnymede* to New Zealand in January 1852 with his wife Eliza on board as a passenger. The *Flying Childers*, helmed by his brother James, was already operating in these waters having left Hobart Town a few weeks earlier. Despite the emerging complexities of the whaling industry and the major changes it was then undergoing, due to overfishing, lack of crew, and a slightly reduced need for its products, both Charles and James had continued their quest to source these large mammals; the effort involved being a risk both financially and personally. Unfortunately, the inherent danger of the profession was no more realised when reports filtered back to Hobart Town regarding an accident that had occurred with regards to the *Flying Childers*. On 25 June 1852 *The Hobart Town Advertiser* reported, 'Intelligence has been brought to town by the Highlander of a fatal accident which occurred to one of the boats of the Flying Childers, off the coast of New Zealand. The boat was fast to a whale, and the line fouled Captain Bailey [sic] and Robert Bush, a son of Mr. R. Bush, of this city, and both were carried overboard. Captain Bailey [sic] was picked up after having been in the water for some time, but we regret to add that the other was never seen again'.

Though James Bayley had been saved from drowning, he had lost an essential member of his crew. It had also been the second near-death experience to befell the two brothers; Charles lucky to survive his boat overturning and hours subsequently spent in southern New Zealand's cold hypothermia-inducing waters in December 1846. How long could they both continue to be involved with this pursuit? With so many factors to consider, including the increasing difficulty of resourcing and fitting out vessels for individual voyages, was it time to diversify their interests and switch to a different industry? One change had already occurred: the *Fortitude*, of which Charles Bayley retained a quarter share, was no longer a whaler.[2] Since its return from the Bering Strait it had been laid up, awaiting a new fate like many other whalers that operated out of Hobart Town.[3]

Charles and James Bayley's brother-in-law Alexander McGregor was also suffering a similar situation with the shipbuilding industry. Major changes were occurring and there was a need to adapt or find an alternate source of employment. It is therefore of no surprise to learn that on 30 April 1852 Alexander and his younger brother John sailed as cabin passengers on board the brig *Dart* to Geelong.[4] They were headed to the Victorian goldfields hoping to dig up a fortune. While John returned to Hobart Town in mid-October per the brigantine *Montezuma*, Alexander remained in Victoria, not arriving back in Hobart Town until 6 December 1852 as a passenger on

---

[2] *The Hobart Town Advertiser*, 2 July 1852.
[3] *The Hobart Town Advertiser*, 26 October, 30 November 1852.
[4] *The Courier*, 1 May 1852; Tasmanian Archives (CUS36/1/141).

board the steamer *Yarra Yarra*.[1] Along with fellow Scottish-born shipwright Donald MacMillan, the trio had undertaken diggings in and around the Forest Creek, Bendigo and Mount Korong regions of rural Victoria.[2] Successfully finding some of the lucrative metal, they conceivably sold part of their bounty locally and then sent more to England. For instance, the ship *Roxburgh Castle* sailed from Melbourne to London in November 1852 with 163 ounces and three pennyweights of gold consigned to a '*McGregor*', assumed to belong to the two brothers.[3] Given gold sold for over £3 per ounce in Melbourne at the time, this amount would have been valued at around £500, a significant windfall for the two brothers and their partner.

A few weeks after Alexander McGregor's return to Hobart Town, the barque *Runnymede* sailed up the River Derwent with Charles Bayley at the helm. After nearly 12 months at sea, the vessel had accrued 40 tuns of sperm whale oil and 30 tuns of black whale oil, worth around £3,880.[4] Evidently sailing in company with one another, on 18 January 1853 the *Flying Childers* under the command of James Bayley also sailed into Hobart Town, having secured on board 60 tuns of sperm whale oil, valued at £4,020; this commodity now selling for £67 per tun while black whale oil was at £40 per tun.[5]

After six weeks spent in port, the *Runnymede* departed Hobart Town on 14 February 1853 heading back to the south seas whaling grounds.[6] A month later the *Fortitude* was being readied to resume service, this time being placed in the freight and passenger trade sailing between Hobart Town and Hokianga in New Zealand, another location then in the midst of a boom though this time due to the presence of vast Kauri forests which were being logged.[7] However, perhaps because of lack of interest, the vessel remained in port until 4 April when it set sail for Singapore under the management of Captain Brydge White.[8] A few weeks later the barque *Flying Childers*, with James Bayley at the helm, left the River Derwent, this time en route to Mauritius.[9] It returned to Hobart Town on 2 August loaded with sugar and sundries.[10] The *Flying Childers* then sailed back down the River Derwent on 31 August, heading for China.[11] In a series of comings and goings, that same day saw the *Fortitude* return to Hobart Town from Batavia with a cargo of sugar, coffee, furniture, rum, spices and cedar. Demand for these products was high. Hobart Town's upper and middle classes had expanded greatly over the previous two decades, becoming eager consumers of imported goods, including foodstuffs, alcohol, household items, fashion, books and music. The *Flying Childers* sailed back to Mauritius on 1 October 1853 for more sugar.[12]

While these relatively quick voyages to procure cargo from Asia and Mauritius were proving profitable for the vessel owners and its captains, Charles Bayley stoically remained on board the *Runnymede* in search of whales, after six months spent at sea only having caught one animal.[13] Unrelenting from the task, the *Runnymede* returned to Hobart Town on 24 December 1853 with 950 barrels of sperm whale oil on board, equivalent to 119 tuns, with a value of £7,970.[14]

---

[1] *The Tasmanian Colonist*, 18 October 1852; *Launceston Examiner*, 8 December 1852.
[2] *The Mercury*, 18 October 1901.
[3] *The Argus*, 11 December 1852.
[4] *The Courier*, 3 January 1853.
[5] *Colonial Times*, 18 January 1853; *The Courier*, 19 February 1853.
[6] *The Courier*, 15 February 1853.
[7] *The Courier*, 5 March 1853.
[8] *The Courier*, 5 April 1853.
[9] *The Tasmanian Colonist*, 28 April 1853.
[10] *The Courier*, 3 August 1853.
[11] *The Courier*, 31 August 1853.
[12] *The Courier*, 3 October 1853.
[13] *The Courier*, 8 October 1853.
[14] *The Tasmanian Colonist*, 26 December 1853.

Meanwhile Alexander McGregor was also making several significant life changes. Since his return from Melbourne and buoyed by several hundreds of pounds in his pocket, he had not only purchased residential land at Battery Point but had also established a shipyard, possibly at a site between Castray Esplanade and the Secheron estate, where he began undertaking repair, refit and overhaul work of large commercial vessels, including the barques *General Wool* and *Canton* in October and November 1853.[15] With regards to his personal real estate transactions, Alexander had purchased a small allotment of 50 feet by 100 feet on 4 April 1853 from Askin Morrison that was located on Runnymede Street, just below its intersection with Cross Street (now called McGregor Street), for the price of £100 (see 'land conveyed' in below diagram).[16] Significantly, it was situated next door to a similarly-sized property that had been purchased by his brother-in-law James Bayley only three days prior.[17] Nearly four years later, on 17 February 1857, Alexander McGregor would purchase the adjacent allotment located on the corner of Runnymede and Cross streets from Thomas Reed Wilson for the sum of £150.[18]

Superimposed map showing location of 'land conveyed' to Alexander McGregor on Runnymede Street, Battery Point.
Google Earth (2025) and www.thelist.tas.gov.au (Historic Deed 03/7836).

---
[15] *The Hobart Town Advertiser*, 20 October 1853; *Colonial Times*, 19 November 1853.
[16] www.thelist.tas.gov.au (Historic Deed 03/7836).
[17] www.thelist.tas.gov.au (Historic Deed 03/7835).
[18] www.thelist.tas.gov.au (Historic Deed 04/4001).

With Charles Bayley and his crew of the *Runnymede* back in port for the warmer months of early 1854, they enjoyed success in the whaleboat races at both the Kangaroo Point and Sandy Bay regattas, Charles also helping to organise the latter event.[1] He was also in town to witness the arrival of the *Fortitude* on 18 January with a cargo of 4,300 bags of sugar and 2,000 coconuts from Mauritius.[2] However, still determined to source whales, Charles once more sailed the *Runnymede* out of the Derwent on 11 February 1854, headed for the south seas whaling grounds.[3]

The remainder of the year 1854 was a plethora of arrivals and departures for the Bayley brothers and their vessels. The *Flying Childers* helmed by James Bayley returned to Hobart Town from Hong Kong via Adelaide on 1 March 1854 with a general cargo.[4] Six days later the *Fortitude* sailed by Captain White left the River Derwent for Guam in ballast.[5] On 7 April the *Flying Childers* once more cleared out, sailing to China in ballast.[6] On 1 July the *Fortitude* sailed back into Hobart Town with a load of sugar from Mauritius and two passengers on board.[7] It cleared out a month later headed back to Mauritius.[8] Next into Hobart Town was the *Flying Childers*, captained by James Bayley, which arrived on 24 September from the Philippines carrying a load of tea, coffee, sugar and rope.[9]

International voyages to procure cargo were proving more and more lucrative. They also relied on significantly less crew (around half of that compared to a commercial whaling vessel) thereby reducing the cost of rations and crew pay. More trips could also be taken on an annual basis as opposed to waiting for a ship to accrue enough whale oil to make the voyage worthwhile before it returned to port. Commercial vessels were also able to ply more reliable trading routes and conceivably take on less risk, though there remained the dangers of weather, crew sickness and injury, on board fires, as well as wrecks, mutinies and piracy. For Charles Bayley, however, he was hedging his bets, being part-owner of the *Fortitude* and still commanding his faithful whaler the *Runnymede*. After a voyage of 11 months, he too sailed back into Hobart Town, this time with 100 tuns of sperm whale on board.[10] Expecting another robust paycheck, he was likely shocked when told of the scarcity of whale oil in both Australia and Europe and just how much his precious cargo was worth, with sperm whale oil selling for £100 per tun and black whale oil for £70 per tun in Van Diemen's Land alone.[11] The local press reported on the conundrum Charles now faced.

The Hobarton Mercury, 29 November 1854.

---

[1] *Hobarton Guardian, or, True Friend of Tasmania*, 7 January 1854; *Colonial Times*, 14 January 1854; *The Courier*, 19 January 1854.
[2] *The Courier*, 19 January 1854.
[3] *The Tasmanian Colonist*, 13 February 1854.
[4] *The Hobart Town Advertiser*, 3 March 1854.
[5] *Colonial Times*, 9 March 1854.
[6] *The Hobart Town Advertiser*, 8 April 1854.
[7] *The Tasmanian Colonist*, 3 July 1854; *The Courier*, 4 July 1854.
[8] *The Courier*, 31 July 1854.
[9] *The Tasmanian Colonist*, 25 September 1854.
[10] *The Hobart Town Advertiser*, 27 September 1854.
[11] *The Cornwall Chronicle*, 30 September 1854; *Colonial Times*, 24 November 1854.

Given the extreme price of whale oil, Charles Bayley and his business partner Askin Morrison made several important decisions. First, the barque *Fortitude,* which had arrived back in Hobart Town on 4 December 1854 with another cargo of sugar from Mauritius, was taken off this route.[12] Next, the *Flying Childers* was also removed from the sugar trade and refitted for a whaling voyage, leaving Hobart Town under the command of James McGregor on 4 January 1855.[13] Third, James Bayley was given charge of the *Runnymede* and navigated the vessel out of the River Derwent en route to the south seas whaling grounds on 16 January.[14] Finally, Charles Bayley, by now 42 years of age, resumed command of the *Fortitude* and cleared Hobart Town on 14 February 1855.[15] His destination was London. On board were his wife Eliza and their 10-year-old daughter Jane Mary.[16] Stored safely in the holds were 82 casks of sperm whale oil that Charles was hoping to gain a tremendous price for once they landed in England, as well as 224 barrels of wool from one or more of Askin Morrison's farming properties, and other sundries.[17]

With both of her brothers again at sea Harriet McGregor remained in Hobart Town, likely disappointed to not be returning to England to see her parents and sisters once more. Her husband Alexander was making more plans for their future, however. With the purchase of property in Runnymede Street, Battery Point, the couple had built a small cottage on the site. Professionally, Alexander was also making his mark.

View of Hobart Town's New Wharf and Battery Point. Shows Alexander and Harriet McGregor's cottage and fenced allotment (c1857).
Tasmanian Archives (NS1013/1/926).

[12] *The Tasmanian Colonist*, 4 December 1854.
[13] *The Hobart Town Advertiser*, 4 January 1855.
[14] *The Courier*, 17 January 1855.
[15] *The Hobart Town Advertiser*, 14 February 1855.
[16] *The Hobart Town Advertiser*, 14 February 1855.
[17] *The Courier*, 14 February 1855.

Having spent a year or two managing his own shipyard at Battery Point, in mid-1855 he partnered with Askin Morrison to purchase the lease of a three-acre shipyard property situated on the edge of the River Derwent at the Government Domain.[1] Officially executing the agreement on 23 August 1855, the pair paid the substantial price of £4,200 for the site's 99-year lease from the date of 1 December 1854, along with an annual payment of one shilling.[2] Another stipulation of the lease was that a patent slip that Captain Edward Goldsmith had imported from England be installed on the property within two years.[3] Just how this piece of infrastructure came to be in Hobart Town is an interesting story.

Captain Edward Goldsmith, along with his wife Elizabeth and their infant son Richard, had first arrived in Hobart Town from Western Australia's Swan River settlement as passengers on board the ship *Bombay* in July 1830.[4] The couple and their yet-to-be-born child had originally departed Liverpool, England, on board the 196-ton brig *James* in mid-December 1829, of which Edward was master, loaded with passengers and their belongings intended for the newly-established settlement.[5] However, the *James* had become stranded upon arrival in Western Australia and subsequently wrecked such that the Goldsmith family sailed to Hobart Town per the *Bombay* and then onto Sydney by the brig *Elizabeth*.[6] They returned to London on board the brig *Norval* in April 1831 with Captain Goldsmith at the helm.[7]

Over the next decade Captain Goldsmith made nearly annual trips between England and Van Diemen's Land, including as master of the brig *Waterloo* which arrived in Hobart Town from Liverpool in August 1832, and the barque *Wave* which arrived in November 1833, March 1835, December 1836, July 1838 and again in September 1839.[8] Sensing potential for the establishment of additional shipyard services to supply the Port of Hobart Town, in October 1839 he partnered with George Bilton, John Meaburn, Andrew Haig and William Williamson to purchase two neighbouring allotments at Battery Point lying between Napoleon Street and the River Derwent.[9] At this site it was the intention of the business partners to not only establish a shipyard to be managed by William Williamson, already a leading shipbuilder of Hobart Town, but also to install a patent slip which Edward Goldsmith would procure in England and trans-ship back to Hobart Town.[10] Operating as the Derwent Ship Building Company the group built several vessels, including the 36-ton schooner *Queen,* launched in September 1840, and the 162-ton brig *Diana*, launched a few months later.[11] Unfortunately the viability of the company was short-lived. On 3 March 1841, less than 18 months after its formation, it was dissolved, likely a combination of its directors suffering financial hardship, a general lack of interest in the building of new craft, the slow sale of vessels built on speculation, and the poorly performing colonial economy.[12] In addition, though Edward Goldsmith had arrived back in Hobart Town from London in December 1840 at the helm of the *Wave*, he had not yet managed to purchase a patent slip which would have been an asset for the company's services.[13]

---

[1] www.thelist.tas.gov.au (Historic Deed 04/1871).
[2] www.thelist.tas.gov.au (Historic Deed 04/1871).
[3] www.thelist.tas.gov.au (Historic Deed 04/1871).
[4] *The Tasmanian*, 30 July 1830.
[5] *Liverpool Albion*, 21 September 1829; *Lloyd's List*, 22 December 1829.
[6] *The Hobart Town Courier*, 31 July 1830; *Colonial Times*, 17 September 1830.
[7] *The Sydney Gazette and New South Wales Advertiser*, 13 January, 19 April 1831.
[8] *The Colonist and Van Diemen's Land Commercial and Agricultural Advertiser*, 10 August 1832; *The Tasmanian*, 15 November 1833, 9 December 1836, 27 September 1839; *Colonial Times*, 10 March 1835; *Bent's News and Tasmanian Register*, 20 July 1838.
[9] www.thelist.tas.gov.au (Historic Deed 02/3002); *Colonial Times*, 29 October 1839.
[10] *The Hobart Town Advertiser*, 4 October 1839.
[11] *The Courier*, 22 January 1841; *The Hobart Town Advertiser*, 24 July 1840; *Colonial Times*, 5 January 1841.
[12] *The Austral-Asiatic Review, Tasmanian and Australian Advertiser*, 9 March 1841.
[13] *The Courier*, 1 December 1840.

Undeterred, Edward Goldsmith then made annual voyages between London and Hobart Town in the 1840s, mostly at the helm of the barque *Rattler*, on one occasion with his wife on board as a passenger.[14] Sticking to such a regular schedule during this period, Edward thus developed both personal and business relationships in Hobart Town such that in 1849 he was induced to bring his wife and their two sons to the colony where they intended to settle.[15] Earlier that year he had also been compelled to bring a patent slip out from England that would be installed near the Old Wharf though the press reported, *'The site for the patent slip chosen by Capt. Goldsmith is at the back of the Commissariat Stores; but we suspect that when he comes he will find other situations more eligible, as the room which would be spared would be insufficient for the works necessary in conjunction with the slip'*.[16] The materials for the slip were on board the *Rattler* when it moored in Hobart Town on 26 November 1849.[17]

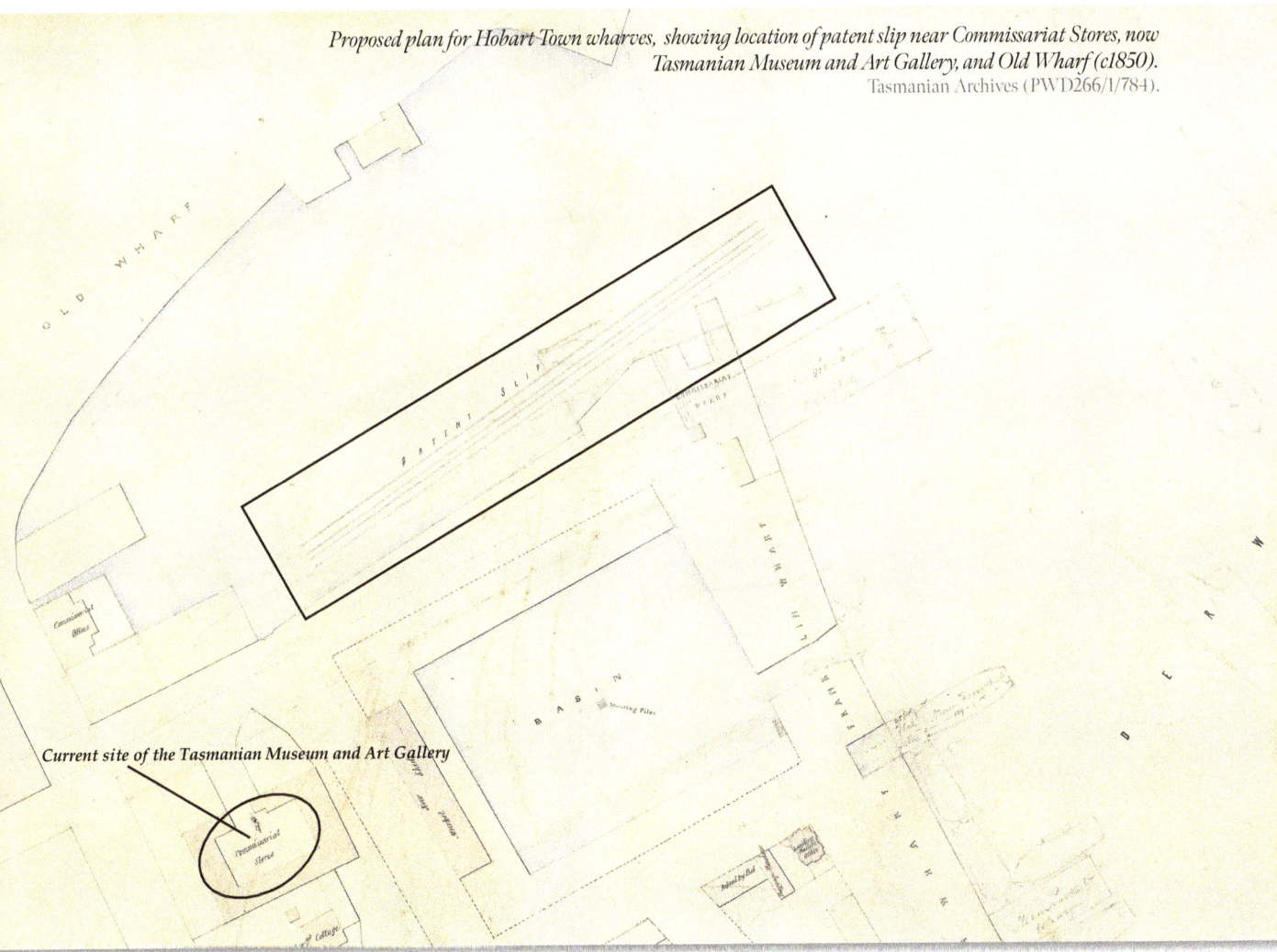

Proposed plan for Hobart Town wharves, showing location of patent slip near Commissariat Stores, now Tasmanian Museum and Art Gallery, and Old Wharf (c1850).
Tasmanian Archives (PWD266/1/784).

Current site of the Tasmanian Museum and Art Gallery

[14] *The Hobart Town Advertiser*, 28 October 1842, 12 November 1847; *Colonial Times*, 19 December 1843, 27 November 1849; *The Courier*, 17 December 1844, 24 December 1845, 14 November 1846, 6 December 1848; *The Britannia and Trades' Advocate*, 19 November 1846.
[15] *Colonial Times*, 27 November 1849; *Hobarton Guardian, or, True Friend of Tasmania*, 28 November 1849.
[16] *The Courier*, 24 February 1849; *The Hobart Town Advertiser*, 13 July 1849.
[17] *The Courier*, 28 November 1849.

Capable of accommodating steamers of up to 1,000 tons burthen or vessels up to 800 tons, the patent slip was expected to be the first of its kind in Van Diemen's Land though not in Australia as one had been operational in Sydney's Darling Harbour since the early 1830s.[1] Unfortunately its installation in Hobart Town was delayed for two reasons. First, Edward Goldsmith was tasked with sailing the *Rattler* back to London, clearing out of the River Derwent on 23 February 1850.[2] Second, he was still waiting to receive a land grant from the Government of Van Diemen's Land on which the patent slip could be installed, believed to have been one of the stipulations for his commitment to procure the slip in the first place.[3]

On 13 December 1850 Edward Goldsmith navigated the *Rattler* back into Hobart Town from London likely expecting to receive positive news from the Colonial Government with regards to a site where he could install his patent slip.[4] Though he had been away for nearly 10 months, there had frustratingly been no action undertaken on the issue. Disappointed, the local press also chastised the regulatory procrastination, not only on behalf of the enterprising captain but also with regards to the lost revenue that would benefit the local economy if the Port of Hobart Town was able to refit, repair and overhaul large commercial vessels, including steamers.[5] However, the cost involved in establishing a patent slip was tremendous. A site was needed close to the port with a reasonable amount of water depth, as well as access to a large piece of gently sloping ground. There was also the infrastructure itself. Once an allotment was selected, piles would need to be driven into the ground at a substantial depth to not only secure the slip but also withstand the large vessels which would be hauled upon it. Though Captain Goldsmith had initially applied to the government for the use of land located between the commissariat store (i.e., the current site of the Tasmanian Museum and Art Gallery) and the Old Wharf, it was found to be too rocky such that the cost to install the piles and the slip was estimated at £10,000.[6]

Pressing on with the issue and delaying his annual departure back to London, on 12 February 1851 the first pile was driven into the ground on a new site at the Government Domain granted to Captain Goldsmith by Lieutenant-Governor Sir William Denison for the purpose of erecting the patent slip.[7] A month later the *Rattler* cleared Hobart Town en route to England without him at the helm; Captain Goldsmith opting to remain in Hobart Town to oversee his patent slip project.[8] In his presence progress quickened with *The Hobart Town Advertiser* of 4 July 1851 reporting that construction of the slip had commenced with the ground fenced off, two cottages built for the use of workmen and several more piles driven into the ground. A few days later Captain Goldsmith published a tender for the work of laying down the slip. Not everyone was happy about the new location, however, with the Hobart Town Bathers' Association remonstrating that the land they had previously rented at the Domain had been appropriated for the patent slip. A solution was then implemented whereby the dressing rooms used by the bathers would be moved 200 yards to the south.[9]

Simultaneous with the construction of the patent slip, Captain Goldsmith established a shipyard on the site, from May 1852 through to mid-1854 receiving income for the repair of boats

---

[1] *The Currency Lad*, 27 April 1833; *The Sydney Gazette and New South Wales Advertiser*, 23 May 1833; *The Courier*, 28 November 1833.
[2] *Colonial Times*, 26 February 1850.
[3] *Launceston Examiner*, 13 February 1850; *The Courier*, 20 February 1850.
[4] *Colonial Times*, 17 December 1850.
[5] *Launceston Examiner*, 11 January 1851; *The Hobart Town Advertiser*, 24 January 1851.
[6] *The Hobart Town Advertiser*, 24 January 1851.
[7] *Hobarton Guardian, or, True Friend of Tasmania*, 15 January, 11 October 1851.
[8] *The Britannia and Trades' Advocate*, 20 March 1851.
[9] *The Hobart Town Advertiser*, 19 December 1851.

View of the Domain Shipyards from Government House (c1860s).
Tasmanian Archives (PH1/1/30).

and punts owned by the government.[10] His yard, with Duncan McGuinnis as foreman, was also noted as repairing and overhauling commercial craft during this period such as river barges and intercolonial barques, including the *Fortitude* upon its return from the Bering Strait.[11]

Frustratingly, by early 1853 construction of the patent slip had been significantly delayed due to the mass exodus of working-aged men to the Victorian goldfields.[12] There were also issues with the lease agreement for the land itself, the legal covenants and conditions of breach deemed not mutual by representatives acting on behalf of the Government of Van Diemen's Land. In particular, there was concern that should Edward Goldsmith become insolvent, leave the colony, otherwise break the lease or die, there were no legal provisions for the Crown to seek redress or to sue for damages.[13] Still, during this period the shipyard remained busy with repair work, as well as launching a new schooner of 25 tons in February 1854.[14]

Continuing to lobby the government for work and assistance with his patent slip, in mid-1854 it was announced that Edward Goldsmith's shipyard had been tasked with building a twin engine paddle steamer to ply as a ferry between Hobart Town and Kangaroo Point on the eastern shore of the River Derwent; Askin Morrison providing surety for the contract.[15] With £5,000 allocated to the project several years earlier, the scheme was by this time several years in the making before construction of the vessel, measuring 110 feet, had even started. However, personal tragedy struck the Goldsmith family two months later with the death of Captain Goldsmith's eldest son Richard

---

[10] *The Hobart Town Advertiser*, 21 May 1852, 13 April 1853; *The Courier*, 14 June, 26 July, 6 December 1853, 1 February, 4 April, 14 June 1854.
[11] *The Tasmanian Colonist*, 10 June 1852; *The Hobart Town Advertiser*, 10 August 1852.
[12] *The Courier*, 3 January 1853; *Colonial Times*, 4 January 1853.
[13] *The Courier*, 26 August 1853; *The Hobart Town Advertiser*, 26 August 1853.
[14] *The Courier*, 17 February 1854; *The Hobart Town Advertiser*, 20 November 1854.
[15] *The Tasmanian Colonist*, 29 June 1854; *The Tasmanian Daily News*, 12 July 1856.

at the age of 24 of scarlet fever.[1] The mariner's mindset was thus likely not abetted by the public frustration and criticism that was then directed at him personally in early 1855 owing to delays and costs associated with '*the building of the colonial Noah's Ark, for the steam ferry from Hobart Town to Kangaroo Point*'.[2] Specifically, accusations were lobbed by the press with regard to the fact that no public tender had been issued calling for construction of the vessel. Instead, the contract had been entered into via private treaty.[3] Another point of contention was the cost to build which Captain Goldsmith had specified to be at an exorbitant £10,000.[4] Moreover, the Colonial Government was to supply the materials with which to build the steamer. Additional concern was remonstrated at the outdated design of the vessel, including the use of two 30 horsepower engines to propel one paddle wheel situated in the centre. Combined with the need to build new infrastructure at Kangaroo Point to accommodate the vessel, as well as the salaries of an engineer and several overseers, the entire exercise was thought to be in the realm of £20,000 for the '*useless wooden trunk*', with annual running costs estimated at £5,000.[5] Two weeks after these grievances were published, Edward Goldsmith began selling off his family's furniture and household goods, intent on permanently returning to England.[6]

On 3 April 1855 the hull of the Kangaroo Point paddle steamer was launched from the Domain shipyard of Edward Goldsmith, built under the superintendence of Duncan McGuinnis.[7] Named *Kangaroo*, its engines were installed a few weeks later with the vessel successfully undertaking its trial voyage on the River Derwent on 27 September, the event being followed by a luncheon on board whereby the health of Captain Goldsmith was toasted.[8]

With more of his household effects sold at auction in the months leading up to their departure, as well as several clearance sales held at his shipyard, Captain Edward Goldsmith, his wife Elizabeth and their only surviving child, a son named Edward (Jr), sailed out of Hobart Town for England as passengers on board the ship *Indian Queen* on 20 February 1856 never to return.[9] He had been paid the final expenses associated with construction of the twin steamer ferry *Kangaroo* by the Colonial Government a few weeks prior.[10]

Despite his earnest ambitions for the establishment of the patent slip he had originally imported to Hobart Town in late 1849, Captain Goldsmith likely left the colony disappointed not to have been the one responsible for its initial use and operation; that notoriety was awarded to Alexander McGregor and his business partner Askin Morrison. He was also likely dejected that this reality was superseded by another enterprising free settler, John Ross, who earned the title of being the first to install and operate this much-needed piece of infrastructure in the colony; his patent slip situated at Battery Point was operational by late March 1855.[11] It was also larger. Still, Captain Goldsmith's legacy remains associated with being the first to establish a shipyard at the Domain, as well as the builder of the paddle steamer ferry *Kangaroo* which went on to ply the River Derwent for more than 70 years.

---

[1] Tasmanian Archives (RGD35/1/4 no. 1429); *The Courier*, 15 August 1854.
[2] *Launceston Examiner*, 10 February 1855.
[3] *Launceston Examiner*, 10 February 1855.
[4] *Launceston Examiner*, 10 February 1855.
[5] *Launceston Examiner*, 10 February 1855.
[6] *The Courier*, 26 February 1855.
[7] *Colonial Times*, 4 April 1855; *The Hobart Town Advertiser*, 4 April 1855.
[8] *The Hobart Town Advertiser*, 24 April 1855; *The Tasmanian Daily News*, 28 September 1855; *The Hobartown Mercury*, 1 October 1855; *The Courier*, 1 November 1855; *Colonial Times*, 20 November 1855.
[9] *The Hobart Town Advertiser*, 25 July 1855.
[10] *Colonial Times*, 21 February 1856.
[11] *Colonial Times*, 26 September 1854; *The Courier*, 30 March 1855; *Colonial Times*, 30 March 1855.

Paddle Steamer Kangaroo at the Domain Shipyards (c1910s).
Tasmanian Archives (PH30/1/5623).

As stated, Alexander McGregor and Askin Morrison commenced ownership of Captain Goldsmith's Domain shipyard property on 23 August 1855 with the pair paying £4,200 for the site's lease with the duration being 99 years from the date of 1 December 1854, along with an annual payment of one shilling.[12] Another stipulation of the lease was that the patent slip that Captain Edward Goldsmith had imported from England be installed on the property within two years.[13] Even though Edward Goldsmith remained in Hobart Town for another six months, on 24 August 1855, i.e., just one day after Alexander McGregor and Askin Morrison had signed the lease, the patent slip on the edge of the River Derwent at the Government Domain was officially opened. The Hobarton Mercury reported, 'It is always a pleasing task to the journalist to record the progress both of public and private enterprise, and it was therefore with great satisfaction that we witnessed the launch of a patent slip in the yard of Mr. A. McGreggor [sic], in the Government Domain. This operation took place yesterday afternoon, in the presence of several of our leading citizens; including amongst others, Messrs. McNaughton, Morrison, Allport, Pitcairns, T. Macdowell, Goldsmith, &c.; and was attended with complete success. It is an evidence of the good management of Mr. McGreggor [sic] that the whole of the work from its commencement, to the launch, had been performed in two months, and he anticipates that the slip will be ready for the reception of vessels within a similar time from the present date'.[14]

---

[12] www.thelist.tas.gov.au (Historic Deed 04/1871).
[13] www.thelist.tas.gov.au (Historic Deed 04/1871).
[14] *The Hobarton Mercury*, 24 August 1855.

It was an interesting time in the history of Van Diemen's Land to start a new business venture. After 50 years of European settlement, the colony was looking to the future with the hope of transitioning from its convict past. From a rudimentary outpost where Britain's notorious though generally petty criminals were banished, along with those government and military personnel needed to administer and police the felons, Van Diemen's Land had outgrown its original use. Assisted and unassisted free settlers had been induced to the island colony, whether through desperation, ambition or a combination of the two, and the convicts had mostly served their time and gone on to live productive lives. Children had been born to both convicts and free settlers alike such that there were by now second and third generations of families living in the colony intent on calling it 'home' as opposed to those of previous generations still pining for Britain.

With this advancement, the pioneer administrators and businessmen of Van Diemen's Lands' early years had also passed on, leading to a more fair, democratic and judicious governing system. Of course there remained social, economic and political problems inherent from its early systems and processes, whereby political, land grant and economic liberalities had been hijacked by those in power, but on the whole the populous was becoming more educated and more inclined to expect reasonable outcomes from their political representatives, particularly those men that were able to vote in elections. The colony was also becoming self-sustaining, its industries and exports driven by wheat, wool, whale oil, timber, jam and fruit. Several decades later, a mining boom would occur to buoy the local economy even more.

From a crude camp of a few hundred Europeans, Van Diemen's Lands' population by the early 1850s stood at more than 70,000 people, with the convicts and ex-convicts slowly but surely being outnumbered by those considered 'free'. The middle and upper classes had also

View of Hobart Town (circa 1857). Alexander and Harriet McGregor's cottage shown in the square.
Tasmanian Archives (NS1013/1/922).

greatly expanded over the decades to become fervent ambassadors for the colony, promoting its opportunities and advantages as opposed to its history and liabilities. With this maturity Van Diemen's Lands' two major centres, Hobart Town and Launceston, had also grown into bastions representative of burgeoning and organised citizenries. Banks, schools, churches and hospitals had been established, government and commercial buildings were by now constructed to architectural designs and high standards, and commerce and private enterprises were changing the landscape of the towns with new buildings and developments. This growth in turn had spurred the upper and middle classes to build homes in the surrounding neighbourhoods on the expectation that roads, footpaths, lighting, water, sewage and other infrastructure would be built to accommodate them. There was also art and culture to explore and enjoy, with theatres, libraries, museums and parks becoming established.

Moreover, Van Diemen's Lands' upward trajectory came during the early decades of Queen Victoria's reign. The 18-year-old monarch had first ascended the throne on 20 June 1837 following the death of King William IV. Two years later Queen Victoria had become engaged to her first cousin Albert and the couple married on 10 February 1840. Her reign was indicative of a period of industrial, political, scientific and military change within the United Kingdom, including Australia and its colonies. It was also a time of social and moral reform within the class system, with the ever-expanding middle class placing firm expectations on religion, respectability, self discipline, morals and behaviour.

All of these factors coalesced to produce changes in Van Diemen's Land, the major ones being the development and implementation of its own constitution, including parliamentary systems and processes for governance, and the cessation of convict labour; both occurring in the early 1850s.

In addition, with the approval of Queen Victoria, Van Diemen's Land officially became known as Tasmania on 1 January 1856, a hope that the re-branding would help shrug off the colony's convict past and hold it in good stead for a prosperous future.

It was in this context that Alexander McGregor found himself, the child of working-class Scottish immigrants who had arrived in Hobart Town with his family at the age of 10 in 1831. By now aged 34, Alexander had capitalised on his own hard work and ambition and that of his two brothers-in-law, Charles and James Bayley, to start his own shipyard business. The new enterprise came at the right place and the right time. Having purchased and exported the patent slip to Van Diemen's Land from England, Captain Edward Goldsmith had been plagued by bureaucracy and personal grief, unable to see the project to fruition. Instead, Alexander McGregor had taken the opportunity to partner with one of Hobart Town's more wealthy merchants and businessmen to successfully navigate the red tape and construction process to have the slip operational within a two month span. He soon set to work establishing his business.

Having been officially opened on 24 August 1855, Alexander McGregor's patent slip commenced operations on 10 October.[1] As opposed to having been built on timber supports, the slip was constructed into a portion of ground at the Government Domain that had been excavated such that it was firmly anchored into rock. With a length of 600 feet, additional strength was given by iron rails laid on timber beams running the entire distance.[2] Its cradle was constructed of Macquarie pine and measured 120 feet in length, with the possibility of an extension to 175 feet.[3] Powered by a 23 horsepower engine, the slip was now deemed capable of hauling up a vessel of up to 1,000 tons burthen.[4]

With 200 hundred people present to witness the auspicious event, including many of Hobart Town's politicians and leading maritime merchants, shipowners and masters, amongst them Askin Morrison and Captain Goldsmith, the first vessel hauled up on Alexander McGregor's patent slip was the 134-ton brig *Dart*.[5] Within days it was followed by the barque *Flying Cloud* and the schooners *Harp* and *Adelaide Packet* a week or two later.[6] With demand high, these were the first of hundreds and hundreds of vessels that would utilise the slip over the coming decades.

---

[1] *The Hobart Town Advertiser*, 9 October 1855.
[2] *The Tasmanian Daily News*, 10 October 1855.
[3] *The Tasmanian Daily News*, 10 October 1855; *Colonial Times*, 10 October 1855.
[4] *The Tasmanian Daily News*, 10 October 1855.
[5] *Colonial Times*, 10 October 1855.
[6] *Colonial Times*, 16, 29 October 1855.

Travel & Tasmania

Charles Bayley, his wife Eliza and their daughter Jane Mary arrived back in Hobart Town on 14 February 1856 as passengers per the ship *Mercia*, exactly one year after they had departed the River Derwent on board the barque *Fortitude*.[7] After a voyage just shy of four months, the *Fortitude* had arrived in London on 11 June 1855 whereby Charles Bayley soon set about disposing of its cargo of whale oil and wool and finding a buyer for the vessel of which he was a quarter owner.[8] Enlisting the help of his distant relative George Bayley (Jr), a London-based surveyor for Lloyd's, the *Fortitude* was advertised for sale by auction a month later, if not sold beforehand.

> At LLOYD'S CAPTAINS' ROOM, ROYAL EXCHANGE,
> On THURSDAY, JULY 12, 1855, at Half-past Two o'Clock
> (Unless previously disposed of by private contract),
> THE substantial Barque FORTITUDE,
> 255 tons O.M.; built at Newcastle, in 1832, and originally classed nine A 1; is copper-fastened, and sheathed with yellow metal; has always been well kept up, and has just discharged a cargo from Hobart Town in excellent condition; this vessel carries a large cargo at an easy draught of water, shifts without ballast, and is well found in stores. Now lying in the London Dock.
> Apply to Messrs RYAN and DALE, 6s, Old Broad-street; or to GEO. BAYLEY and WM. RIDLEY, 2, Cowper's-court, Cornhill

Shipping & Mercantile Gazette, 21 June 1855.

No doubt remaining in London until the *Fortitude* was sold, reportedly for £1,000, Charles Bayley and his family then ventured to Essex where they visited with his parents Charles and Mary Bull in Burnham-on-Crouch, his father by now in his early 70s and his mother aged 67.[9] The trio then would have travelled further north to visit with other relatives, including the celebrated shipbuilder James Bayley (Jr²) and his two sons William Sage Bayley and James Rogers Bayley at their yard in Ipswich. Time would have also been allocated to calling on Charles' sisters Mary and Emmaretta, the latter and her family living in Poplar, London, where Emmaretta's husband Isaac Rogers worked as a sail maker.[10]

It was the first time Charles had been back in England for several decades and he would have noticed significant changes. The Industrial Revolution had spurred the establishment of factories

---

[7] Tasmanian Archives (MB2/39/1/19 p489).
[8] *The Public Ledger*, 12 June 1855.
[9] *Colonial Times*, 15 February 1856.
[10] 1851 England Census for Emmaretta Rogers.

for textile making, tools, machinery and other manufactured products, resulting in a seismic shift in the population from agricultural to urban areas. With this change and the development of steam technologies and iron and steel production, railways had been constructed linking major and minor areas across the country, as well as small and large steamships to service a growing demand for local, domestic and international trade and passenger transport. Technologies for communication, including the electrical telegraph, had also been introduced, making it easier to convey messages between distant locations.

Having been living in Hobart Town since at least the mid-1830s and spending the bulk of his time sailing the southern seas in search of whales, Charles Bayley would have perhaps been overwhelmed by all of the alterations that had taken place in England, as well as the increase in the population of London and other areas he was previously familiar with. However, he was likely impressed with the great strides in shipbuilding then underway, with iron-hulled ships fitted with steam engines and screw propellers set to revolutionise his trade.

Charles and Mary Bayley Bull.
LINC Tasmania eHeritage Database (2012).

The Bayley family thus experienced a whirlwind though short-lived adventure in England, balancing visits with family and friends with tourist and other activities. After six months spent in the country, on 6 November 1855 Charles and Eliza Bayley and their daughter Jane Mary set sail for home, departing London as cabin passengers on board the ship *Mercia*.[1]

Arriving back in what was now called Tasmania in mid-February 1856, Charles Bayley undoubtedly wasted no time in catching up on all of the business news he had missed, including the establishment of his brother-in-law Alexander McGregor's patent slip at the Domain. Of note, Charles' brother James was also back in Hobart Town having sailed the *Runnymede* up the River Derwent, coincidentally not only on the same day but during the same hour that Charles and his family arrived. The press reported on the occurrence. Though it made for a good story, the *Runnymede* had in fact departed the River Derwent on 16 February 1855.[2] '*Captain Bailey [sic], of the Runnymede, parted with his brother on the morning of the 14th February, 1855,—Captain Bailey [sic], of the Runnymede, on a whaling voyage to the South Sea, the other brother on a voyage to England. Strange to say the ships about the same hour entered the Heads yesterday, the 14th February,—the one, the Mercia, from London, containing Capt Bailey [sic] who went to England; the other, the Runnymede, Captain Bailey [sic], from his whaling cruise, both brothers meeting at the same hour on the very spot at which they parted exactly twelve months since.*'[3]

After 12 months spent hunting in the southern whaling grounds, the *Runnymede* had 70 tuns of sperm whale oil in its holds valued at £5,700, considering the price per tun in Hobart Town was £85 at the time.[4] Another family reunion, this time for the McGregor family, took place a few days later with the arrival in Hobart Town of the *Flying Childers*, also from the whaling grounds.

---

[1] Tasmanian Archives (MB2/39/1/19 p489).
[2] *The Courier*, 17 January 1855.
[3] *The Tasmanian Daily News*, 15 February 1856.
[4] *Colonial Times*, 1 February 1856; *The Courier*, 15 February 1856.

Helmed by James McGregor, the vessel had 58 tuns of sperm whale oil in its holds after a voyage of 13 months.[5] Both the *Runnymede* and *Flying Childers* were then placed in succession on Alexander McGregor's patent slip to undergo repair and overhaul.[6]

With regards to their living situations during this time, the 1856 Hobart Town Electoral Roll notes Charles Bayley and his family as living in Kelly Street, Battery Point.[7] Alexander and Harriet McGregor were living nearby, at their home on Cross Street, Battery Point (now McGregor Street), at its corner with Runnymede Street, as well as operating a shop out of the same location.[8] Possibly a small grocer, it was likely that this business was managed by Harriet.[9] James Bayley is not noted on the roll even though he owned land in Runnymede Street.

The two Bayley brothers were not home for long, however. Following a respite of two months Charles resumed command of the *Runnymede* and sailed it out of the River Derwent on 4 April 1856. Three days later he would officially become the vessel's half owner with his brother James purchasing the other half share from Askin Morrison.[10] Now joint owners, James was also on board the *Runnymede* as it slipped out of the Derwent, serving as the vessel's chief officer.[11]

Searching mostly in waters off New Zealand's west coast, in company with the *Flying Childers* helmed by James McGregor, before heading to the east coast of Australia and the waters off Lord Howe Island, the *Runnymede* returned to Hobart Town on 22 December 1856 with 77 tuns of sperm whale oil on board valued at £7,084 since the commodity was now worth £92 per tun.[12]

Personally, apart from the marriage of James McGregor to Elizabeth Drake in the days prior to the departure of the *Flying Childers* in April 1856, there were few other noteworthy events for members of the McGregor family during this year.[13] Alexander McGregor's patent slip continued to be a success with a steady stream of vessels engaged on it. He also won the sailing boat race at that year's Hobart Town Regatta, competing in the *Heather Bell*.[14]

With regards to the Bayley family, however, there is one major event that needs to be detailed. On 30 December 1856, just eight days after returning home on board the *Runnymede*, James Bayley, aged 33, married Emma Elizabeth Butchard, aged 18, at the Battery Point home of Alexander and Harriet McGregor.[15] Witnesses were Alexander McGregor and Charles Bayley.[16]

Marriage registration of James Bayley and Emma Elizabeth Butchard, 30 December 1856.
Tasmanian Archives (RGD37/1/15 no. 374).

---

[5] *The Hobart Town Advertiser*, 19 February 1856.
[6] *Colonial Times*, 27 February 1856.
[7] *The Courier*, 5 April 1856.
[8] *The Courier*, 5 April 1856.
[9] *The Courier*, 5 April 1856.
[10] National Archives of Australia, Register of British Ships: Main Register (with continuation entries), Port of Hobart [contains Volumes 7, 8, 9 (part)].
[11] R. Richards (2014). *Captain Charles Bayley: Whaling Master 1813-1875*.
[12] *Colonial Times*, 16 July, 21 October, 14 November, 23 December 1856; *The Courier*, 22 August, 24 October 1856; *The Hobarton Mercury*, 22 December 1856.
[13] Tasmanian Archives (RGD37/1/15 no. 309).
[14] *The Tasmanian Daily News*, 5 December 1856.
[15] Tasmanian Archives (RGD37/1/15 no. 374).
[16] Tasmanian Archives (RGD37/1/15 no. 374).

Born in Stepney, London, on 10 February 1838, Emma Elizabeth Butchard was the second eldest child and only daughter of David Butchard, a master mariner, and his wife Elizabeth (nee Judy).[1] Emma's father had spent most of her early years sailing between England and Sydney at the helm of the intercolonial trading barques *Spartan* and *Andromache*.[2] For reasons not known but assumed to be because of the death of her mother, by 1853 Emma was based in Australia, frequently accompanying her father on voyages he undertook at the helm of the intercolonial trading schooner *Elizabeth Jane* operating between Hobart Town and Geelong.[3] It is also likely that her eldest brother Thomas worked on board the vessel in some capacity during this period.

By early 1855 Emma Butchard was sailing with her father and possibly her brother on board the schooner *Surf* operating between Chile, the Pacific Islands and Hobart Town.[4] Sadly, Captain David Butchard died in Hobart Town after a short illness on 14 September 1855 at the age of 58.[5] His death occurred at the residence of Reverend William Day. It is likely that Emma, now an orphan, remained living with the Day family or another family familiar to her up until her marriage to James Bayley some 15 months later. She would have then moved in with James and his relatives at Battery Point, possibly with his sister Harriet and Harriet's husband Alexander McGregor.

Uncharacteristically, but assumed to be because of this union, there was time for the newly married couple to settle into life with one another. James did not depart on board the *Runnymede* on 10 February 1857 with his brother Charles at the helm.[6] Instead, he is noted as being present in Hobart Town in early March where he testified as part of a law suit involving one of the *Runnymede*'s wayward crew members.[7]

Emma and James Bayley (nee Butchard).
Napier/Atkinson Family Tree on Ancestry.com.

With his patent slip proving profitable, it was during this period that Alexander McGregor began significantly expanding his property portfolio at Battery Point. As previously stated, on 17 February 1856 he purchased additional land on the corner of Cross and Runnymede streets from Thomas Reed Wilson, paying £150 for the 53 feet by 51 feet parcel.[8] A few months later Alexander wrote to the Hobart Town Municipal Council requesting that water lines be extended to his premises.[9] He also requested that improvements be made to drainage as flooding of a nearby creek had caused damage to the foundations of his home.[10] In the decades to come Alexander would purchase more and more residential, commercial and farming properties throughout Hobart Town and southern Tasmania more generally.

---

[1] London, England, Church of England Births and Baptisms, 1813-1924 for Emma Elizabeth Butcher.
[2] *The Sydney Monitor and Commercial Advertiser*, 13 May 1839, 3 July, 29 September 1840; *The Sydney Herald*, 28 August 1839; *Sydney Free Press*, 12 April 1842.
[3] *The Courier*, 17 October 1853; *Colonial Times*, 1 November 1853; *The Hobart Town Advertiser*, 26 April 1854.
[4] *The Courier*, 17 April 1855.
[5] *The Courier*, 14 September 1855.
[6] *The Courier*, 10 February 1857.
[7] *The Hobart Town Advertiser*, 6 March 1857; *The Tasmanian Daily News*, 6 March 1857.
[8] www.thelist.tas.gov.au (Historic Deed 04/4001).
[9] *The Hobart Town Advertiser*, 22 May 1857.
[10] *The Hobart Town Advertiser*, 14 July 1857.

The two Bayley brothers were also building wealth for their respective families. After six months spent sailing in the south sea whaling grounds off the coast of New Zealand with Charles at the helm, the *Runnymede* returned to the mouth of the River Derwent in mid-August 1857, noted to be moored off Passage Point (i.e., Tinderbox).[11] However, despite the close proximity it did not enter into Hobart Town, Charles instead opting to sail the vessel to waters off Tasmania's east coast and then to those off mainland Australia in search of more whales before returning to New Zealand waters.[12] After a voyage totalling 13 months the *Runnymede* sailed into Hobart Town on 7 March 1858 with 63 tuns of sperm whale oil on board and an undisclosed amount of whale bone, valued at more than £4,800 considering the local price per tun of sperm whale oil was £75 at the time.[13]

After a turnaround of just one month, the *Runnymede* cleared the River Derwent on 8 April 1858 headed back to the west coast of New Zealand, once more with Charles Bayley at the helm.[14] James Bayley had also cleared the Derwent just a few weeks earlier, this time as a cabin passenger on board the ship *Aurora Australis*. Heading in an opposite direction, he had sailed to London with his wife Emma and his sister Harriet McGregor on 26 March.[15] James was no doubt planning to introduce his bride to his parents Charles and Mary Bull, with Harriet keen to be reunited with this couple, both advancing in age, as well as her two elder sisters and their families whom she had not seen in 12 years.

Sea travel between Tasmania and England was lengthy and expensive. There were very few members of Hobart Town's community who had both the time and the funds to make the journey. The Bayley brothers and their sister were fortunate that they could travel to England and be united with family members; it was a luxury not many could partake in. It was also likely one that they never thought possible considering the circumstances in which they had grown up. However, like his elder brother Charles, the maritime industry had been kind to James Bayley, particularly his involvement in the whaling industry. He now not only had the funds to return to England but also the time as Charles had once again taken command of the *Runnymede* while James and his wife Emma were away. Harriet's husband Alexander McGregor was also rising in the wealth ranks, his steady industriousness and perseverance with the patent slip, where he was involved in not only overhauling but caulking, coppering, repairing and other maintenance efforts of international, intercolonial, coastal and local commercial craft, had resulted in a significant increase in their income stream. During the year 1858 alone 35 vessels, including several steamers, had been engaged on the slip equating to an aggregate tonnage of 7,000 tons, whilst 70 vessels had been repaired at a cost of £12,000.[16] These figures put Alexander's shipyard as the highest grossing of the three yards that were fitted with patent slips in Hobart Town.[17] Mixing business with pleasure Alexander was additionally becoming a stalwart of the local racing scene, finishing a commendable third in the yacht race at the 1859 Hobart Town Regatta held on 5 January in the *Blue Bell*.[18] He and his younger brother John Gibson McGregor had also built several smaller craft for these events.

---

[11] R. Richards (2014). *Captain Charles Bayley: Whaling Master 1813-1875*; The Hobart Town Advertiser, 14 August 1857.
[12] R. Richards (2014). *Captain Charles Bayley: Whaling Master 1813-1875*; The Hobart Town Advertiser, 30 September 1857.
[13] The Hobart Town Advertiser, 8 March 1858; The Courier, 8 March 1858; Tasmanian Weekly News, 27 March 1858.
[14] The Hobart Town Advertiser, 9 April 1858; The Hobart Town Daily Mercury, 20 May, 8 June 1858.
[15] The Hobart Town Advertiser, 27 March 1858; The Hobart Town Daily Mercury, 27 March 1858.
[16] The Hobart Town Daily Mercury, 18 January 1859.
[17] The Hobart Town Daily Mercury, 18 January 1859.
[18] The Courier, 5 January 1859.

Harriet and Alexander McGregor (late 1850s).
Lenna of Hobart Heritage Hotel.

With regards to James and Emma Bayley and Harriet McGregor, the *Aurora Australis* arrived at Gravesend on the River Thames on 22 June 1858 after a voyage of 88 days.[1] Harriet then returned on board the same vessel, arriving in Hobart Town on 30 December 1858 after clearing London on 24 September.[2] In total, she had spent three months in England, one assumes the bulk of this time in the company of her family in Essex, Suffolk and London. On 8 March 1859, just over two months after Harriet's return, the *Runnymede* also arrived in Hobart Town with Charles Bayley at the helm. Its voyage of exactly 11 months had produced 65 tuns of sperm whale oil valued at £4,745; the local price being at a low of £73 per tun due to oversupply and reduced demand.[3] Though profitable the *Runnymede*'s voyage had proved disastrous in terms of personnel, however. Three crew members had been drowned after their boat was overturned during a squall while they were searching for two additional crew members who had deserted in the vicinity of Thompson Sound in New Zealand's fiordland region.[4] The deaths included the vessel's second mate Henry Struggles.[5] Charles Bayley was also of the opinion that the two deserters had also drowned, '*as they were both unaccustomed to boating, and no tidings could be obtained of them along the coast*'.[6]

Undeterred by the incidents of the previous voyage and his advancing age Charles Bayley, who was by now 46 years old, sailed the *Runnymede* out of Hobart Town on another whaling voyage after one month in port.[7] The vessel travelled to the southern whaling grounds off New Zealand, including the Chatham Islands.[8] It returned to Hobart Town on 1 August 1860 after nearly 15 months spent at sea, one of the longest stints Charles had undertaken in many years.[9] In its holds were 74 tuns of sperm whale oil and two tuns of black whale oil, with a combined value of £6,000, given sperm whale oil was selling locally at £80 per tun and black whale oil at £30.[10]

Several events of note had taken place in Charles Bayley's absence. First, James Bayley and his wife Emma had arrived back in Hobart Town from London per the ship *Isles of the South* on 23 October 1859.[11] All told the pair had been away for over 19 months. Second, on 6 December 1859 Alexander McGregor purchased the property owned by James Bayley at Battery Point in the vicinity of Runnymede and Cross streets, thus expanding his allotment significantly.[12] That same day, assumed to be protecting their home from any future bankruptcy or business proceedings that he may become involved in, Alexander signed the parcel over to his wife Harriet to be placed in trust '*during her life for her sole and separate use and free from the debts control and engagements of her said husband*'.[13] Several months later, on 13 March 1860, Alexander purchased the whaling barque *Flying Childers* in partnership with his two brothers James and John.[14] Owned by Askin Morrison, James had been master of the vessel since early 1855, undertaking annual voyages to the southern whaling grounds.

---

[1] *Lloyd's List*, 22 June 1859.
[2] *The Courier*, 30 December 1858; *The Hobart Town Advertiser*, 31 December 1858; Tasmanian Archives (MB2/39/1/23 P123).
[3] *The Courier*, 8 March 1859; *The Hobart Town Daily Mercury*, 5 March 1859.
[4] *The Hobart Town Advertiser*, 11 October 1858; *The Courier*, 11 October, 17 November 1858.
[5] *The Hobart Town Advertiser*, 11 October 1858; *The Courier*, 11 October, 17 November 1858.
[6] *The Hobart Town Advertiser*, 11 October 1858; *The Courier*, 11 October, 17 November 1858.
[7] *The Courier*, 9 April 1859.
[8] *The Hobart Town Advertiser*, 23 June 1860.
[9] *Launceston Examiner*, 21 August 1860; *The Mercury*, 21 August 1860.
[10] *The Mercury*, 21 August 1860.
[11] *The Hobart Town Advertiser*, 24 October 1859.
[12] www.thelist.tas.gov.au (Historic Deed 04/8030).
[13] www.thelist.tas.gov.au (Historic Deed 04/8031).
[14] National Archives of Australia, HOBART, Continuation [Transactions] Register, Volume 7, 1855-1949, Folio Tr 106.

By becoming shipowners, the three McGregor brothers were looking to capitalise on the potential profits that could be generated from the trade, though the price of whale oil was not as high as in previous years. Still, considering Alexander and John were both shipwrights with the former owning the patent slip, the three men could also leverage their resources with regards to vessel maintenance, repair and overhaul, resulting in significant cost savings.

On 12 September 1860 the *Runnymede* sailed out of the River Derwent on another whaling voyage.[1] This time at the helm was its joint owner James Bayley; Charles giving up command after undertaking several successive voyages in the vessel.[2] Also on board was James' wife Emma. Charles did not remain idle for long, however. A week after the *Runnymede* departed Hobart Town, he sailed with his wife Eliza, their daughter Jane Mary and his sister Harriet McGregor to Sydney as passengers on board the steamer *Tasmania*.[3] After three months of travelling, the foursome returned to Hobart Town on 21 December 1860 via Melbourne on board the steamer *City of Hobart*.[4]

Upon his homecoming Charles Bayley appears to have focused his attention on expanding his own business interests and portfolio, likely as a way to divest his personal time and efforts away from being at the helm of whaling vessels. The 387-ton American whaling barque *North America*, for example, had limped into Hobart Town on 3 February 1860 under the command of Captain Chappell to repair significant damage it had received during a violent gale that occurred off the coast of New Zealand.[5] In the weeks that followed, its cargo of 17 casks of black whale oil were advertised for sale by auction and several members of its crew deserted.[6] Still, with its damage repaired, the *North America* sailed out of the River Derwent on 12 March.[7]

The *North America* returned to Hobart Town exactly one year later, this time for provisions as well as to investigate the source of a leak.[8] However, instead of heading back to the whaling grounds, the vessel was placed on Alexander McGregor's patent slip and subsequently advertised for sale by auction without reserve.[9] On 5 April 1861 it was sold to John Lucas, shipbuilder of Battery Point, for £600.[10] This purchase appears to have fallen through, however, and the *North America* was advertised for sale by auction a few weeks later on account of its insurance underwriters.[11] Sold to John McGregor for £390, it was then officially purchased by Charles Bayley and Alexander McGregor on 8 July 1861 as joint owners, after having undergone considerable alterations and repairs.[12] Renaming it *Derwent Hunter*, it was the intention of the pair to place the vessel in intercolonial trade as opposed to the whaling industry.[13]

The *Derwent Hunter* was refitted and brought round to the New Wharf, expected to sail for Newcastle

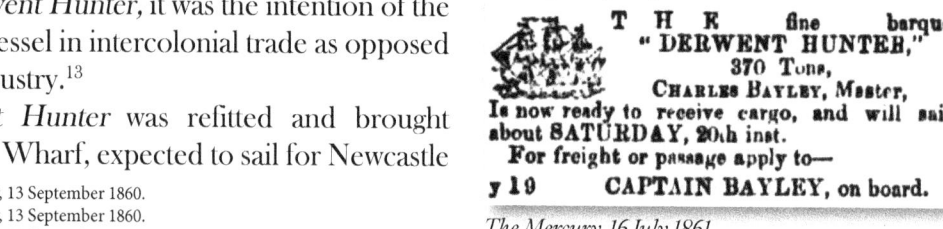

The Mercury, 16 July 1861.

[1] *The Hobart Town Advertiser*, 13 September 1860.
[2] *The Hobart Town Advertiser*, 13 September 1860.
[3] *The Hobart Town Advertiser*, 20 September 1860.
[4] *The Hobart Town Advertiser*, 22 December 1860.
[5] *The Hobart Town Daily Mercury*, 4 February 1860.
[6] *The Hobart Town Advertiser*, 18, 29 February 1860; *The Hobart Town Daily Mercury*, 5 March 1860.
[7] *The Hobart Town Daily Mercury*, 13 March 1860.
[8] *The Hobart Town Advertiser*, 12 March 1861.
[9] *The Hobart Town Advertiser*, 3 April 1861.
[10] *The Hobart Town Advertiser*, 6 April 1861.
[11] *The Mercury*, 6 April 1861.
[12] *The Hobart Town Advertiser*, 23 April 1861; National Archives of Australia (HOBART, Register of ships, Volume 8, 1865-1877, Folio 107); *The Mercury*, 5 July 1861.
[13] *The Mercury*, 5 July 1861; *The Hobart Town Advertiser*, 22 July 1861.

on 20 July 1861 and possibly Sydney with Charles Bayley at the helm.[14] Sadly, a melancholy event took place two days later that impacted his departure with massive consequences for the entire Bayley family; Charles' daughter Jane Mary died.

The only surviving child of Charles Bayley and his wife Eliza, Jane Mary Bayley died at the age of 17 years and nine days on 22 July 1861 at the family's Kelly Street home.[15] Her cause of death was consumption, i.e., tuberculous, a highly contagious bacterial disease of the lungs common for the period, especially in young adults, that the medical field knew very little about. Spread through the air by mucous droplets transferred from an infected person via coughing, sneezing, kissing or speaking, there was no known cure for the disease in the 1860s with most people infected with tuberculous treated with rest, good nutrition and clean air. It was an unkind pathway to death, however, with a significantly high mortality rate, often taking several years to progress from its onset until the patient's demise. Symptoms included fever, chest pain, night sweats, weight loss, and a cough producing sputum or blood, often interspersed with periods of remission.

Jane Mary, Charles and Eliza Bayley (late 1850s).
LINC Tasmania eHeritage Database (2012).

Jane Mary's death notice published in *The Mercury* notes that she died '*after a long and painful illness*', suggesting she had been ill for some time. Thus the family's recent trip to Sydney may have been to seek medical opinion or a change in climate.

Jane Mary Bayley was buried on 25 July 1861, possibly at the Presbyterian burial ground in Church Street, North Hobart, where her grandparents James and Jean Inglis had been buried.

On 5 August the *Derwent Hunter* sailed out of the River Derwent en route to Sydney with Charles Bayley at the helm, loaded with potatoes, onions, hay, fruit and jam.[16] His grieving wife Eliza was also on board.[17]

---

[14] *The Hobart Town Advertiser*, 22 July 1861.
[15] Tasmanian Archives (RGD35/1/6 no. 2879).
[16] *The Mercury*, 6 August 1861.
[17] *The Mercury*, 6 August 1861.

View from North Hobart showing the Presbyterian Burial Ground in Church Street (c1890s).
Tasmanian Archives (NS1013/1/973).

Passengers & Properties

By coincidence, in mid-November 1861 the whaling barque *Runnymede* and the intercolonial trading vessel *Derwent Hunter* both sailed into Spring Bay on Tasmania's east coast; the former to clean ship before sailing back into Hobart Town, the latter to shelter from bad weather.[1] It was a somewhat serendipitous reunion for Charles Bayley and his brother James and their wives Eliza and Emma. The couples had not seen one another since James had navigated the *Runnymede* out of the River Derwent on 12 September 1860 heading for the southern whaling grounds.[2] Thus James and Emma were perhaps unaware that Charles and Eliza's only child Jane Mary had died four months prior, while Charles and Eliza were commensurately unaware that Emma had given birth to a baby girl eight months earlier. There was much to lament and much to celebrate; life's successes punctuated with its deepest cuts.

Named Harriet Louisa and nicknamed Hally, James and Emma Bayley's first child was born on 21 March 1861 while the *Runnymede* was operating in waters between Tasmania and New Zealand's west coast.[3] It was an interesting decision to give birth to a child on board a whaling vessel sailing in remote and isolated waters, particularly one that did not have any other women on board nor anyone experienced in midwifery or even skilled medical care. Emma Bayley had obviously sailed on board large vessels previously, including with her father at the helm of craft employed in intercolonial trade. However, it was a brave decision that she made to board the *Runnymede* when it left Hobart Town in September 1860, at the time three months' pregnant, though one that fortunately ended in a successful birth and recovery.

Though considered a significant personal risk, it was not uncommon at the time for wives to sail with their husbands on board commercial vessels. Certain arms of the Bayley and McGregor families were part of a collective of couples and their young children preferencing the dangers and challenges of shipboard life as opposed to spending months or even years apart. While Charles Bayley and his wife Eliza had chosen to remain separated for the bulk of Charles' whaling career, balancing the lack of opportunity to have more children with a more mundane home life, other couples like James and Emma Bayley, as well as James McGregor and his wife Elizabeth on board the *Flying Childers* (and their young children), were determined to sail together.[4]

Several days after their chance encounter in Spring Bay, Charles Bayley sailed the *Derwent Hunter* into Hobart Town.[5] The *Runnymede*, with his brother James and family on board,

[1] *The Mercury*, 18 November 1861.
[2] *The Hobart Town Advertiser*, 13 September 1860.
[3] Tasmanian Archives (RGD33/1/8 no. 4777); *The Mercury*, 12 March 1861; *The Hobart Town Advertiser*, 9 May 1861.
[4] Tasmanian Archives (MB2/39/1/23 P128, MB2/39/1/26 P103).
[5] *The Hobart Town Advertiser*, 18 November 1861.

followed on 22 November 1861 with 78 tuns of sperm whale oil on board, valued at £6,084, after notably the '*best voyage of this season, of any whaler sailing out from Hobart Town*'.[1] Also in Hobart Town was the Scottish-built 201-ton schooner *Camilla*, recently operating out of Sydney as a whaler before being placed in intercolonial trade.[2] Purchased by Captain John Clinch in June 1861 for £850, the vessel had been sailed to Hobart Town by Captain Brydge White with a cargo of coal.[3] Upon arrival, Captain Clinch sold three by one-quarter shares in the vessel with Alexander McGregor purchasing one share, Charles Bayley (though absent at the time) purchasing another share, and Captain White purchasing the remaining share.[4] Its new owners, intent on placing the *Camilla* in intercolonial trade, then carried out repairs on Alexander McGregor's patent slip, in the process converting the craft into a brigantine.[5]

It was a strategic choice for Charles Bayley and Alexander McGregor to place a second vessel that they jointly owned in intercolonial trade. The whaling industry was obviously still profitable though an educated speculator could see that it would be waning in the decades to come, with coal and petroleum products beginning to significantly supersede whale oil as an energy and lighting source. In contrast, demand for the movement of agricultural products and other commodities between the Australian and New Zealand colonies, now becoming largely self-sufficient, was only increasing, as was the movement of passengers.

On 26 September 1861, commanded by Captain White, the *Camilla* cleared the River Derwent for Auckland taking 19 bales of hops and several passengers.[6] It then sailed to Newcastle, returning to Hobart Town on 7 December with coal.[7] Three weeks later it sailed for Auckland, this time taking 25 tons of stone, 25,000 palings, various posts and rails, books, jam and other sundries.[8]

On 3 December 1861, four days before the *Camilla* sailed, Charles Bayley helmed the *Derwent Hunter*

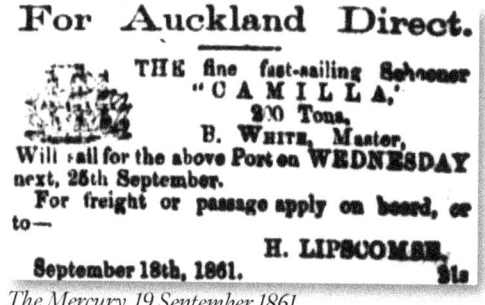

The Mercury, 19 September 1861.

out of the River Derwent also headed for New Zealand, this time with a cargo of sheep, though without his wife Eliza on board.[9] Still, it must have been a new experience for the couple, accustomed to the routine of whaling vessels at sea for long periods of time, to be part of a trading route with such regularity and to see and hear of vessels they now owned coming and going with similar frequency.

Alexander McGregor was also travelling, regularly taking on insurance work involving journeys to remote areas of Tasmania's coastline and the mainland to assess vessels that had become stranded or wrecked.[10] Steadily and with calculated risk, the Bayley and McGregor families were becoming stalwarts of multiple facets of the Tasmanian maritime industry. Included amongst this brethren was James Bayley who once more sailed the barque *Runnymede* out of Hobart Town en route to the south seas in search of whales. The vessel left port on 7 January 1862, perhaps understandably without his wife Emma and baby daughter Hally on board.[11]

---

[1] *The Mercury*, 22 November 1861.
[2] *The Shipping Gazette and Sydney General Trade List*, 30 January 1860; *Empire*, 21 February, 21 December 1860.
[3] *The Sydney Morning Herald*, 13 June 1861; *The Hobart Town Advertiser*, 20 August 1861.
[4] National Archives of Australia (HOBART, Register of ships, Volume 8, 1865-1877, Folio 109).
[5] *The Hobart Town Advertiser*, 2 September 1861.
[6] *The Mercury*, 30 September 1861.
[7] *The Mercury*, 19 November, 9, 31 December 1861.
[8] *The Mercury*, 1 January 1862.
[9] *The Hobart Town Advertiser*, 4 December 1862.
[10] *Launceston Examiner*, 26 October 1861; *The Hobart Town Advertiser*, 30 October 1861.
[11] *The Mercury*, 8 January 1862.

Brigantine Camilla.
Maritime Museum of Tasmania (POMJ23a).

For Harriet McGregor and her two sisters-in-law Eliza and Emma Bayley, the year 1862 was another series of vessel comings and goings. The ladies lived within close proximity to one another at Battery Point, no doubt sharing part of their days in each others company. Though the loss of Jane Mary Bayley, at the age of 17, would have still been raw, the presence of baby Hally Bayley would have brought much needed joy to the families. Interestingly, James and Emma Bayley had also adopted a young son by this period with Charles William Bayley born to unknown parents in early 1860.[1] The child was doted on by all of his relatives. For Harriet in particular, with no children of her own, there were also nieces and nephews on the McGregor side that lived close by and would have often visited, including those belonging to her husband's brothers James and John and sisters Jean (now Horne) and Elizabeth (now Mason). Of note, Harriet was informant to the birth of Elizabeth and her husband Alfred Mason's daughter Janet who was born in Hobart Town on 1 December 1861.[2] Also still living was the McGregor family's matriarch Janet. However, she sadly died on 6 May 1862 at the age of 64 from paralysis.[3] She was living at 1 Cross Street, Battery Point, at the time of her death, i.e., the home of Alexander and Harriet located on the corner of Cross and Runnymede streets.[4] Janet McGregor was buried four days later at the Davey Street Congregational Cemetery in Wellesley Street, South Hobart.[5] As a mark of respect, vessels moored in the Port of Hobart Town lowered their flags to half-mast.[6]

With regards to vessel movements, the *Derwent Hunter* returned to Hobart Town on 13 January 1862 having departed Kaikoura, New Zealand, in ballast on 23 December 1861, commanded by Charles Bayley.[7] He reported that of the 2,170 sheep the vessel carried to New Zealand, 156 died which was considerably below average. It soon loaded more sheep, this time 2,200 animals for Lyttelton, leaving Hobart Town on 23 January. The *Derwent Hunter* arrived back in Hobart Town on 4 March 1862 in ballast, indicating that the trade was a one-way route.[8] The vessel then left Hobart Town on 17 March with 2,100 sheep for Kaikoura.[9] The livestock were being shipped by W. Knight of Tasmania to George Anstey as part of a flock of 20,000 sent in total.[10] Having to maintain the health of such a large number of animals on board his barque must have been quite the contrast for Charles Bayley compared to his days on board a whaler.

Barque Derwent Hunter.
Maritime Museum of Tasmania (POMD 13a).

---

[1] *The Mercury*, 8 January 1862; *The Advertiser*, 29, 31 August 1863; Tasmanian Archives (RGD35/1/6 no. 4050).
[2] Tasmanian Archives (RGD33/1/8 no. 4794).
[3] Tasmanian Archives (RGD35/1/6 no. 3329).
[4] *The Mercury*, 8 May 1862.
[5] *The Mercury*, 9 May 1862; https://www.findagrave.com/memorial/234425959/janet-mcgregor.
[6] *The Advertiser*, 8 May 1862.
[7] *The Mercury*, 14, 23 January 1862; *The Hobart Town Advertiser*, 18 January 1862; *The Advertiser*, 23 January 1862.
[8] *The Mercury*, 5 March 1862.
[9] *The Mercury*, 18 March 1862.
[10] *The Mercury*, 18 March 1862.

With Charles Bayley at the helm, the *Derwent Hunter* arrived back in Hobart Town from New Zealand on 22 April 1862 and moored off Alexander McGregor's shipyard to be overhauled.[11] It was relaunched a month later and immediately laid on for Newcastle via Sydney, sailing out of the River Derwent on 26 May.[12] On board were Charles' wife Eliza, their adopted nephew Charles Bayley, as well as Alexander and Harriet McGregor.[13] The foursome remained on the *Derwent Hunter* for the entire trip, arriving back in Hobart Town exactly two months later with a load of coal in addition to 150 dozen oranges and one case of drugs.[14] Three weeks later, on 15 August, Charles Bayley navigated the *Derwent Hunter* back out of the Derwent, this time en route to Otago, New Zealand, with 19 passengers and a cargo of sundries.[15] In a rather quick turnaround, the craft arrived back in Hobart Town on 19 September.[16] Significantly, this was the last trip Charles Bayley made at the helm of a commercial vessel. He was 49 years of age.

All told, between 1839 and 1862 Charles Bayley had undertaken five voyages at the helm of the whaling barque *Wallaby*; seven voyages at the helm of the whaling barque *Fortitude*, of which he was a part-owner for three of the voyages; 10 voyages at the helm of the whaling barque *Runnymede* which he also part-owned; and six voyages at the helm of the intercolonial trader *Derwent Hunter*. During this period he had amassed a great deal of wealth, conservatively estimated to be well over £20,000. Still, he and his wife Eliza had lived modestly in a cottage in Kelly Street, Battery Point, since the early 1840s and they had endured significant periods away from one another at the expense of building a family. They had also buried their two children.

Despite retirement from the helm, Charles Bayley did not give up the vocation altogether. He remained a half-share owner in the whaling barque *Runnymede* with his brother James, a half-share owner in the intercolonial trader *Derwent Hunter* with his brother-in-law Alexander McGregor, and a quarter-share owner of the intercolonial brigantine *Camilla* with Alexander McGregor, Brydge White, William Belbin and Charles Dowdell. Acting as a shipping agent for these vessels, he began working out of his home in Kelly Street.[17] He would continue to expand his fleet of commercial vessels in the years to come. Meanwhile, on 16 December Charles cleared out of the Derwent, this time in charge of the cutter yacht *Surprise*, purchased by Alexander McGregor from Sydney-based owners in early 1862.[18] Accompanied by captains McArthur, Chamberlain (Sr), Chamberlain (Jr), Lucas and G. S. Wilson, the group were headed to Port Davey and Tasmania's south-

Painting of Charles Bayley.
LINC Tasmania eHeritage Database (2012).

[11] *The Mercury*, 23 April 1862.
[12] *The Advertiser*, 22 April 1862; *The Mercury*, 27 May 1862.
[13] *The Mercury*, 29 April 1862; *Hobart Town Advertiser*, 31 May 1862.
[14] *The Advertiser*, 24 July 1862; *The Mercury*, 28 July 1862.
[15] *The Advertiser*, 16 August 1862; *The Mercury*, 21 August 1862.
[16] *The Mercury*, 20 September 1862.
[17] *The Mercury*, 27 February 1863.
[18] *The Mercury*, 9 January 1862; *Launceston Examiner*, 11 January 1862.

west coast on a fishing excursion.¹ Charles Bayley was finally ready for some much-needed downtime. In addition to expanding his recreational pursuits, retirement saw Charles take up charitable work and other benevolent causes, including joining the committee to raise funds for those affected by the wreck of HMSS *Orpheus*, as well as organising the Hobart Town Regatta.²

Continuing to summarise vessel movements, on 27 January 1863 the barque *Runnymede* made a brief return from another whaling voyage commanded by James Bayley. The 60 tuns of sperm whale oil stored on board appears not to have been discharged, however.³ Instead the vessel left Hobart Town a few days later, this time with James' wife Emma and their daughter Hally on board. It returned on 18 June 1863 having secured another 12 tuns of sperm whale oil; its 72 tuns of oil now valued at £5,904 with the local price being £82 per tun.⁴

The *Runnymede* remained in port for several months, undergoing extensive repairs at Alexander McGregor's shipyard.⁵ During the interim the Bayley family dealt with the loss of another child. On 27 August 1863, at the Kelly Street home of his uncle and aunt Charles and Eliza Bayley, Charles William Bayley died of infantile cholera.⁶ The adopted son of James and Emma Bayley, he was four years and eight months old at the time of his death.⁷ As a mark of respect, vessels in the Port of Hobart lowered their flags to half-mast.

The result of ingesting water or food contaminated with the bacterium *Vibrio cholerae*, symptoms of cholera include severe diarrhoea, vomiting and dehydration. The infection was so acute and life-threatening at the time that patients, particularly infants and children, often died within hours of the first symptoms appearing. Unfortunately the bacterium thrived in unsanitary environments and with Hobart Town's limited capabilities to treat its drinking water supply and manage its sewage, it was common for outbreaks to occur and be widespread.

On 2 October 1863, a month after the death of his young son, James Bayley sailed out of Hobart Town on board the *Runnymede* to begin another voyage to the south seas in search of whales.⁸ His wife Emma and daughter Hally did not accompany James this time; Emma was by now five months' pregnant.

With the impending arrival of another niece or nephew, Charles Bayley and his wife Eliza made the decision to relocate from Battery Point and its incessant water supply and public health issues, to a home further away from town. It was also a property that offered the larger Bayley family a lot more space and better sanitary conditions.

> BISHOPSTOWE.—For Sale, with immediate possession, BISHOPSTOWE, the well-known residence of the Bishop of Tasmania, who is unable through continued ill-health to return to the Colony. The house stands on a block of land of five acres, rising in a gentle slope from New Town Bay, and commanding scenery of the most beautiful and varied description. The house is most substantially built of stone, containing fifteen rooms, with the usual compliment of stable, coach houses, offices, outbuildings, &c. The gardens are plentifully stocked with fruit trees of the best description, and are in a high state of cultivation. Distance from Hobart Town 2 ¼ miles.
> Title—Crown Grant.
> For further particulars and terms, apply to
> W KNIGHT, & Co.,
> New Wharf.
> Also—A paddock of one and a half acres, half of which consists of an orchard of the choicest fruit trees. t † 30o

The Mercury, 16 October 1863.

---

¹ *The Mercury*, 17 December 1862.
² *The Advertiser*, 17 April, 7 November 1863.
³ *The Mercury*, 19 January 1863; *The Advertiser*, 23 June 1863.
⁴ *The Mercury*, 19 January, 18 June 1863; *The Advertiser*, 28 January 1863.
⁵ *The Advertiser*, 4 September 1863.
⁶ *The Mercury*, 29 August 1863; *The Advertiser*, 29 August 1863; Tasmanian Archives (RGD35/1/6 no. 4050).
⁷ *The Mercury*, 29 August 1863; *The Advertiser*, 29 August 1863; Tasmanian Archives (RGD35/1/6 no. 4050).
⁸ *Hobart Town Advertiser: Weekly Edt*, 10 October 1863.

On 27 November 1863 the couple purchased the 'Bishopstowe' estate belonging to Francis Russell Nixon, the first Bishop of Tasmania.[9] Situated at New Town overlooking both Cornelian and New Town bays, the five-acre property was acquired at auction for £2,300.[10] It included a substantial 15-room Regency-era 'marine villa' that had been built by Robert Pitcairn, a prominent Hobart Town solicitor, and his wife Dorothea in the mid-1830s.[11] After purchasing the estate in 1849, Bishop Nixon had expanded the home, adding a drawing room in a new western wing.[12]

Renaming the property 'Runnymede' after his whaling barque, it was an idyllic location, less than three miles from Hobart Town, though offering the vastness of a country estate, including its sanitation and health benefits. While the stone house and immediate grounds are still in existence, since 1965 leased by the National Trust (Tasmania) from the State Government of Tasmania, the surrounding area has undergone substantial change since its construction, including the establishment of Cornelian Bay Cemetery which was formally opened in 1872 and vast reclamation works of New Town Bay which began in 1915 such that the property no longer shares a boundary with this water body. The area is now also dissected by the Brooker Highway and surrounded by sports ovals and the Tasmanian Hockey Centre, much of its fruit trees, gardens and bushland being superseded. 'Runnymede' now also lies within the suburb of New Town which underwent much subdivision of land into smaller and smaller allotments in the decades after the Bayley family purchased the property, including the development of a railway line and train station.

New Town Bay showing 'Bishopstowe' (1850s).
Tasmanian Archives (PH30/1/343).

[9] *The Advertiser*, 27, 30 November 1863.
[10] *The Hobart Town Courier*, 6 May 1836; *The Advertiser*, 27 November 1863; https://heritage.tas.gov.au/Documents/THR12100%20Permanent%20entry%20Datasheet%20%26%20CPR%20combined.pdf.
[11] www.thelist.tas.gov.au (Historic Deed 02/0022).
[12] www.thelist.tas.gov.au (Historic Deed 02/0022); *Hobarton Guardian, or, True Friend of Tasmania*, 7 November 1849.

1930s map showing location of the 'Runnymede' estate in relation to a map of New Town (prior to reclamation works) and Cornelian Bay overlayed with 2025 map.

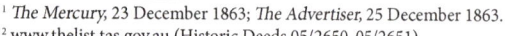

View of 'Runnymede' from New Town Bay (c1910s).
Tasmanian Archives (NS1013/1/1169).

Charles Bayley and his wife Eliza were noted as living at 'Runnymede' in the lead-up to Christmas 1863.[1] In February 1864 the couple also purchased a separate one-acre allotment bordering New Town Bay and adjacent to their new estate.[2] That same month the barque *Runnymede* was sighted at Fortescue Bay though it only briefly entered the River Derwent to take on supplies and likely receive news and family updates before James Bayley sailed the vessel to New Zealand's Chatham Island region in search of more whales.[3]

With her husband at sea, Emma Bayley moved into 'Runnymede' with their young daughter Hally. It was here that Emma gave birth to a son named William Inglis Bayley on 27 May 1864.[4] Sadly, the newborn died just nine days later on 5 June, also at 'Runnymede'. Cause of death was jaundice and erysipelas, i.e., an infection affecting the skin caused by *Streptococcus* bacteria.[5] Another death would befall Emma several months later with the loss of her elder brother Thomas David Butchard at 'Runnymede' on 1 September 1864.[6] Cause of death was tuberculosis.[7] He was 27 years of age.

James, Emma and Hally Bayley (c1863).
LINC Tasmania eHeritage Database (2012).

[1] *The Mercury*, 23 December 1863; *The Advertiser*, 25 December 1863.
[2] www.thelist.tas.gov.au (Historic Deeds 05/2650, 05/2651).
[3] *The Mercury*, 23 December 1863; *The Advertiser*, 5, 22 February 1864.
[4] *The Advertiser*, 31 May 1864.
[5] *The Advertiser*, 7 June 1864; Tasmanian Archives (RGD35/1/7 no. 4477).
[6] *The Advertiser*, 5 September 1864.
[7] Tasmanian Archives (RGD35/1/7 no. 4637).

The larger Bayley family endured a third death in 1864 with the passing of its patriarch Charles Bull on 21 October, though it would have taken several months to receive the news by letter from England. He was 82 years of age and buried at St Mary the Virgin Church in Burnham-on-Crouch in a headstone paid for and erected by his youngest daughter Harriet McGregor.[8]

Despite the upheaval to his family situation and the loss of several loved ones, Charles Bayley remained busy in retirement. In addition to managing his new estate of 'Runnymede', including its ornamental and vegetable gardens, Charles maintained his association with the Hobart Town Regatta. He also volunteered with the staging and administration of other local and regional regattas, including acting as a judge at the New Norfolk Regatta held on 27 December 1864.[9] However, he was fortunate to escape serious injury when, as a passenger on board the evening coach from New Norfolk to Hobart Town, he was flung from the vehicle along with all of the other occupants, including his brother-in-law Alexander McGregor.[10] The accident had occurred while the coach was navigating a bend in the road and encountered an oncoming horse and cart.[11] A few weeks earlier Charles Bayley had been elected a director of the Derwent and Tamar Fire and Marine Assurance Company.[12]

The *Runnymede* commanded by James Bayley returned to Hobart Town on 21 January 1865 after a 16-month voyage encompassing waters off New Zealand, Tasmania's east coast and the south-east coast of mainland Australia.[13] On board was 80 tuns of sperm whale oil, valued at £5,040 considering the local price for the commodity at the time was rather low at £63 per tun.[14]

Grave of Charles Bull, St Mary the Virgin Church, Burnham-on-Crouch, Essex, England.
https://www.findagrave.com/memorial/214296471 (photo added by Bill Evans).

After one month spent in port, James Bayley sailed the *Runnymede* out of the River Derwent on 21 February 1865.[15] He returned briefly in late July to recharge supplies, though the vessel's departure from Hobart Town was delayed owing to difficulty with several crew members

---

[8] Essex, England, Church of England Deaths and Burials, 1813-1996; UK and Ireland, Find a Grave Index, 1300s-Current.
[9] *The Advertiser*, 28 December 1864.
[10] *The Mercury*, 28 December 1864; *The Advertiser*, 28 December 1864.
[11] *The Advertiser*, 28 December 1864.
[12] *The Mercury*, 13 December 1864.
[13] *The Mercury*, 23 January 1865.
[14] *The Advertiser*, 20 January 1865.
[15] *The Mercury*, 22 February 1865.

absconding.[1] The interlude gave the opportunity for James' wife Emma and their now four-year-old daughter Hally to embark as passengers.[2]

The *Runnymede* returned to port after another successful voyage on 2 December 1865. After 10 months at sea, the vessel held 65 tuns of sperm whale oil in its holds.[3] The commodity was trans-shipped to London owing to the '*extraordinary advance in the price of sperm oil in the home market*', despite the product selling locally for £100 per tun.[4]

While his brother James had been at sea on board the *Runnymede* for the bulk of 1865, Charles Bayley had expanded his business enterprises, becoming an agent for the barque *Bella Mary* which he and his brother-in-law Alexander McGregor had purchased quarter shares in.[5] The vessel was placed in intercolonial trade, sailing between New Zealand and Hobart Town. Charles had also established an office at the New Wharf, i.e., Salamanca, where he oversaw administrative and agent duties associated with the *Runnymede* and the other vessels in which he owned part-shares, including the *Camilla* and *Derwent Hunter*. Meanwhile, in addition to major repair and overhaul work carried out at his shipyard at the Government Domain, Alexander McGregor was also branching into shipbuilding. On 12 December 1865, the 59-ton schooner *Petrel* was launched from his yard with little Hally Bayley performing the customary christening honours.[6] The craft was intended for the Launceston to Hobart Town trade, built primarily by the yard's apprentices.[7] Alexander was also continuing to build his own vessel portfolio, by late 1865 being owner or part-owner of the barques *Flying Childers*, *Prince Regent* and *Emily Downing*.[8] Not satisfied with vessels alone, in July 1865 he also purchased the Lord Rodney Hotel at the New Wharf for £525.[9]

Lord Rodney Hotel (c1890s).
Tasmanian Archives (PH30/1/9165).

[1] *The Advertiser,* 25, 29 July, 1 August 1865.
[2] Tasmanian Archives (MB2/39/1/30 p210).
[3] *Tasmanian Morning Herald,* 4 December 1865.
[4] *The Mercury,* 23 December 1865, 23 January 1866.
[5] *The Advertiser,* 8 February 1865; National Archives of Australia (HOBART, Register of ships, Volume 9, 1865-1877, [pages 1-173, continues on film roll 2], Folio 6).
[6] *The Mercury,* 13 December 1865.
[7] *The Mercury,* 13 December 1865.
[8] *The Mercury,* 25 February 1864; *The Advertiser,* 23 June, 23 September 1864.
[9] *The Mercury,* 27 July 1864.

Whale Oil & Waves

The year 1866 began with another industrious period for the Bayley and McGregor families. With the price of sperm whale oil still high, the barque *Runnymede* had cleared out of the River Derwent on 28 December 1865 almost immediately after discharging its latest cargo of oil.[10] With James Bayley remaining at the helm, his wife Emma and their daughter Hally were also on board; the couple and their young child opting to spend time together at sea as opposed to months apart. Alexander McGregor was also making plans, advertising the lease of his shipyard, including the infamous patent slip, for sale by auction in late January. It had been 11 years since he had taken over the yard from Captain Edward Goldsmith, in partnership with Askin Morrison, paying £4,200 for the site's 99-year lease beginning on 1 December 1854, along with an annual payment of one shilling.[11] Since this time the slip had become an essential piece of infrastructure for commercial vessels belonging to and visiting the Port of Hobart Town where large and small-scale overhaul, repair and refit services were performed. In recent years the shipyard had also expanded into shipbuilding. Thus with 88 years left on the lease, the auction for the yard was spirited though it was ultimately purchased by George Wilson for the price of £3,200.[12] However, while Alexander McGregor had sold his part of the lease, he had purchased Askin Morrison's share and also remained the shipyard's operator, thus likely paying an annual sum to George Wilson as a sub-lessee.[13]

Coinciding with the sale of his shipyard's lease, Alexander McGregor was appointed a director of the Tasmanian Steam Navigation (TSN) Company that operated passenger and cargo

The Mercury, 1 January 1866.

---

[10] *The Mercury*, 29 December 1865.
[11] www.thelist.tas.gov.au (Historic Deed 04/1871).
[12] *The Mercury*, 1 February 1866.
[13] www.thelist.tas.gov.au (Historic Deed 05/3955); *The Mercury*, 1 June 1876.

services between Tasmania and various mainland ports.[1] A few weeks later, on 2 April 1866, his new schooner *Petrel*, of which Alexander was the agent, arrived in Launceston on its maiden voyage carrying a cargo of tea and sugar.[2]

With their vessels engaged in various trades, Charles Bayley and Alexander McGregor spent the remainder of 1866 dutifully managing the routes, passengers, cargoes, crew, clearances, customs and other administrative duties associated with the numerous craft they by now owned. The pair also continued their director roles with various business enterprises, as well as their committee responsibilities associated with the Hobart Town Regatta. On the home front, Alexander and his wife Harriet travelled to Melbourne in mid-1866 very likely mixing business responsibilities with a holiday.[3] However, another illness would soon strike the wider family unit.

While away at sea on board the *Runnymede* Emma Bayley became ill with the latter stages of tuberculous, the same disease that had most recently killed her brother, and she was slowly but surely becoming more and more plagued by the serious illness. It is therefore not happenstance that the *Runnymede* returned to port with James at the helm and a sick Emma on board on 30 July 1866 after a voyage of only seven months.[4] The vessel carried 25 tuns of sperm whale oil, valued locally at £2,500 owing to the price being £100 per tun, though would fetch more if trans-shipped to London.[5]

Upon reaching port, news quickly began to circulate of Emma's health, as well as that of a serious accident that had occurred to James a few weeks prior whereby he had fallen from the topgallant yard of the *Runnymede*, though had fortunately '*struck the braces, which threw him off into the sea* [a startling distance of 90 feet], *from which he was almost immediately rescued*'.[6] His rescuer was the *Runnymede*'s third mate, a courageous Pacific Islander by the name of John Bull whom, upon hearing the splash, had instantly sprang over the side, swimming to James' assistance and keeping him afloat until a boat could be lowered and the pair subsequently picked up.[7] Relieved to only have been badly bruised from the ordeal, upon the *Runnymede*'s return to Hobart Town, James presented John Bull with a gold watch and chain as a token of appreciation for saving his life.[8]

After a month in port the *Runnymede* once more sailed out of the River Derwent headed back to the south seas whaling grounds on 29 August 1866, this time with Captain H. F. Hill at the helm, formerly its chief mate.[9] It was the first time in 17 years that neither Charles nor James Bayley were in command of their vessel. It was the right decision. On 4 December 1866 Emma Bayley passed away at the Battery Point home

Emma Bayley (c1865).
LINC Tasmania eHeritage Database (2012).

---

[1] *The Cornwall Chronicle*, 17 March 1866.
[2] *Launceston Examiner*, 3 April 1866; *The Mercury*, 4 April 1866.
[3] Tasmanian Archives (MB2/39/1/30 p347).
[4] *The Mercury*, 25, 30 July 1866; Tasmanian Archives (MB2/39/1/30 p353).
[5] *The Mercury*, 25, 30 July 1866; *Tasmanian Morning Herald*, 31 July, 25 August 1866.
[6] *Tasmanian Morning Herald*, 30 July 1866; *The Mercury*, 7 August 1866.
[7] *Launceston Examiner*, 31 July 1866.
[8] *The Mercury*, 7 August 1866.
[9] *The Mercury*, 28, 30 August 1866.

View of Hobart Town's New Wharf and Battery Point c1866). Directly in front of Alexander and Harriet McGregor's cottage on the hill is the barque Runnymede (shown in the square).
Tasmanian Archives (NS1013/1/1622).

of Alexander and Harriet McGregor.[1] She was 27 years of age and left behind her husband James and their five-year-old daughter Hally. Ships in port lowered their flags to half-mast as a mark of respect.[2]

Following the death of his wife, James Bayley and his daughter Hally moved in with Charles and Eliza Bayley at their expansive 'Runnymede' estate, with the former likely taking on a mothering role.[3] However, the move was only temporary. On 26 February 1867 James and Hally left Hobart Town as passengers on board the 621-ton ship *Windward* bound for London.[4] Also on board were 21 bundles of whalebone consigned to James.[5] It would be another five years before the duo sailed back to Hobart Town.

In James' absence, Charles Bayley and his brother-in-law Alexander McGregor purchased another commercial vessel, this time the Clyde-built 342-ton barque *Helen*. Charles travelled to Sydney to complete the transaction, arriving back in Hobart Town as a passenger on board the steamer *Tasmania* on 1 April 1867.[6] The *Helen* had only been launched two years prior and was classed by Lloyd's as A1 13 years.[7] It was intended that it would take the place of the *Derwent Hunter* in intercolonial trade, with the *Derwent Hunter* instead fitted out once more for whaling. However, instead of operating out of the Port of Hobart Town, the *Helen* was based out of Sydney during the first few years of Charles Bayley and Alexander McGregor's ownership, trading between that city and various Asian ports, including Bangkok and Fuzhou.[8]

By this point in time the business interests of Charles Bayley and Alexander McGregor were very much aligned, being joint or part-owners and thereby agents of the barque *Derwent Hunter*, the brigantine *Camilla*, the barque *Bella Mary*, and now the barque *Helen*. Meanwhile Charles and James Bayley remained joint owners of the *Runnymede*. Conversely, Alexander McGregor was sole owner of the barque *Emily Downing* and schooner *Petrel*, and part-owner of the barques *Flying Childers* and *India*.

Continuing to be the proprietor of the principal shipyard in the colony, Alexander McGregor had also relaid his patent slip in mid-1867 at the substantial cost of £4,000, likely using the money generated from the sale of the site's long-term lease to fund the works.[9] The driving wheel for the slip, weighing eight tons, was manufactured locally by Messrs Clark and Son of Collins Street and was highlighted in the Hobart Town press as evidence of the engineering capabilities and ingenuity of local manufacturers, as opposed to importing a comparable piece of equipment from England.[10] The slip was now capable of taking up vessels of up to 800 tons.

Another source of income for Alexander McGregor was his role as a director of the TSN Company, including often travelling to the mainland on behalf of this organisation to inspect vessels that had been damaged, wrecked or otherwise needed to be sighted. His wife often travelled with him during these trips too. For instance, Alexander and Harriet proceeded to Melbourne on behalf of the TSN Company in mid-March 1868; the couple travelling as cabin passengers on board the steamer *Tasmania*.[11]

[1] *Tasmanian Morning Herald*, 5 December 1866.
[2] *The Mercury*, 5 December 1866.
[3] *The Mercury*, 26 January 1867.
[4] *The Mercury*, 27 February 1867.
[5] *The Mercury*, 27 February 1867.
[6] *The Mercury*, 2 April 1867.
[7] *The Mercury*, 20 March 1867.
[8] *The Mercury*, 3 August 1871.
[9] *The Mercury*, 12 April 1867.
[10] *The Tasmanian Times*, 25 June, 6, 25 July, 24 August 1867.
[11] *The Tasmanian*, 25 July 1867; *The Mercury*, 16 March 1868.

There were of course social, sporting and recreational events and attractions to entertain all members of the Bayley and McGregor families during this period. One such diversion was the highly anticipated arrival of His Royal Highness, Prince Alfred, the Duke of Edinburgh, who was expected to visit Hobart Town in early 1868. Notably the first ever visit to Australia by a member of the Royal Family, the Prince had left England at the command of HMS *Galatea* in January 1867, first visiting the Mediterranean and South America. The vessel then reached Adelaide on 31 October to commence a royal tour of Australia.

After spending several weeks in South Australia the Prince's party sailed to Melbourne before arriving in Hobart Town on 6 January 1868. The population of Van Diemen's Land was buzzing. Numerous formal events and festivities, including receptions, tours, dinners and balls, had been organised to showcase the colony and its growing populace. Hobart Town had also been extensively decorated with flags and bunting to welcome the Prince and his contingent.

H.R.H. THE DUKE OF EDINBURGH, K.G.
PHOTOGRAPHED BY
JOHNSTONE, O'SHANNESSY & C°

Tasmanian Archives (NS1013/1/1980).

The official State Landing took place on 7 January 1868 starting at the New Wharf. Here a Royal Salute was fired and the Prince was escorted to his carriage by the Governor of Tasmania, Sir Thomas Gore Browne, and other dignitaries, thereupon travelling to a Landing Stage where formal speeches and addresses took place. From there the Prince travelled via carriage to Franklin Square, on the way traversing through three decorative arches. The first arch, the 'Welcome to Tasmania' emblematic arch, featured two whaleboats manned by Tasmanian-born youths dressed in costume, amongst other colonial-produced items and products. Of note, this particular structure had been designed, created and decorated by a committee of local citizens, included amongst them Alexander McGregor who was specifically involved in the arch's development such that he was thanked for '*his unremitting exertions in its construction*'.[12] It was also noted that Alexander not only gave money to the project but his time and attention, as well as the labour of the men in his employment, to ensure the arch was ready in time.[13] In addition he helped with the organisation and staging of a citizen's banquet given to the crew of the Prince's vessel HMS *Galatea*. Held at the Hobart Town Hall the event '*was a sight which will long be remembered by those who were present at it. Never was any similar dinner witnessed in these colonies, and never was such a complete success*

---

[12] *The Tasmanian Times*, 9 January 1868.
[13] *The Tasmanian Times*, 9 January 1868.

'Welcome to Tasmania' emblematic arch at the Hobart Town wharf (January 1868).
Tasmanian Archives (PH30/1/31).

attained'.[1] The article continued. 'The idea originated with the Citizen's Reception Committee, and the arrangements were remitted to a sub-Committee ... As it is only fair that credit should be given where credit is due, and especially as the great trouble taken has resulted in such a noble sight as was witnessed on Saturday, we may mention that the working men of this committee were ... most ably assisted by several members of the General Committee, amongst whom the following were especially prominent in their efforts to advance the affair: ... *Captain Bayley, Mr A. McGregor.*'[2] Obviously staunch and reverent monarchists, Charles Bayley and Alexander McGregor also helped organise the Tasmanian Anniversary Regatta, held on 9 January 1868, which the Prince attended and acted as patron.[3] Moreover, an illumination in honour of the Prince's visit was also organised with many buildings and residences dressed with flags and lights. Noteworthy examples were reported in the press, including '*Mr A. McGregor's residence [which] was beautifully and tastefully illuminated with gas. There was a star surrounded by a crown with the motto "Welcome Prince Alfred", two anchors of gas lights, the verandah was hung with Chinese lanterns, and the whole had a most imposing effect*'.[4]

---
[1] *The Tasmanian Times*, 13 January 1868.
[2] *The Tasmanian Times*, 13 January 1868.
[3] *The Cornwall Chronicle*, 15 January 1868.
[4] *The Tasmanian Times*, 18 January 1868.

With His Royal Highness Prince Alfred's departure from Hobart Town on 18 January 1868 on board HMS *Galatea*, the next vessel of interest to sail up the River Derwent with relevance to the Bayley family was their barque *Runnymede,* which returned from its whaling voyage on 7 February 1868 with 21 tuns of sperm whale oil on board, 24 tuns of black whale oil and 11 hundredweight of whale bone.[5] Under the management of Captain Hill the vessel had not enjoyed its usual success, though had not done poorly. It entered out for another voyage a month later on 6 March 1868, again with Captain H. F. Hill at the helm.[6]

With so many vessels coming and going the Port of Hobart Town was a hive of activity, as were the associated maritime-related support industries established in the colony to accommodate both local and visiting commercial and recreational vessels. Alexander McGregor's patent slip was in high demand and he had profited handsomely from the patronage it had received since he had established the enterprise 13 years prior. However, with Alexander's business interests now heading in the direction of vessel ownership, in April 1868 he relinquished his management of the Domain patent slip and shipyard, sub-letting the site to his very capable younger brother John.

With his time and resources now focused on his fleet of vessels engaged in international and colonial trade and whaling, Alexander McGregor was likely looking forward to the future and expanding his fleet further. Unfortunately less than two months later an incident took place several hundred miles to the north of Hobart Town, at Whirlpool Reach on the River Tamar. Primarily plying between Hobart Town and Launceston, Alexander's 59-ton schooner *Petrel* had departed the latter port on 22 June 1868 under the command of Captain G. P. Harrison.[7] Disastrously, whilst navigating the lower reaches of the River Tamar under tow during low tide and a strong current, the vessel had become unmanageable, drifting onto Whirlpool Rock, becoming embedded and quickly filling with water such that it sunk.[8] Despite several attempts by a steam tug to pull the *Petrel* off the rock, under the guidance of Alexander who had travelled to the site from Hobart Town, the vessel was ultimately declared a wreck, though its cargo of sugar, barley, butter and other sundries was largely saved.[9] Still,

The Tasmanian Times, 9 April 1868.

although Alexander McGregor had registered the vessel, he had not insured it such that the *Petrel*'s demise resulted in a significant financial loss for his business operations.[10] He did, however, recover some money when the hull of the wrecked vessel was advertised for sale a few weeks

---

[5] *The Mercury,* 8 February 1868.
[6] *The Cornwall Chronicle,* 7 March 1868.
[7] *Launceston Examiner,* 23 June 1868.
[8] *The Cornwall Chronicle,* 24 June 1868; *Launceston Examiner,* 25 June 1868.
[9] *The Mercury,* 24 June 1868; *Launceston Examiner,* 25 June 1868.
[10] *The Mercury,* 24 June 1868; *Launceston Examiner,* 25 June 1868.

later.¹ Sold for £50 the salvagers were not able to dislodge the wreck of the *Petrel* from the rock such that it was not until almost a year later when currents forced the hull to drift three miles down the river and become beached.²

With the loss of the *Petrel* Alexander McGregor had an immediate need to replace the craft and maintain his presence in the Tasmanian coastal trade. Fortunately he was able to procure the services of his brother John who, within only a few weeks of the wreck, began building a new vessel at his Domain shipyard. By mid-July the new schooner was reported to be in frame with the planking commenced.³ While he awaited for the vessel to be completed Alexander retained his business enterprises and expanded his involvement in other interests. For instance, he was elected to the committee of the Tasmanian Railway and Progress Association in August 1868.⁴ He also continued to be involved in the organisation and staging of the Hobart Town Regatta, along with his brother-in-law Charles Bayley.⁵ Very likely, at the instigation of Alexander, Charles was additionally elected a director of the TSN Company, the two men obviously keen on further consolidating their business pursuits and endeavours.⁶ Moreover, with his reputation as an astute businessman and integral member of the Hobart Town community rising in profile, in late 1868 Alexander was nominated to run for election to become an alderman of the Hobart Town City Council.⁷ However, he graciously declined the offer, not wishing to become engaged in politics at the time.⁸ There were more pressing matters that needed his attention, including his vessel then under construction at the Domain.

On 9 January 1869 Alexander McGregor's new schooner, measuring 90 feet stem to sternpost, with a breadth of 22 feet and a depth of nine feet, was launched from his brother's shipyard. The press reported on the auspicious event and vessel. '*As she now lies to an anchor, she is, without exaggeration, one of the prettiest models of a vessel of her class ever turned out by Tasmanian shipwrights, and the workmanship and materials employed in her construction are in every respect worthy of the excellence of her design*'.⁹ The article continued in much the same praiseworthy prose. '*As regards her workmanship, it may fairly challenge comparison with any that has been, or can be, executed in the Australian colonies, a circumstance not to be wondered at, inasmuch as her builder had made up his mind to spare neither expense nor trouble to render her a specimen of the most finished naval architecture his establishment could turn out. Indeed, so excellent is the carpentry that it requires a minute examination to thoroughly appreciate. She has been built and designed by Mr. John McGregor, for his brother, Mr. Alexander McGregor, the well-known ship-owner of this port.*'¹⁰

The launch itself was also worthy of several paragraphs in multiple papers. The *Tasmanian Times* reported, '*A large number of persons assembled at the patent slip of Mr. McGregor, in the domain, on the afternoon of Saturday, 9th January, to witness the launch of the new vessel for some time on the stocks there. ... Everything being ready at a few minutes past five, and the tide serving, the christening ceremony was performed by Mrs A. McGregor naming this latest addition*

---

¹ *Launceston Examiner*, 30 June 1868.
² *The Mercury*, 8 April 1869.
³ *The Tasmanian Times*, 16 July 1868.
⁴ *The Tasmanian Times*, 19 August 1868.
⁵ *The Tasmanian Times*, 19 August 1868.
⁶ *The Mercury*, 2 February 1869.
⁷ *The Tasmanian Times*, 8 December 1868.
⁸ *The Mercury*, 8 December 1868.
⁹ *The Mercury*, 11 January 1869.
¹⁰ *The Mercury*, 11 January 1869.

Hally Bayley at Hobart's Domain slipyard.
Maritime Museum of Tasmania (PCR50-198).

to our Tasmanian fleet the "Hally Bayley".[1] Disappointingly, its namesake was not present at the launch event. Hally Bayley and her father James had remained in England, living in Burnham-on-Crouch with James' mother Mary Bull and his eldest sister, also named Mary.[2] By now eight years of age, Hally was attending school nearby.

The *Hally Bayley* departed Hobart Town on its maiden voyage on 3 February 1869. With Captain G. P. Harrison at the helm the vessel was loaded with various cargoes, including drapery and furniture, to be unloaded in Launceston.[3] It was the start of a promising career for the schooner in intercolonial trade that would last several decades.

There were more vessel arrivals and departures to report. After nearly a year at sea Charles and James Bayley's barque *Runnymede* returned to port on 22 February 1869 with 63 tuns of sperm whale oil on board.[4] The vessel had predominantly remained in Australian waters, taking in the east coast of Tasmania, Kangaroo Island and the coastal waters of New South Wales and Victoria.[5] Returning with nearly a full cargo, given the market price per tun in London was around £92, all of the *Runnymede*'s oil was quickly trans-shipped and sent to England via the ship *Harrowby*.[6]

Harriet and Alexander McGregor were also finalising plans to travel to England. The same day the *Runnymede* returned to Hobart Town, a complimentary dinner was held as a send-off for Alexander. Indicative of the couple's standing within the local community and the significance of the journey they were about to make, *The Tasmanian Times* reported on the occasion. *'Our worthy townsman Mr. A. McGregor, being about to leave the colony per Southern Cross tomorrow, en route for England, about thirty gentlemen, all old colonists, and personal friends connected also with the commercial and shipping interests of Hobart Town, entertained him at a dinner last evening at the Bird-in-Hand Hotel, Argyle Street. Dr. Crowther occupied the chair, and Mr. Colvin the vice-chair. An excellent dinner, provided in Mr. Oldham's well known style, embracing all the delicacies of the season, having been partaken of, the usual loyal toasts were drank, after which the health of the guest was proposed by the chairman, and enthusiastically responded to. Several other toasts, embracing the commercial agricultural, shipping and whaling interests of the colony, and the health of Mrs McGregor and the ladies of Tasmania, were proposed by the chairman and suitably acknowledged. The party broke up about 10:30 pm.'*[7]

The Tasmanian Times, 25 February 1869.

---

[1] The Tasmanian Times, 30 January 1869.
[2] 1871 England Census for James Bayley Bull.
[3] The Tasmanian Times, 4 February 1869.
[4] The Tasmanian Times, 27 February 1869.
[5] The Mercury, 20, 26 February 1869.
[6] The Mercury, 20, 26 February 1869.
[7] The Tasmanian Times, 27 February 1869.

An address to Alexander McGregor and his wife Harriet was also published in the local press, written by the shipwrights and other employees of the Domain slipyard. Alexander graciously provided the couple's response. The pair then departed Hobart Town on 24 February 1869, sailing as cabin passengers on board the steamer *Southern Cross* to Melbourne.[8] Out of respect for their departure the new schooner *Hally Bayley* had been decorated with bunting and *'nearly all of the vessels in port hoisted their ensigns'*.[9] Uniquely they were proceeding to England via a newly-opened up 'overland route', made possible by construction of the Suez Canal, whereby the couple would sail from Melbourne to Galle (now Ceylon, Sri Lanka), then journey overland to Suez in Egypt. They would then board another ship, sail through the canal to a port in the heel of Italy, followed by a train journey to France and ship to London.[10] All told this new route reduced the time to travel from Melbourne to London from 100 days to around 50 days. It was a significant improvement for those eager to reach their destination as opposed to endure the journey.

Given Alexander and Harriet were expected to be away for a year, Charles Bayley took over the management of Alexander McGregor's businesses, including acting as his shipping agent. Not one to be idle, it was also no coincidence that Alexander had tasked his brother with building another vessel during his absence. With the launch of the *Hally Bayley*, its position on the Domain stocks was quickly taken over by the keel of a larger craft.[11] Focused on steadily adding to his fleet Alexander no doubt also tasked Charles Bayley with overseeing this project too. In addition, Charles was still managing the affairs of his younger brother James, who remained in England with his daughter Hally, including with regard to their whaler *Runnymede*. After another successful voyage the vessel had entered out of the River Derwent on 17 March 1869 under the command of Captain Hill.[12] Not on board, however, was one of the *Runnymede*'s regular crew members.

Recognised as the last 'full-blooded' Aboriginal man in Tasmania, William Lanne, also known as King Billy or William Lane, had died at the Dog and Partridge Hotel in Goulburn Street on 3 March 1869, i.e., 10 days following the *Runnymede*'s return to port, of apparent alcohol poisoning and cholera.[13] Shortly thereafter his body had been conveyed to the General Hospital in Hobart Town whereby three days later it was released to Charles Bayley who had arranged and paid for the funeral. The procession then accompanied the body, contained in a coffin covered with a large possum rug, to St David's Church before it was carried to the nearby burial ground. Chief mourners were Charles Bayley, Captain Hill and the entire crew of the *Runnymede*, many of whom were also the pallbearers, along with Captain John McArthur of the whaling barque *Aladdin*, and a large contingent of leading citizens, comprising *'members of Parliament, City Aldermen, Shipowners, Shipmasters* [and] *Merchants'*.[14] Given William Lanne's standing and significance, the press reported that the ceremony *'was a circumstance long to be remembered by all who took part in it'*. Ironically, more than 150 years later, this statement sadly remains true.[15]

The awful situation that transpired was revealed shortly after the funeral when *'it became known beyond all doubt that the head of King Billy, as well as his hands and feet, had not been buried, but had been abstracted whilst at the Hospital, where the body had been lying'*. With

---

[8] *The Tasmanian Times*, 24 February 1869.
[9] *The Tasmanian Times*, 25 February 1869.
[10] *The Tasmanian Times*, 25 February 1869.
[11] *The Tasmanian Times*, 27 February 1869.
[12] *The Tasmanian Times*, 18 March 1869.
[13] Tasmanian Archives (RGD35/1/7 no. 7779); *The Mercury*, 8 March 1869.
[14] *The Tasmanian Times*, 8 March 1869.
[15] *The Tasmanian Times*, 8 March 1869.

great indignation at the appalling desecration of his employee's body, Charles Bayley immediately formed a deputation with Captain McArthur and Charles Colvin to investigate the circumstances, lobbying the Colonial Secretary, Sir Richard Dry, for an investigation into the tampering that had occurred by those associated with the General Hospital, including Dr William Crowther on behalf of the Royal College of Surgeons, as well as others acting on behalf of the Royal Society of Tasmania.[1] The trio also called for a police watch of the grave site to ensure no further dismemberment could take place. With absolute dismay their efforts were to no avail. The police guard was suspiciously called off during the night and the body further dissected.[2]

The resulting investigation and public enquiry, spurred by high ranking members of the Hobart Town community, including Charles Bayley, and a general public woefully disgusted with the actions that had taken place, did not resolve the situation nor did it result in those involved being held responsible. Sadly, it was not until the 1990s that the University of Edinburgh repatriated a skull believed to be that of William Lanne to the Tasmanian Aboriginal Centre.[3]

Following Charles Bayley's involvement with the death of William Lanne and its subsequent investigations, spanning several months, the circumstances of which likely caused political and social fracture amongst his peers, as well as the departure of the *Runnymede* on another whaling voyage, the remainder of 1869 was largely uneventful for him. While his brother James, sister Harriet, brother-in-law Alexander McGregor and niece Hally were enjoying a family reunion in England, Charles stoically maintained the Bayley and McGregor business affairs. However, he was not without the company of other relatives as his 30-year-old nephew Charles Graveley, the London-born eldest son of his sister Emmaretta, was by now in Hobart Town, staying at his 'Runnymede' estate in New Town.[4]

As the year 1869 came to a close there was further good news for Charles Bayley. The barque *Runnymede* returned to port on 25 October after another successful voyage; the 65 tuns of sperm whale oil stored in its hold valued at £5,850.[5] After a quick turnaround and refit the vessel cleared out of Hobart Town sailing back to the whaling grounds on 15 November.[6]

In addition to his professional dealings, there were other interests to occupy Charles Bayley's time. In September 1869 he was elected vice president of the Southern Tasmanian Cricket Association.[7] He also maintained his involvement with the Hobart Town Regatta, including commissioning Thomas Morland of the Domain shipyard to build a whaleboat to compete for the Tasman Prize.[8] The yacht *Surprise* was also readied to compete.[9] With the regatta held in mid-December the craft successfully won the yacht race with Charles Bayley at the helm.[10] Meanwhile Charles' new whaleboat, aptly named *Runnymede*, also won its event.[11]

More positive news came two days before Christmas with the return of Harriet and Alexander McGregor on board the *Tamar* from Melbourne.[12] After spending several months in Europe, the couple had sailed back to Australia via the overland route.[13]

---

[1] *The Tasmanian Times*, 8 March 1869.
[2] *The Tasmanian Times*, 8 March 1869.
[3] https://en.wikipedia.org/wiki/William_Lanne.
[4] *The Mercury*, 17 April 1869, 14 September 1923.
[5] *The Mercury*, 25 October 1869.
[6] *The Mercury*, 16 November 1869.
[7] *The Mercury*, 28 September 1869.
[8] *The Mercury*, 1 December 1869.
[9] *The Tasmanian Times*, 14 December 1869.
[10] *The Mercury*, 14 December 1869.
[11] *The Tasmanian Times*, 11 December 1869.
[12] *The Mercury*, 24 December 1869.
[13] *The Mercury*, 22 December 1869.

Discretion & Deaths

*I*t is interesting to reconcile the persona of Charles Bayley profiled in this book thus far with the man who is assumed to have fathered at least three children born out of wedlock between 1870 and 1873. The first child, a boy named Albert Ernest Bayley, was born in Hobart Town on 11 January 1870. His mother registered his birth on 8 February giving her name as Bridget Elizabeth Murphy of Elizabeth Street. The child's father is distinctly listed as Charles Bayley, master mariner. There was only one such person living in Hobart Town at the time with this name and occupation such that there is little doubt they are one and the same person.

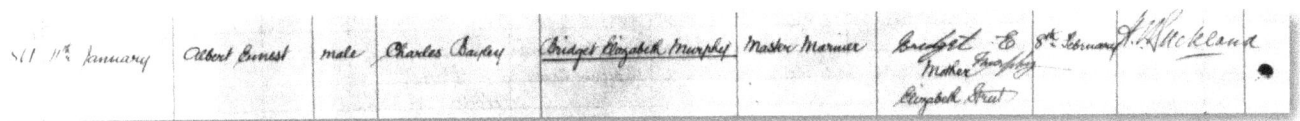

Birth registration of Albert Ernest Bayley, 11 January 1870.
Tasmanian Archives (RGD33/1/10 no. 861).

While it was obviously not unknown for married men to father illegitimate children in Victorian-era Tasmania, the fact that Bridget Murphy had the audacity to register their son with the surname of Bayley is definitely out of the ordinary, particularly since Charles Bayley was both married at the time and an upstanding and prominent citizen of Hobart Town.

Did Charles know about the child's birth, registration and surname and, in doing so, acknowledge the child as his own, or was this weighted administrative act undertaken solely by Bridget? Unfortunately the answers to these questions are not known. What is known, however, is that the child was conceived in mid-to-late April 1869 during a tempestuous period whereby Charles was involved in the investigation and subsequent turmoil of William Lanne's body. It was also a period where 57-year-old Charles was somewhat on his own in Hobart Town, with his sister Harriet and her husband Alexander McGregor, as well as his brother James and James' daughter Hally, all in England.

Still, Charles' wife Eliza, by now in her mid-50s, was very much alive and the couple were jointly living at their 'Runnymede' estate in New Town. However, given Charles kept an office at Salamanca and would have spent the bulk of his time at the Hobart Town wharf area overseeing the vessels that he owned, as well as taking care of Alexander McGregor's fleet, the couple may not have been spending that much time together. They may also have been enduring a somewhat fractured relationship, albeit these circumstances offer no reasoning or excuse for a man of

Charles' standing to go outside the bounds of his marriage and seek comfort with a 20-something-year-old dressmaker of a different class. It is also not known just how common this situation was amongst Hobart Town's gentlemen, merchants, politicians and businessmen. Questions abound. Was Charles one of many men of his cohort to seek a mistress and is it only the fact that the child was registered in his name that we are able to determine this deviance over 150 years later?

Sadly, little Albert Ernest Bayley did not live long enough to pass on any family history. He died on 17 February 1870 at just over one month in age. The cause of death was *convulsions from congenital debility*. His death was registered by Alexander Clarke, an undertaker, this time with the surname of Murphy. It is not known where Albert was buried.

Death registration of Albert Ernest Murphy, 17 February 1870.
Tasmanian Archives (RGD35/1/7 no. 9141).

No doubt keeping the birth and subsequent death of his illegitimate son to himself, a more public acknowledgement of a family member's passing came when the flags of vessels in the Port of Hobart Town were lowered to half-mast as a mark of respect upon the death of Alexander McGregor's sister Jean.[1] Having married Thomas Addison Horne in 1847, a Norwich-born ex-convict who had been transported to Hobart Town per the *Lord William Bentinck* in 1838 after being found guilty of horse stealing, Jean had subsequently given birth to six sons and one daughter (named Harriet). Sadly Jean died on 13 July 1870 at the age of 44 in Hobart Town of stomach and liver cancer.[2] Widowed by the time of her death, the couple's youngest surviving sons very likely moved in with Alexander and his wife Harriet at their home in Runnymede Street, Battery Point, while the older boys, ranging in age from their early twenties to their teens, were sent to sea as apprentices on board vessels Alexander either owned or was associated with.

With all of these family changes going on, both Alexander McGregor and Charles Bayley remained resolute in their commercial endeavours. The pair also set about expanding their fleet, purchasing the barque *Asia* in February 1870, in conjunction with Captain S. Kennedy.[3] The 308-ton vessel arrived in Hobart Town from Melbourne a few weeks later and was subsequently fitted out as a whaler.[4]

The next major event to take place with regards to Alexander McGregor's shipping empire was the launch of his now legendary vessel the *Harriet McGregor* on Saturday 22 October 1870.[5] The significance of the vessel was no less highlighted by the fact that nearly 1,000 people attended the launch event. Having taken 15 months to construct, built by Alexander's brother John, the 331-ton barque was intended for the London to Hobart Town trade. Worthy of repeating, the local press provided extremely detailed reporting on the launch of the vessel, including the role that Alexander's wife Harriet played in her namesake's christening.

[1] *The Mercury*, 14 July 1870.
[2] *The Mercury*, 14 July 1870.
[3] Tasmanian Archives (CON31/1/22 p60, RGD35/1/7 no. 9352).
[4] *The Tasmanian Times*, 26 February 1870;
National Archives of Australia, HOBART, Register of ships, Volume 9, 1865-1877, [pages 1-173, continues on film roll 2], Folio 86.
[5] *The Mercury*, 24 October 1870.

Helen (left), Asia (middle) and Wild Wave (right) at Hobart Town's New Wharf (1880s).
Maritime Museum of Tasmania (POMZ13a).

'Shortly after three o'clock on Saturday afternoon crowds of people began to collect in the vicinity of the Domain, as it had previously been announced that the launch would take place at four o'clock; inside of the yard were congregated a large mustering of shipowners, merchants, shipbuilders, captains of the port and others interested in nautical manners, who carefully examined the vessel and unanimously expressed their admiration of her beautifully formed hull, and the substantial manner in which every part was constructed. From the windows of the different buildings and workshops, numbers of the fair sex might be observed gazing with interest upon the busy scene. During the morning heavy showers of rain had fallen and even in the afternoon the weather was not all that could be desired; this and the dirty state of the Domain walks prevented many from going who otherwise would have been present; as it was, however, the people present inside and outside of the yard could not have numbered less than 1000. The yard itself presented quite a gala appearance, flags fluttering in the breeze and the new barque was gaily decorated with bunting and flowers as was also the barque Runnymede lying alongside the hulk.

A temporary platform had been erected at the bow of the vessel so as to afford accommodation for the lady upon whom devolved the pleasurable duty of performing the ceremony of christening and her companions. Hoisted on poles on deck were a variety of flags, the house flag of the owner flying at the main, the British ensign at the stern, and the Union Jack at the bowsprit end. The butts and stern of the new vessel were strewn with flowers, and from her bow hung a ribbon with the orthodox bottle of champagne suspended from it. After the shores were knocked away the vessel began to move, and Mrs McGregor dashed the bottle of champagne against the bow, and amid loud cheers christened her the "Harriet McGregor." Gathering way, the vessel followed by a parting bottle of wine, glided gracefully into the water and ran out a short distance into the river where an anchor was cast. The workmen employed at the yard then gave three hearty

Harriet McGregor at Hobart Town's New Wharf.
State Library of Victoria, A. C. Green photographer (H91.250/130).

cheers, which were responded to by a number of people who were engaged at work on board. As the vessel slowly veered round with her broadside to the spectators, her fine lines and exquisite proportions were observed to advantage, and the designer and builder, Mr John McGregor, was warmly congratulated by numerous friends who were present.

After the launch the ladies and gentlemen present assembled in the moulding loft, where ample provision in the shape of champagne, &c., was provided. Mr H. B. Tonkin, J.P., Master Warden of the Marine Board, proposed the first toast - "Success to the Harriet McGregor and prosperity to her owners." He congratulated her builder upon the successful launch, and said that he had written to Lloyd's surveyors in London by the last mail in the strongest terms of approval of the vessel, and that he would challenge her against any size in the world in point of material and workmanship. He sincerely trusted she would prove remunerative to her owners, and that they would live long to enjoy the fruits of her success.

The toast was received with three cheers given with great enthusiasm.

Mr Alexander McGregor, in reply, said he was no orator, but he sincerely thanked those present for their good wishes and trusted they would be realised.

Captain Fisher proposed the health of Mr John McGregor, the builder of the Harriet McGregor, He wished her a long and prosperous career, and congratulated her builder upon her appearance, and the successful result of his labours in the beautiful vessel then lying at her anchor near them. He had proposed the health of Mr John McGregor some 18 months before at the launch of the Halley [sic] Bayley, as good a vessel as was to be found among the whole coasting fleet in the Australian waters. He firmly believed the Harriet McGregor would, when Lloyd's surveyors had reported upon her, do credit to Tasmania. He had noticed that a vessel built in New South Wales had obtained in London the highest class ever awarded to vessels built in Australia - A1 for 12 years - and from what he had seen of the Harriet McGregor he was confident she would not in any respect be inferior to the Rachel - the vessel in which he had referred. He had known Mr John McGregor since he was a little boy and he could say with confidence that he would do credit to the old stock. He trusted that the establishment would prosper in his hands, for he believed he was not betraying any secret in informing them that Mr Alexander McGregor had already, or was on the eve of retiring and transferring the business to Mr John McGregor.

The toast having been received with cheers, Mr Alexander McGregor said that his brother was necessarily absent, for on Saturday evenings a good deal of business devolved upon him, but he was sure he would be much gratified with the compliment that had been paid him.

Mr Charles Crosby proposed the health of Mrs A. McGregor and the ladies of Tasmania. There were no words needed from him to secure a hearty response to this toast. He wished the ship and her owners every prosperity.

Mr Alderman Risby had the pleasing duty of acknowledging the toast on the part of Mrs. A McGregor and the ladies of Tasmania. He felt sure the vessel would not have been so successfully launched but for the presence of the ladies. All present must admit that Mrs McGregor did the duty assigned to her of christening the vessel well. On behalf of the ladies he returned them his sincere thanks for the manner in which the toast had been proposed and received.

Mr Charles Dowdell proposed the health of the whaling interest of Tasmania coupled with the name of Capt Charles Bayley (applause). Although the Harriet McGregor was not intended as a whaler, her owners were largely interested in the whaling vessels sailing out of Hobart Town. All present were aware that Captain Bayley had been for many years actively and successfully engaged in whaling; he had been brought up under the auspices of their friend Mr John Watson, whose absence on this occasion he was sure all present would regret.

Captain Bayley returned thanks. As most of them knew he had many years experience of the rough side of a whaler's life; he was now enjoying the smooth. He heartily trusted that the whaling interest in which he was still deeply engaged would continue to prosper, in which case he would endeavour for many years to come still to enjoy the smooth.

Mr. D. McMillan [sic] thought the company should not separate without drinking the health of the shipwrights, blacksmiths, joiners, and other artisans who had been employed in the construction of the beautiful vessel whose launch they had witnessed that afternoon. As a shipwright himself he could speak from experience that no better work in every branch of the trade had ever been turned out in Hobart Town or could be turned out elsewhere.

This toast having been duly honored [sic] the company separated much pleased with the proceedings of the afternoon.'[1]

---

[1] *The Tasmanian Times*, 24 October 1870.

Following the launch event and the subsequent fitting out and rigging of the *Harriet McGregor*, it was announced that Captain Richard Copping, who was then at the helm of the barque *Bella Mary* employed in intercolonial trade and owned by Alexander McGregor and Charles Bayley in partnership with several others, would take command of the new vessel.[1] The *Harriet McGregor* was then loaded with cargo, including tuns and tuns of sperm whale oil that had recently been discharged in Hobart Town by Alexander McGregor and Charles Bayley's new whaler *Asia*.[2] A few weeks later it was announced that the *Harriet McGregor* was ready to be loaded with wool.[3]

On 8 February 1871 the *Harriet McGregor* cleared out of Hobart Town on its maiden voyage to London. Stored on board were various cargoes, including 185 casks of sperm whale oil, two tons of whale bone and 113 bundles of wool, all consigned to Alexander McGregor, along with other quantities of wool, leather and sperm whale oil consigned to other merchants.[4] All told the vessel was reportedly carrying £20,000 worth of freight.[5] The only passenger on board was the captain's wife Susannah Copping.[6]

The *Harriet McGregor* arrived in London on 19 May 1871 after a voyage of 99 days. However, instead of sailing from Hobart Town across the Indian Ocean to South Africa and then north to Europe, the vessel took the 'clipper route', first heading to New Zealand, then around Cape Horn before sailing along the coast of South America and into the North Atlantic Ocean.

Captain Copping provided the details in a letter sent to Alexander McGregor whereby he summarised the vessel's journey. '*After leaving Hobart Town we had strong winds until passing New Zealand; passed the Snares in five days. After leaving New Zealand had fine weather, but not so many fair winds as might naturally have been expected, but saw no ice. Passed Cape Horn 12 March, 32 days out. On 21st March experienced a very heavy gale of wind, and had to heave the ship to, a very heavy sea running, and the ship behaved remarkably well throughout the gale. On the 23rd kept the ship away again, and at 6 p.m. Inkerman Featherstone, while in the act of going aloft to help to secure the main-topsail, which had partly blown adrift, fell off the rail overboard, and was not seen again. He was in the act of speaking to and laughing with one of the fellow apprentices at the time. I immediately brought the ship to the wind, but there was not the remotest possibility of doing anything to save him. In rounding the ship to we very narrowly*

Susannah and Captain Richard Copping.
Maritime Museum of Tasmania (PGSL089).

---
[1] *The Tasmanian Times*, 26 November 1870.
[2] *The Tasmanian Times*, 22 December 1870.
[3] *The Mercury*, 12 January 1871.
[4] *The Mercury*, 7 February 1871.
[5] *The Mercury*, 7 February 1871.
[6] *The Mercury*, 7 February 1871.

escaped shipping a very heavy sea, which, if it had struck us, would have swept the decks. We crossed the equator on the 9th April, 60 days out. Passed the Western Islands on the 30th April, experiencing nothing but gales and strong easterly winds into the Channel, arriving at Gravesend on the 18th, and at London Docks, on the 19th May, after a passage of 99 days.'[7]

The *Harriet McGregor* arrived back in Hobart Town on 11 October 1871 after circumnavigating the globe in a total of eight months and three days, during this period discharging and taking on full cargoes in London, as well as being placed on the slip to have its copper removed and the barque subjected to a thorough inspection by surveyors acting on behalf of Lloyd's of London, a process that itself took several weeks.[8] The outcome of this scrutiny: the *Harriet McGregor* was classified as A1 for nine years, the highest period accorded to a vessel built of blue gum to date.[9]

The *Harriet McGregor* sailed from Gravesend on 8 July and then forth to the island of Maderia which it passed on 25 July.[10] It crossed the equator on 30 August and the meridian of the Cape of Good Hope four days later. Though next experiencing a succession of violent gales and heavy seas for most of its passage east across the Indian Ocean, the *Harriet McGregor* was none the worse for wear when it sighted land at Port Davey on Tasmania's south-west coast on 10 October, arriving off Hobart Town's Domain shipyard a day later.[11] It was the end of the vessel's first round-trip between Hobart Town and London and the start of a very promising career during which it would be highly praised for both its reliability and capabilities as a safe and fast sailer.

Wagoola (left) and Harriet McGregor (right) at Hobart Town's New Wharf (1877).
State Library of Victoria, A. C. Green photographer (H91.108/2644).

[7] The Mercury, 6 July 1871.
[8] The Mercury, 12 October 1871.
[9] The Mercury, 12 October 1871.
[10] The Mercury, 12 October 1871.
[11] The Mercury, 12 October 1871.

While Alexander McGregor and his new vessel were both enjoying commercial success, Charles Bayley, being eight years older than the former and approaching his 60th year of age, was very much mixing his business interests with the 'smoother' side of life, including the social, sporting and recreational aspects of semi-retirement. The early 1870s, for example, saw him elected president of the Wellington Cricket Club, as well as maintaining his role as vice president of the Southern Tasmanian Cricket Association.[1] He would continue in both of these capacities up until his death.[2] Charitable with his time and also his money, in late 1870 Charles donated funds to the Kennerley Boys Home to help fund the purchase of a flag pole.[3] He additionally provided funds to the New Town Public School for their annual prize giving ceremony.[4] The Hobart Town Regatta remained an organisation and event that Charles Bayley continued to support; in 1871 acting as a judge and umpire as well as being on the committee.[5]

In terms of his business dealings Charles Bayley remained the part-owner of many vessels, and a director of both the TSN Company and the Derwent and Tamar Marine Insurance Company.[6] By the early 1870s he had also begun investing in mining ventures, including being a large shareholder of the Tasmanian Mineral Exploration Company.[7] He was perhaps looking to diversify his portfolio given the price of whale oil, along with agricultural and pastoral commodities, had all experienced large declines in value, resulting in a depressed Tasmanian economy more generally. Charles Bayley and Alexander McGregor's whaling barque *Derwent Hunter*, for example, had returned to Hobart Town in September 1871 after seven months at sea. Its large cargo of 87 tuns of sperm whale oil, however, was only valued at £5,829 given the price per tun was at a low of £67.[8] Similarly, the following month the *Runnymede* returned to Hobart Town from the whaling grounds; its 12-month cruise resulting in the accumulation of only 40 tuns of sperm whale oil valued at £2,680.[9] A day after the *Runnymede* arrived the *Flying Childers* also appeared on the River Derwent; its eight month voyage only equating to 23 tuns of sperm whale oil. Despite the contraction of the sperm whale oil market, the whales were obviously also getting harder to source and secure. However, by early 1872 the price of the commodity would again rise to £80 per tun.[10]

On a personal level Charles Bayley appears to have carried on his extra-marital affair with Hobart Town dressmaker Bridget Elizabeth Murphy. She gave birth to a daughter named Emma Gertrude Bayley on 14 September 1871. Once again the child's birth was registered by her mother, now living in Campbell Street, with her father noted as Charles Bayley, master mariner.

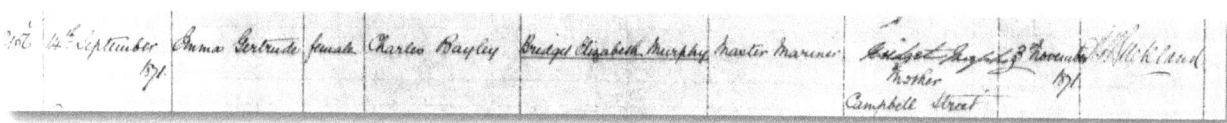

Birth registration of Emma Gertrude Bayley, 14 September 1871.
Tasmanian Archives (RGD33/1/10 no. 2156).

---

[1] *The Mercury*, 13, 17 September 1870.
[2] *The Mercury*, 20 September, 6 October 1871, 10, 28 September 1872, 29 September 1874.
[3] *The Tasmanian Times*, 26 December 1870.
[4] *The Mercury*, 29 December 1870.
[5] *The Mercury*, 25 January 1871, 30 January 1872.
[6] *Launceston Examiner*, 2 December 1871.
[7] *The Mercury*, 17 August 1871.
[8] *The Mercury*, 6 September 1871.
[9] *The Mercury*, 30 September 1871.
[10] *The Mercury*, 23 March 1872.

It was around the time of the birth of Charles Bayley's second illegitimate child that he and his sister Harriet McGregor would have received news in Hobart Town from their brother James in England of their mother's death. Mary Bull had died on 26 April 1871 at Burnham-on-Crouch, Essex, aged 83. She was buried seven days later at the nearby St Mary the Virgin Churchyard in the same grave as her late husband.[11]

James Bayley and his daughter Hally had spent five years in England, assumed to be living with or in close proximity to his parents and other relatives during this period. His daughter Hally had attended school in Burnham-on-Crouch and was now 10 years of age. With the death of his only surviving parent, James felt the need to return to Tasmania, likely to be closer to his brother Charles and sister Harriet. Fortunately passage to Hobart Town from London was readily available, with the vessel very aptly named after his sister.

Having left Hobart Town on 6 November 1871 Alexander McGregor's new barque *Harriet McGregor* had sailed into London on its second voyage on 21 March 1872.[12] It departed Gravesend just over a month later, on 30 April, after discharging and loading another large load of various cargoes. On board as the only passengers were James and Hally Bayley and James' 32-year-old cousin Elizabeth Bayley.[13] The trio arrived in Hobart Town on 18 August 1872, undoubtedly receiving an extremely warm welcome from Charles and Eliza Bayley and Harriet and her husband Alexander McGregor.[14]

With the return of James and Hally Bayley and the arrival of Elizabeth Bayley, the Bayley family's 'Runnymede' estate at New Town immediately became more lively; the trio no doubt giving Charles and Eliza Bayley a welcome reprieve from several years spent wandering the rooms and halls of their large home alone. There was also much to catch up on, including personal news, gossip, business dealings, the status of their jointly-owned vessel, the *Runnymede*, and the state of whaling and other colonial industries. There was also the estate itself, with Charles occupying his time farming the property and several neighbouring fields which he leased.[15] He had additionally set about stocking it with animals, including albino pheasants he had imported from New Zealand on board his barque *Bella Mary*.[16] With a similar focus on community events and volunteering, James Bayley joined his brother to act as a judge at the Hobart Town Regatta held in early 1873.[17] The pair also became members of a committee to establish a Sailors' Home in Hobart Town.[18]

Despite the arrival of his brother back from England, Charles Bayley appears to have maintained his liaison with Bridget Elizabeth Murphy. On 14 June 1873 she gave birth to another daughter, named Henrietta Bayley. The birth was registered by her mother, now living in Elizabeth Street, and the father was listed as Charles Bayley, master mariner.

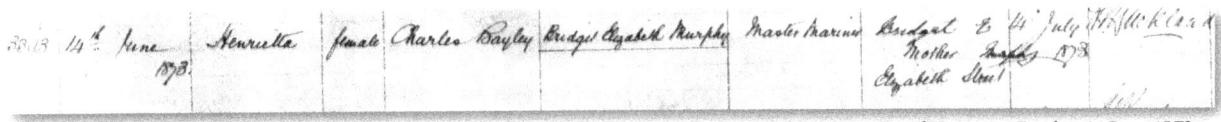

Birth registration of Henrietta Bayley, 14 June 1873.
Tasmanian Archives (RGD33/1/10 no. 3393).

---

[11] UK and Ireland, Find a Grave® Index, 1300s-Current for Mary Rogers Bull.
[12] *The Mercury*, 7 November 1871; *Lloyd's List*, 22 March 1872.
[13] *The Mercury*, 19 August 1872.
[14] *The Mercury*, 19 August 1872.
[15] *The Mercury*, 8 February 1875.
[16] *The Mercury*, 12 October 1872.
[17] *Launceston Examiner*, 8 February 1873.
[18] *The Cornwall Chronicle*, 30 September 1874.

Sadly, baby Henrietta died at six months of age on 18 December 1873. The cause of death was noted as '*chronic hydrocephalus*', i.e., fluid on the brain apparently brought on by teething.[1] Henrietta, with the surname of Murphy, was buried at Cornelian Bay Cemetery.

The year 1874 was marked with more illnesses and ultimately deaths for Charles Bayley and his family. His wife Eliza developed a disease of the kidneys that ultimately progressed to serious renal failure over a matter of months resulting in her death. She died on 2 December at 'Runnymede' at the age of 56.[2] The official cause of death was '*apoplexy and granular degeneration of the kidneys*'. Out of respect all of the vessels in port at Hobart Town lowered their flags to half-mast.[3] Eliza was buried at Cornelian Bay Cemetery. Sensing their own demise and coinciding with the closure of the St Andrews Presbyterian Church Burial Ground in North Hobart two years prior, in August 1874 Charles and Eliza had organised for the removal of the remains of their two deceased children, Jane Mary and Eliza (Jr), their two nephews Charles and William Bayley, James Bayley's first wife Emma, as well as those of Eliza's parents James and Jean Inglis and brother William, to a new family vault at Cornelian Bay.[4] It was here that Eliza Bayley was buried two days following her death.[5]

For reasons not confirmed, but perhaps because of Eliza Bayley's illness or disapproval, several weeks after her death James Bayley married his 34-year-old cousin Elizabeth Bayley. The wedding took place at St Andrews Church on 21 December 1874.[6] Witnesses were Joseph E. Risby and Daniel Stanfield, both associates of James'.

Born in Burnham-on-Crouch in 1840, Elizabeth was the daughter of the late Rogers James Bayley, a shipbuilder who had worked as foreman at the yard of his very successful brother William Bayley (Jr²) in both Ipswich and Burnham-on-Crouch. She had arrived with James per the *Harriet McGregor* in July 1872, possibly undertaking a governess role in charge of his daughter Hally. It is interesting to note that Elizabeth was heavily pregnant at the time of their wedding, a state that would have been considered socially awkward at the time.

The newlyweds had little time to enjoy their honeymoon period, however. Adding to a series of deaths Charles Bayley also died. On 20 January 1875, a month after the wedding, he passed away at 'Runnymede'.[7] The cause of death was '*effusion into the left pleura*', i.e., fluid in the lungs, possibly a symptom of lung cancer.[8]

Eliza Bayley (c1860s).
LINC Tasmania eHeritage Database (2012).

---

[1] Tasmanian Archives (RGD35/1/8 no. 1798A, AF35/1/1 p15).
[2] Tasmanian Archives (RGD35/1/8 no. 2358); *The Mercury*, 8 December 1874.
[3] *The Mercury*, 3 December 1874.
[4] Tasmanian Archives (AF35/1/1 p21).
[5] Tasmanian Archives (AF70/1/1 p430).
[6] Tasmanian Archives (RGD37/1/33 no. 204).
[7] *The Mercury*, 21 January 1875.
[8] Tasmanian Archives (RGD35/1/8 no. 2431).

Charles Bayley was buried two days following his death at Cornelian Bay in the newly-erected family vault. He was 62 years of age. Given his standing in the Hobart Town community, several obituaries summarising his life and commending his industriousness, integrity, discipline, resolve and spirit were published in the local press, one of which is copied here.

Knowing that he was facing death, in July 1874 Charles had transferred ownership of all of his vessels, including the *Runnymede, Asia, Camilla, Bella Mary, Derwent Hunter* and *Helen*, to his brother James. At a previous time point, he had also transferred ownership of his 'Runnymede' estate to James. Charles' will, signed just four days prior to his death, therefore bequeathed only a portion of his actual real and personal estate, valued at £435.[9]

One issue that Charles Bayley did not take care of in the lead-up to his demise was the maintenance of his only surviving child, three-year-old Emma Gertrude Murphy. Two months following his death, the child's mother, Bridget Elizabeth Murphy, was charged by Superintendent Propsting of the Hobart Town Police with '*using abusive language to him in Collins-street, and with having spat upon his trousers*'.[10] According to Propsting, Bridget had '*called him such names as were calculated to disturb the peace, besides spitting on him*'.[11] The press further noted that Propsting believed Bridget to be '*in the habit of insulting him on account of his having been compelled to discontinue some payments of money which he was formerly authorised to hand to her, the gentleman from whom it came being now deceased*'.[12] Being found guilty, Bridget was fined 5s and costs, though in default was imprisoned for a week.[13]

THE LATE CAPT. CHARLES BAYLEY.

Yesterday was consigned to the grave the body of one who in a quiet, unostentatious way has done much for the advancement of Tasmania. Captain Charles Bayley was no ordinary man. Of great perseverance and indomitable energy, he was successful in whatever he undertook; while so long as the acquisition of fortune was a necessity or an object, his enterprising spirit was seldom at a loss for a new field of industry, which he pursued with such unflinching integrity and honesty of purpose, that no one ever grudged Charles Bayley his good fortune; certainly no one ever had occasion to complain that he had attained his end to the disadvantage of any with whom he had dealings.

Captain Bayley was a native of Essex, and at an early age devoted himself to a seafaring life. He came to Tasmania when a mere boy. He speedily worked his way to the height of the ambition that guided his young life, and commenced sailing from Tasmania as a master and part owner so long back as the year 1838. In that or the following year he commenced what he for some time continued at, conveying to Port Phillip in his ship, the Wallaby, stock and produce for the early settlers in Victoria from Tasmania, and other places. He was early, long, and closely mixed up with the first settlement of Victoria, and had he chosen he might have had his pick of some of the choicest lots where now stands the city of Melbourne, or of fine properties in the country for a merely nominal consideration, but he preferred retaining his home in Tasmania, that has not dealt unkindly with him.

He left the intercolonial trade to enter on that of whaling, which he did as master and part owner. His career in this capacity was one of singular and almost uninterrupted success. He sailed in the Fortitude as part owner, and while in command of her, made a most miraculous escape. A boat in which he was, was swamped and capsized. All hands clung to the boat, till one after another the crew were washed away, he having been saved by getting his finger into a plug-hole in the boat, to which, his finger swollen, he was found clinging in an insensible condition, after he had floated for hours in the cold latitudes off the south coast of New Zealand. He next commanded the Runnymede, which was built for him, and of which he was part owner for many years. He then, with his brother, became sole owners, and remained so at the time of his death. While pursuing his own occupation as a whaler, and afterwards, he continued increasing his interest in shipping, and was part owner of several whalers, and of a number of other vessels. He abandoned a seafaring life some twenty years ago; and on the departure of Bishop Nixon, he became owner of the beautiful residence of Runnymede, where he died. To the last he retained a large interest in shipping, and no man in Hobart Town has perhaps done more towards promoting the shipping of Hobart Town and increasing the importance of the port. When a master in command, his vessels were always remarkable for their admirable fitting, and justified the pride he took in them. As an owner he was equally anxious to have everything connected with his vessels neat, taut, and reliable. Both as a master and as an owner he was remarkable for his considerate care for the seamen under him, and while laxity of discipline was the last thing he would have tolerated, he was respected and beloved by those under him. He commanded without authority, and he was obeyed without fear. Captain Bayley studiously avoided all interference with public affairs. His private life was exemplary, and secured him general esteem. As a man of business he was punctual and systematic, never doing anything in a hurry; always doing everything well. His tact and discrimination pointed him out as invaluable in the management of such commercial companies as he was connected with. He never rushed hastily to conclusions; but, if slow to decide, he was firm of purpose when once he had made up his mind, and thus, Captain Bayley, who has been for years a member of the Executive directory of the Derwent and Tamar Insurance Company, and of the Tasmanian Steam Navigation Company, commanded the confidence of the shareholders, and contributed in no small degree to the present position of their successful enterprises. For some months he has been missed from his usual haunts. His medical attendants had long despaired of his life, yet his wife preceded him, she having died some seven weeks ago. They had several children, all of whom are dead. He retained his faculties to the last, and though for some days the end was hourly looked for, his consciousness never deserted him. A few hours before his death on Wednesday afternoon, he took a formal leave of his friends, and departed as if proceeding on an ordinary journey. Death had no terrors for him, and when he passed away, he left few peers in his walk of life. His presence and assistance will be missed at the event of next week. He was foremost in the first getting up of the annual regattas, and for some thirty years has been uninterruptedly a member of committee, and has generally discharged all or some of the duties of starter, judge, or umpire, and in this, as in everything else, he was never satisfied with anything short of complete success.

The Mercury, 23 January 1874.

Bridget Murphy's Convict Record (1875).
Tasmanian Archives (CON105/1/2 p119).

[9] Tasmanian Archives (AD960/1/10 no. 1784).
[10] *The Tasmanian Tribune*, 1 April 1875.
[11] *The Tasmanian Tribune*, 1 April 1875.
[12] *The Tasmanian Tribune*, 1 April 1875.
[13] *The Tasmanian Tribune*, 1 April 1875.

Charles Bayley.
Tasmanian Archives (NS1013/1/849).

Legacies & 'Lenna'

As stated, following the death of Charles Bayley his business interests were taken over by his younger brother James Bayley, by now 51 years of age, in conjunction with their brother-in-law Alexander McGregor. The bulk of Charles' assets, including real estate, shares, money and personal effects, had previously been transferred to James in the months before Charles' death such that there was very little of his estate remaining by the time probate occurred.

With James, his wife Elizabeth and James' daughter Hally continuing to live at 'Runnymede' in New Town, just over a month after Charles' death Elizabeth gave birth. On 25 February 1875 a daughter named Bessie Mary Bayley was born.[1] Sadly, indicative of the true nature of infant mortality at the time, and like many of her half-siblings and cousins previously, the child did not survive infancy, dying three weeks later on 17 March of diarrhoea.[2] Little Bessie was buried in the Bayley family's vault at Cornelian Bay Cemetery.

Though James and Elizabeth Bayley did not have any additional children, they both appear to have settled into a comfortable life at 'Runnymede' where, assisted by several servants and gardeners, they judiciously raised James' daughter Hally, by now a teenager, as well as tended to the grounds and gardens. Appearing to enjoy the lifestyle of a gentleman farmer, James also expanded the estate over the coming years by purchasing several surrounding paddocks and fields, constituting many additional acres. Nurturing his interest in agriculture, he won prizes for the pheasants he exhibited at Tasmanian Poultry Society shows and provided funds towards the Hobart Town Cottage Garden Society.[3] Also sharing his late brother's interest in sport, James was additionally elected president of the Wellington Cricket Club, acting as Charles' replacement from October 1875.[4] In time, he would be elected to the Southern Tasmanian Cricket Association and be voted vice president of the newly-formed New Town Cricket Association as well as the New Town Football Association.[5] James would continue in many of these roles for decades.[6] With a keen interest in the development of his local community, in May 1878 James was also appointed a trustee of the Hobart Town Public Cemetery at Cornelian Bay.[7]

With specific regards to his commercial activities, in February 1875 James took over Charles Bayley's vacancy to become a director of the TSN Company.[8] Alexander McGregor also remained

---

[1] Tasmanian Archives (RGD33/1/11 no. 1044).
[2] Tasmanian Archives (RGD35/1/8 no. 2549).
[3] *The Mercury*, 21 August 1879, 4 September 1879.
[4] *The Mercury*, 1 October 1875.
[5] *The Mercury, 16 August 1878*, 8 September 1880, 14 April 1881, 21 September 1883, 27 September 1884.
[6] *The Mercury*, 19 September 1876.
[7] *The Mercury*, 28 May 1878.
[8] *The Mercury*, 9 February 1875.

Elizabeth and James Bayley at 'Runnymede', New Town.
Tasmanian Archives (NS1619/1/106).

an ongoing director of this organisation; the pair by this point in time aligning many aspects of their business activities.[1]

Some time around this period James Bayley's eldest sister Mary Rogers Bayley Bull, whose marriage to Stephen Park near London in 1839 was unsuccessful, also appears to have arrived from England and moved in to 'Runnymede'. It was undoubtedly a very welcome reunion for both James and his youngest sister Harriet McGregor to be reunited with another sibling in Hobart Town. It is Harriet and her husband Alexander that we must now focus on.

With regards to their own property situated on the corner of Cross and Runnymede streets in Battery Point, the wealth generated by Alexander's many maritime and commercial business dealings over the decades had resulted in the pair significantly improving the small cottage that they had built on their plot of land in the mid-1850s, as well as its surrounding gardens. By mid-1875 the couple had also purchased several more adjoining parcels of land such that they now owned a large allotment extending along Runnymede Street between the New Wharf and Cross Street. However, the width of the combined parcel was only around 100 feet before the boundary with a reserve comprising the flagstaff, signal station and Prince of Wales' Battery was reached; an issue that would come to the forefront many years later.[2]

Still, with the need to secure the property and shelter it from the impact of continued drainage problems, Alexander McGregor set about building a stone fence across the bottom part of its perimeter. Uniquely the wall was somewhat of a novelty, built of ashlar stone laid to mimic the planking of a ship such that a curve shape was produced, with Huon pine used for posts.[3] With the work undertaken by E. Messiter of Harrington Street, the entire project was expected to cost £400.[4] Its construction coincided with the completion of Runnymede Street by the Hobart City Council which had previously been a limited access thoroughfare owing to the mountainous rock located on the site.[5]

With his house sitting in a prominent position overlooking Hobart Town's New Wharf, Alexander McGregor set about populating the port with more of his vessels. In July 1874 he and his wife Harriet travelled to Adelaide via Melbourne to purchase the clipper ship *Lufra* at a substantial cost of £11,000.[6] Significantly, the acquisition made Alexander the largest shipowner in Tasmania with his fleet (as sole or joint owner) by now encompassing the international traders *Harriet McGregor* and *Helen*; the intercolonial traders *Hally Bayley, Isle of France, Bella Mary* and *Camilla*; and the whalers *Emily Downing, Asia, Derwent Hunter* and *Flying Childers*.[7]

The 672-ton Scottish-built *Lufra* joined the *Harriet McGregor* in the London to Hobart Town trade, first clearing the River Derwent on 1 December 1874 under the command of Captain Richard Copping.[8] A strong and patriotic advocate for Tasmanian industry, employment and trade, Alexander ensured that all of the vessel's officers and crew were local men and boys.[9] Also by now plying between Hobart Town and London was Alexander's barque *Helen*, which had first sailed up the Derwent in late 1872, five years after it had been jointly purchased by Alexander

---
[1] *The Cornwall Chronicle*, 9 February 1875.
[2] www.thelist.tas.gov.au (Historic Deeds 06/0797, 06/0798, 06/0992).
[3] *The Mercury*, 3 March 1875.
[4] *The Mercury*, 3 March 1875.
[5] *The Tasmanian Tribune*, 1 September 1874.
[6] *The Mercury*, 8 July 1874; *Launceston Examiner*, 23 July 1874.
[7] *The Mercury*, 11 July 1874.
[8] *The Tasmanian Tribune*, 2 December 1874.
[9] *The Mercury*, 20 August 1874.

Legacies & 'Lenna'

View of Alexander and Harriet McGregor's cottage at Runnymede Street, Battery Point (early 1870s).
Tasmanian Archives (NS1013/1/63).

and Charles Bayley in half-shares.[1] Not satisfied with this contingent, in June 1875 Alexander purchased a part-share in the 236-ton whaling barque *Water Witch* along with his brother-in-law James Bayley.[2]

While Alexander McGregor's prosperity was on the rise, his brother Captain James McGregor and his family were facing a personal battle. On 14 January 1875 at their home in Kelly Street, Battery Point, James' wife Elizabeth died of a stomach ulcer.[3] She was 41 years of age. Out of respect, the vessels in port dropped their flags to half-mast.[4]

By now at the helm of the whaling barque *Emily Downing*, James McGregor had only arrived back in port in early November 1874 after an extensive 15-month voyage.[5] The vessel had then entered out of the River Derwent on another whaling voyage on 4 January 1875.[6] With James absent from home during his wife's sickness and subsequent death 10 days later, the responsibility of taking care of the couple's four children would have fallen to relatives, specifically Alexander and Harriet McGregor. Moreover, as James was likely to be away for upwards of a year, immediately following his wife's death their children would have moved in with Alexander and Harriet at their home in Runnymede Street. Given James would continue in his role as captain of a whaling vessel for the bulk of the years ahead, his three daughters, i.e., Janet (17 years old), Elizabeth (15 years old) and Amy (9 years of age) and their only son Alexander James (11 years old), were thus under

---

[1] *The Tasmanian Tribune*, 23 December 1872.
[2] *The Mercury*, 10 June 1875.
[3] *The Mercury*, 19 January 1875; Tasmanian Archives (RGD35/1/8 no. 2426).
[4] *The Mercury*, 16 January 1875.
[5] *The Tasmanian Tribune*, 9 November 1874.
[6] *The Mercury*, 5 January 1875.

the guardianship of their uncle and aunt for the foreseeable future. With four additional people now living in the couple's small house, the home very quickly became too small such that Alexander sought to expand the property. However, given his high standing in the community and the wealth he had by now amassed, he opted to build quite a large and substantial new dwelling, befitting of his stature as well as the needs of his now-enlarged family. Alexander had also leased a narrow strip of adjacent land from the Government of Tasmania's Land Office. Running the entire length of the south-east boundary of his existing property, it was part of the Flagstaff Reserve and Prince of Wales' Battery.[7] He also purchased more residential and commercial properties along the New Wharf, steadily continuing to build his real estate portfolio.[8]

Hobart Town master builder James Gregory, with more than 20 years of experience, was contracted to design and construct the first stage of Harriet and Alexander's new home, having first met in March 1876 to discuss the project.[9] A few days later, Alexander showed James Gregory 'a rough plan of a building which he proposed to have erected'.[10] The pair then met with prominent Hobart Town architect and ex-convict Edward Casson Rowntree who had previously designed the Hobart Town Savings Bank, still in existence at 26 Murray Street, as well as the Congregational Church at Richmond.[11] However, none of Rowntree's plans were deemed suitable such that James Gregory and Alexander McGregor jointly developed the design and plan, with some

View of Hobart Town's New Wharf and Battery Point, shows Alexander and Harriet McGregor's home and the completion of Runnymede Street, as well as two of his vessels (c1875).
W L Crowther Library, State Library of Tasmania.

---

[7] *The Tasmanian Tribune*, 30 May 1876; *The Mercury*, 2 August 1876.
[8] *The Tasmanian Tribune*, 30 May 1876; *The Mercury*, 2 August 1876.
[9] *Tribune*, 26 June 1878.
[10] *Tribune*, 26 June 1878.
[11] *Tribune*, 26 June 1878.

Alexander and Harriet McGregor's cottage at Runnymede Street, Battery Point (c1875). Harriet McGregor is seated on the fountain's foundation, second from right. It is assumed that the two women located on the left are Janet and Elizabeth McGregor, with Amy and Alexander James McGregor located in front of the fountain. It is not known who the teenage girl is on the far right, though given her more refined outfit, it may be Hally Bayley who would have been around 14 years old at the time.
Tasmanian Archives (PH30/1/7563).

ideas taken from Rowntree's designs.[1] James Gregory then provided a rough estimate of around £4,000 for the building's construction.[2] Works began on 4 April 1876 under the constant superintendence of both Alexander and Harriet McGregor who remained living in their existing cottage while their new home was built immediately adjacent, bordering on Runnymede Street.[3] With installment payments made at regular intervals, the roof was commenced in September 1877 after almost 18 months of construction.[4] The building was thus nearing completion in mid-December 1877, with some external cementing and plastering needed, and the construction of a verandah still remaining, estimated to cost an additional £2,000.[5] However, it was at this point in time that Alexander McGregor sacked James Gregory with the latter then initiating a civil suit against Alexander for money owed. Heard in the Supreme Court of Hobart Town in June 1878, proceedings of the case, which took place over several days and also involved the jury taking a tour of the home, revealed that £324 remained owing on Alexander McGregor's invoice, for work, labour and materials associated with the new home; with £4,000 having already been paid.[6]

Published in the local press, the proceedings also relay important details with regard to the original part of the building known as 'Lenna', including that overages had occurred due to an

---
[1] *The Mercury*, 26 June 1878; *Tribune*, 27 June 1878.
[2] *The Mercury*, 26 June 1878.
[3] *The Mercury*, 26 June 1878.
[4] *Tribune*, 26 June 1878.
[5] *The Mercury*, 26 June 1878.
[6] *Tribune*, 26, 27 June 1876.

additional third storey (described as a plain attic with windows to improve the roofline) and a tower being added that were not within the original scope of works.[7] There had also been no accounting for the erection of outbuildings in the quote, nor terraced walls or a carriage drive, all of which had been completed.[8] However some ornamental embellishments to the upper windows had been taken out, as well as balustrades removed from the lower windows.

The court case additionally reveals a level of animosity between the two parties mostly stemming from Alexander McGregor's scrupulous micro-management of the project, indicative of all of his business affairs, to ensure that he always received the best deal out of transactions, regardless of how menial. Two additional and rather startling artefacts significantly impacting the works and thereby the civil case that followed were that there had been no formal contract established between the two parties prior to construction and that there had been no architect nor a clerk of works employed to oversee the works despite the magnitude of the project.[9]

After several hours of deliberations the jury reached a verdict, ruling for the plaintiff with Alexander McGregor ordered to pay James Gregory £324 without interest.[10] With his ego very likely bruised and Alexander McGregor gruff from the court case experience, he contracted with other tradesmen to have the works associated with his home, 'Lenna', completed.

View of 'Lenna' from the Hobart Town wharf (c1878).
Tasmanian Archives (PH6/1/65).

[7] *The Mercury*, 26 June 1878; *Tribune*, 26, 27 June 1876.
[8] *Tribune*, 27 June 1878.
[9] *Tribune*, 27 June 1878.
[10] *Tribune*, 28 June 1878.

While his new home was under construction between 1876 and 1878, Alexander McGregor had remained resolute in his commercial operations. He also dealt with several matters that affected his shipping interests. For instance, the whaling barque *Flying Childers,* which he jointly owned with his brother Captain James McGregor, became stranded at Port Davey during heavy weather in mid-June 1877. With James at the helm and leading recovery efforts, it was initially believed that the uninsured vessel would be salvaged without damage.[1] However, several days later it was reported that the *Flying Childers* had become a complete wreck in heavy weather, though its crew, gear and cargo of oil were saved.[2] Despite valiant efforts, the loss of such a large and important vessel would have been disastrous.

More bad news came a few months later coinciding with the wreck of another vessel owned by Alexander McGregor, the *Isle of France*.[3] Having left Port Esperance with a full load of timber, the barque had been sailing to South Australia when it became stuck on a reef near Eddystone Point on Tasmania's north-east coast and ultimately wrecked.[4] At the time under the command of Captain William Lebrant, all crew managed to make it safely to shore. However, the vessel and its cargo were only partly insured such that it was another financial loss for Alexander McGregor, along with the *Isle of France*'s joint owner Edward Lucas.[5]

There were technological advances that were at the time being implemented that would have had a profoundly positive impact on Alexander McGregor's business communications, however. The increasing use of telegrams for communication meant that he was able to keep up to date with the movements of his vessels to and from England, New Zealand and other Australian ports, via messages sent along submarine cables, as well as within Tasmania via overland cables. He was thus more immediately informed if they were in danger or had become wrecked as had been the case with both the *Flying Childers* and the *Isle of France*.

With an immediate need to replace at least one of the vessels, Alexander McGregor placed an order with his brother John for construction of a new barque. Built at the Domain shipyard, it would be another year before it was ready for launching. During the interim, there remained the ongoing work involving Alexander and Harriet's new home, as well as one other associated issue causing much grief: ownership of the land that Alexander had leased from the Colonial Government between his property and the Prince of Wales' Battery and flagstaff. While Alexander had first written to the Colonial Government requesting permission to purchase the strip in February 1876, i.e., two months before construction of his new home began, and had received a letter from William Moore, the Minister for Lands, the following day approving his occupation of the allotment at a '*peppercorn rent*', it was soon determined that the land in question did not actually belong to the Colonial Government and instead was owned by the Crown.[6] Despite this fact representatives of the Government of Tasmania had continued to process the transaction, apparently contrary to law, issuing Alexander with a lease agreement with no restrictions, also including the proviso that should the property become available for sale, Alexander could purchase it at the going rate.[7] Assuming that the lease was solid, Alexander had thus fenced in the property, incorporating it within the bounds of his own, and building an extension to his

---

[1] *Launceston Examiner*, 30 June 1877.
[2] *The Mercury*, 7 July 1877.
[3] *Tribune*, 3 November 1877.
[4] *Tribune*, 3 November 1877.
[5] *Tribune*, 3 November 1877; National Archives of Australia, HOBART, Register of ships, Volume 9, 1865-1877, [pages 1-173, continues on film roll 2], Folio 100.
[6] *Tribune*, 26 October 1877.
[7] *Tribune*, 26 October 1877.

existing cottage on it.⁸ The ensuing issue eventually came to a head in Parliament where, during discussions amongst members, Alexander McGregor was stated to have been misled and unfairly treated by government authorities, though may have used his influence at the political level to gain a favourable outcome. A Select Committee was thus established to further investigate the matter, with a conveyance also sent to the Secretary of State in England.⁹ It would be some years before the issue was resolved, the debate ultimately thwarted by the decommissioning of the Prince of Wales' Battery and the transfer of that land to the Government of Tasmania. In time, Alexander McGregor would become outright owner of the property.

⁸ *Tribune*, 26 October 1877.
⁹ *Tribune*, 26 October 1877; *Launceston Examiner*, 10 November 1877.

View of 'Lenna' from Hobart (c1878).
Tasmanian Archives (NS1013/1/526).

With his schedule taken up dealing with multiple business and personal circumstances and events, the latter half of 1878 very likely marked the highs and lows of life in general for Alexander McGregor and his wider family, the contrast signified by two celebrations and one death. First, after taking over guardianship of his brother James' four children, Alexander was witness to the marriage of James' eldest daughter on 4 July 1878. Aged 21 years of age, Janet Smith McGregor married 24-year-old South Australian James Matthews at the Chalmers Free Church in Harrington Street, Hobart Town.[1] Sensing a need to document the occasion, perhaps because the newlyweds were near-immediately moving to Adelaide, as well as pictorialise the completion of their new home, Alexander and Harriet organised for two photographs to be taken: one of the wedding party seated, which included themselves, and one of the wedding party on the balcony of 'Lenna'. Both are striking for different reasons, most notably one is the last documented photo of Harriet.

Assumed to be the wedding party photo of Janet McGregor and James Matthews who married in Hobart Town on 4 July 1878. Harriet McGregor is seated on the groom's left and Alexander McGregor seated on the bride's right.
Tasmanian Archives (PH30/1/7561).

Next, just over a month later, Alexander McGregor's new barque was launched on 10 August 1878 from his brother John's Domain shipyard. With the weather agreeable, '*some thousands of spectators*' made their way to the Domain to witness the event, according to the press.[2] The article

[1] *The Mercury*, 11 July 1878.
[2] *The Mercury*, 12 August 1878.

Assumed to be the wedding party photo of Janet McGregor and James Matthews, taken at 'Lenna' on 4 July 1878.
Tasmanian Archives (PH30/1/7362).

continued. 'Every available space was occupied. Amongst those who repaired to the vicinity of the ship, which was arrayed in bunting, the house flag of Mr. Alex. McGregor surmounting all—were Members of both Houses of the Legislature, and prominent representatives of the shipping and mercantile interests. Everything having been in readiness, a posse of artisans went through the interesting performance of clearing away all the impediments, and as the shores were removed, at a signal the vessel began to move, when Miss McGregor, daughter of the builder, went through the customary ceremony, and having dashed against the bow of the vessel the usual bottle of wine, gave the pretty vessel her name as amid ringing cheers, she glided gracefully and easily into the bosom of the broad Derwent where she floated bird-like, her handsome proportions evoking

Loongana at the New Wharf, Hobart Town (c1880).
Maritime Museum of Tasmania (POMD75c).

renewed cheering. She was named the "Loongana," which is, we learn, an aboriginal word signifying swift or fleet. The ship throughout is an admirable example of the perfection to which the art of ship building has been brought. As she was spoken of afterwards at the launch which followed, she is a credit to the builder, the owner, the port and the Colony.'[1]

The article went on to describe the dimensions of the 283-ton *Loongana*, along with the materials used in its construction. It then continued, 'The workmanship throughout, which cannot be surpassed, reflects great credit upon the shipwrights, joiners, blacksmiths, and other artisans employed in the construction of the vessel. She is a beautiful model of a clipper barque, having moderate rise and length of floor. She has an elliptic stern which has a remarkably neat appearance, appropriately ornamented with carved work. Her figure-head represents a young and handsome female of "modern fashion". The vessel may

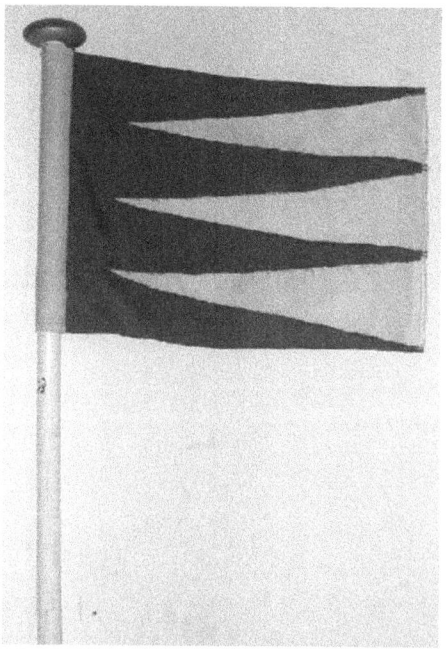

Alexander McGregor's house flag (miniature).
Maritime Museum of Tasmania (A1990033).

[1] *The Mercury*, 12 August 1878.

be regarded as one of the most handsome, strong, and symmetrical of the many fine vessels that now form our colonial fleet.'[2]

Immediately after the launch a number of gentlemen adjourned to partake of refreshments, which had been laid out in the moulding loft. With their glasses raised, toasts were proposed to the builder John McGregor, the owner Alexander McGregor, the artisans, the mercantile and shipping interests of the port, the ladies and the press. All were graciously received.[3] One person notably present at the launch event and its celebrations was Harriet McGregor, though she did not christen the vessel. This time the honour went to one of John McGregor's daughters. She was by now, however, declining in health.

Harriet McGregor died just over two months later on 23 October 1878. The cause of death was '*chronic hepatitis and peritonitis*', the latter referring to inflammation of the lining of the stomach or abdomen.[4] She was 49 years of age.

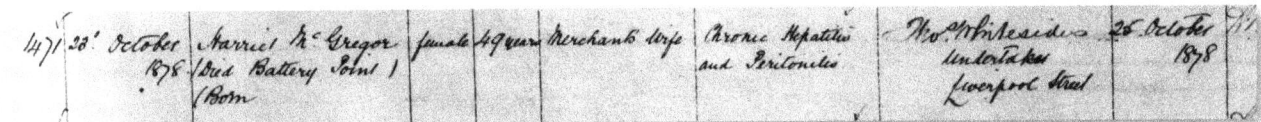

Death registration of Harriet McGregor, 23 October 1878.
Tasmanian Archives (RGD35/1/9 no. 1471).

Not only were the flags of vessels in port displayed at half-mast the day following Harriet's death as a mark of respect, an extensive eulogy was published twice in *The Mercury*, at the time quite unusual for a woman but obviously one befitting of Harriet's standing in the community.[5] The text reveals that Harriet was quite a remarkable benefactor within her local community and an avid supporter of the poor, indicating that there is so much of her life story that has yet to be discovered. She was sadly missed.

Harriet McGregor was buried at Cornelian Bay Cemetery in a private vault three days following her death.[6] In time, the remains of her husband Alexander would also be buried there.

> With deep regret we have to record the death of Mrs. M'Gregor, the wife of the well-known ship-owner, Mr. Alex. M'Gregor, Battery Point, which occurred on the 23rd inst. Outside the family, the relatives, and intimate friends, the most poignant regret will perhaps be felt among that humble class whom what the newspaper says will perhaps never reach. In Mrs. McGregor the poor have lost a kind benefactor. Essentially retiring and unobtrusive in her manners, hers was the true nobility that, in the sorrows and privations of others, always took a part; and yet, except the recipients of her bounty, few knew the good she did. Nor was that bounty indiscriminate. Her heart was open to all, but to the really deserving she was a friend indeed. Of her it may be truly said, she went about doing good. She has been long in declining health. Her last appearance in public was on the occasion of the launch of the latest addition to her husband's fleet, the Loongana; but it was not till Sunday, 20th inst., that all hope of her recovery was given up. The tidings of her death caused a feeling of deep and general regret throughout the colony, and it was felt that in her death, the poor had lost a kind and considerate friend. In her own circle, among her friends and acquaintances, they who knew her best esteemed her most.

The Mercury, 29 October 1878.

---

[2] *The Mercury*, 12 August 1878.
[3] *The Mercury*, 12 August 1878.
[4] Tasmanian Archives (RGD35/1/9 no. 1471).
[5] *The Mercury*, 24, 29 October 1878.
[6] Tasmanian Archives (AF35/1/1 p71).

Alexander McGregor (c 1870s).
Tasmanian Archives (NS6192/1/7).

Rifts & Romance

Harriet and Alexander McGregor had been married for 31 years before her death in October 1878 at the age of 49. During this period the couple had experienced somewhat of a 'rags to riches' storyline due to their association with Harriet's brothers Charles and James Bayley, as well as Alexander's business acumen and shrewdness. By the time of his widowhood, 57-year-old Alexander was Tasmania's largest shipowner and one of its wealthiest merchants. He was not content on stopping this traction.

A month following Harriet's death, rumours within Tasmania's political factions began circulating that Alexander McGregor could be convinced to run for office in the upcoming Legislative Council election with *The Mercury* reporting, '*Should Mr. McGregor be so persuaded, we feel assured that all opposition to his return would be withdrawn, and that he would have a walk over*'.[1] While he mulled over the decision, Alexander remained engaged in his various commercial and mercantile enterprises, with his involvement in the whaling industry likely occupying the bulk of his time. Between dealing with crew insubordination issues and declining prices for whale oil, there was much to consider. Was it time to reduce his stake in this endeavour? Alexander had been very fortunate during his many decades involved in this industry as the owner or part-owner of several whaling vessels; the outcome of many voyages always appearing to result in a profit. Yet, it was still a speculation and there were many risks involved. The press provided a summary of Alexander's stake. '*Mr. McGregor has invested a very large capital in the "whaling trade." He may be regarded as the first among our speculators in this precarious venture of fortune, and he has certainly always had the reputation of sending his "whaling fleet" to sea, equipped in all respects quite as completely as any that has ever left this port*'.[2] It continued, '*The "whaling trade" of late years has not been one in which capitalists like to engage, but Mr. McGregor having been for years so largely interested in it, does not wish, it would appear, to abandon it.*'[3]

Obviously not willing to forgo his wager entirely, at least for the near distant future, Alexander was also looking to invest in other industries. From the late 1870s, for example, he became a large shareholder in several mining ventures located in the north-west region of Tasmania.[4] Still, he was certainly looking to lessen his future prospects in the whaling industry. The whaling barque *Emily Downing*, of which Alexander McGregor had been sole owner since 1864, had been built in 1841 by convict labour at Port Arthur and launched under the original name of *Lady Franklin*.

---

[1] *The Mercury*, 20 November 1878.
[2] *Tribune*, 22 February 1879.
[3] *Tribune*, 22 February 1879.
[4] *The Cornwall Chronicle*, 24 September 1877.

View of New Town Bay from Hobart Town's Domain showing Runnymede laid up (1880).
State Library of Victoria (FL1304_29).

Initially used to transport convicts and stores between Hobart Town and Norfolk Island, for over two decades it had been employed as a whaler. However, given its age and years of service, it was starting to show significant signs of deterioration such that any large-scale repairs would ultimately be cost prohibitive.[1] The low price for whale oil at the time additionally meant that the *Emily Downing* was not financially viable to be fitted out for voyages. Was it time to reconsider the vessel's future?

Similarly, another long-time whaler, the 30-year-old barque *Runnymede* owned by James Bayley, was also experiencing a dubious future. By now captained by Alexander McGregor's brother John, the vessel had arrived in Hobart Town on 2 April 1879 with 58 tuns of whale oil on board after cruising waters off the Great Australian Bight into Western Australia over a nine-month period.[2] The cargo was valued at £3,480, with sperm whale oil then priced at around £60 per tun.[3] A previous voyage taken under the management of Captain Thomas Davis, however, had resulted in several inquiries and court cases owing to a crew member being unlawfully forced ashore at Frenchman Bay, Western Australia. Captain Davis was subsequently found guilty and sentenced to five months' imprisonment.[4] It was the last straw for James Bayley. He had the *Runnymede* towed to New Town Bay near his 'Runnymede' estate and put out of use.[5]

While the whaling industry was obviously in decline, mercantile trade was certainly experiencing a continued upward trajectory. Alexander McGregor's new barque *Loongana*, intended for the clipper trade, had been surveyed in Hobart Town by a representative from Lloyd's of London and

[1] *The Mercury*, 29 September 1879.
[2] *Tribune*, 11 April 1879.
[3] *The Mercury*, 25 November 1879; *Launceston Examiner*, 15 November 1879.
[4] *Launceston Examiner*, 2 October 1877.
[5] *The Mercury*, 9 June 1879.

given the class A1 for 10 years.⁶ With seven vessels now sailing in international or intercolonial trade, i.e., *Harriet McGregor, Helen, Lufra, Hally Bayley, Bella Mary, Camilla* and *Loongana*, albeit several were starting to show their age after many years of service, Alexander was also looking to increase the type of cargoes that could be shipped out of Tasmania. Not simply satisfied with the export of wheat, wool and whale oil, there was increasing interest in sending mining products and fruit to other colonies, as well as Europe. With his consistent need for innovation and to be at the forefront of his commercial pursuits, Alexander researched how other regions were handling the shipment of various products, including by importing Californian apples to Hobart Town, the local press cheerfully announcing that, '*All the apples were packed separately*'. Offering advice to exporters, the article continued, '*in this fact lies the secret of the remarkable state of preservation in which they have arrived. This is a hint which Tasmanian exporters should not fail to take advantage of*'.⁷ Alexander had no doubt already taken the idea on board.

Looking to expand and modernise his businesses, in late January 1880 Alexander McGregor removed his office from the New Wharf to premises at 1 Elizabeth Street, opposite the Telegraph Office. He also formalised his enterprises into one company, going by the name of Alex. McGregor & Company, and became an agent for the New Zealand Fire and Marine Insurance Company.⁸ The general populace of the colony of Tasmania was also looking to the future and a more contemporary purview, in the process sensing a need to elect new leaders that could facilitate this transition. It was in this context that Alexander agreed to run for election.

Announcing his candidacy for the Legislative Council representing the District of Hobart, owing to the death of Sir James Milne Wilson, Alexander McGregor placed a letter in *The*

Alex. McGregor and Co. offices (marked by the letter A). Located near the corner of Elizabeth and Macquarie streets, Hobart Town. Now the site of the Hobart General Post Office.
Launceston Manuscript Collection (LPIC147/3/191).

---

⁶ *The Mercury*, 28 August 1879.
⁷ *The Mercury*, 17 December 1879.
⁸ *The Mercury*, 18 February, 31 May 1880.

Mercury stating that his constituents could '*rely on my* [him] *honestly supporting all progressive measures calculated to open up the country, develop its resources, foster its commerce, and sustain its prosperity*'.[1] Nominated by John Lord, George Salier, E. L. Crowther, J. Watchorn, W. Burgess, Thomas Frosham and John Gleeson, the election was held on 22 March 1880 with Alexander defeating the other candidate, Russell Young, a Hobart Town solicitor, by a margin of 279 votes to 195.[2] Following the announcement of his success, Alexander thanked his committee and his friends for working so hard to get him elected. As a member of the Legislative Council, i.e., the Upper House, his term was for six years.

The next session of the Parliament of Tasmania, however, did not occur until August 1880, giving Alexander McGregor more time to adjust to his new status and role, as well as concentrate on his business activities. First taking his seat as one of 16 members of the Legislative Council on 10 August, he was one of three new members officially sworn in that day.[3] It was ultimately a short sitting, however, with more ceremonial and dignitary tasks undertaken as opposed to official business.

Parliament House, Hobart Town (c1880s).
Tasmanian Archives (PH1/1/5).

Independent of the Tasmanian political sphere, there still remained much volatility in the whaling industry, with both Alexander McGregor and his brother-in-law James Bayley remaining two of Hobart Town's primary participants. Having laid up the *Runnymede* in New Town Bay since mid-1879, in late 1880 the vessel was once more being overhauled on the Domain slip in preparation for being refitted for another voyage; the price of whale oil then on the rise.[4]

On 8 February 1881 the *Runnymede* cleared out of Hobart (Hobart Town officially becoming known as Hobart on 1 January 1881) under the command of Captain J. B. Travis.[5] Revealing the

---
[1] *The Mercury*, 16 March 1880.
[2] *The Mercury*, 18, 23 March 1880.
[3] *The Mercury*, 11 August 1880.
[4] *The Mercury*, 22 December 1880.
[5] *The Mercury*, 8 February 1881.

true state of the industry, however, several weeks later the *Derwent Hunter* arrived back in Hobart after 18 months spent in search of whales though, owing to bad weather, it had only accumulated 18 tuns of oil in its holds.[6] Still jointly owned by James Bayley and Alexander McGregor in partnership, the voyage would have resulted in a significant loss for the pair. Undeterred by the hit to his pocketbook, Alexander purchased a two-storey brick home in Macquarie Street, one of many properties he would purchase over the coming months and years.[7]

With his interest in real estate expanding and his stake in maritime trade appearing to lessen, in November 1881 Alexander McGregor sold the barque *Bella Mary,* which had been involved in intercolonial trade for many years, to Messrs Stone Bros. of Auckland, New Zealand.[8] He had owned the vessel outright since October 1880 after purchasing shares then owned by James Bayley, Richard Copping and Frederick Salier.[9] A few weeks after finalising the sale Alexander McGregor and James Bayley also advertised their shares in the brigantine *Camilla* for sale. The vessel had been laid up for nearly two years off the Hobart Domain and was thereby costing money as opposed to generating a profit.[10] It was soon sold to Messrs Belbin and Co. for £520.[11]

As well as business partners, Alexander McGregor and James Bayley had obviously remained close friends despite the death of Alexander's wife and James' sister Harriet. The duo socialised amongst the same cohort and appear to have often visited with one another at their respective homes, 'Lenna' and 'Runnymede'. However, both Alexander and James nearly met with an accident in December 1881 after the buggy they were in almost came to grief while being driven along the Domain owing to their horse being frightened by the sound of a nearby train whistle. Fortunately, the pair were able to disembark from the buggy without injury after the horse fell.[12] The event nonetheless no doubt served as an indication to Alexander and James of the increasing role railway transport was having in the colony, particularly as a mode to move passengers and freight at the expense of shipping. It was perhaps another reason for the sale of several of their old and tired vessels that had previously been involved in intracolonial and intercolonial trade.

Possibly a photo of James Bayley's wife Elizabeth and his daughter Hally in the garden at 'Lenna' (c1880).
Tasmanian Archives (PH30/1/2956).

[6] *Launceston Examiner*, 7 March 1881.
[7] www.thelist.tas.gov.au (e.g., Historic Deeds 06/6364, 06/6559, 06/6616, 06/6911, 06/7836).
[8] *The Mercury*, 15 November 1881.
[9] National Archives of Australia, HOBART, Register of ships, Volume 9, 1865-1877, [pages 1-173, continues on film roll 2], Folio 115.
[10] *The Mercury*, 9 December 1881.
[11] *The Mercury*, 9 December 1881; HOBART, Register of ships, Volume 9, 1865-1877, [pages 1-173, continues on film roll 2], Folio 196.
[12] *Launceston Examiner*, 5 December 1881.

With competing modes of transport, including the introduction of railways and iron steamships, combined with low demand for whale oil, owing to the increasing availability of alternate energy sources, it was definitely a time of change within the maritime industry. For James Bayley, the future of his whaling barque *Runnymede* was a decision he did not have to make. The fate of the vessel was ultimately determined with its loss at Frenchman Bay, near Albany in Western Australia, on 19 December 1881; all crew saved.[1] The vessel had parted from its anchor during a gale and became a total wreck after being driven ashore. Calling on help from the wider McGregor family, James Bayley arranged for Captain James McGregor to sail the whaling barque *Emily Downing* to the site of the wreck to undertake salvage operations. The vessel departed Hobart Town on 7 January 1882, returning on 19 March after a successful mission whereby the *Runnymede* was stripped of everything of value, including stores, boats, casks, 16 tuns of oil, spars, rigging and gear.[2] Of note, the kauri pine mast from the wrecked vessel was ultimately fitted to the brig *Chieftan* in Hobart in April 1883.[3]

The loss of the *Runnymede* and the sale of several vessels within his fleet meant that James Bayley had more time to devote to other activities. As such, in late December 1881 he was appointed a warden of the Hobart Marine Board, a highly respected position within Hobart's maritime community that also came with a small stipend.[4] Coinciding with this tenure James was also a member of the Hobart Chamber of Commerce.[5]

For Alexander McGregor the year 1882 began with him providing a fireworks display from the grounds of 'Lenna' to welcome in the new year.[6] In time, the exhibition would become an annual event with many of Hobart's citizens flocking to the wharf area to witness the spectacle. While his wife Harriet had been dead for some years now, Alexander was not living alone at his large home. Several of his brother James' children remained living at 'Lenna', as did James himself when not at sea. Alexander was also the children's guardian during James' lengthy voyages, including one he took at the helm of the whaler *Emily Downing* which departed Hobart on 11 May 1882.[7]

In terms of his commercial ventures, Alexander McGregor continued to develop his interest in mining. He was also using his larger vessels to ship the product to England; the barque *Lufra*, for instance, taking 20 tons of tin shipped by Alex. McGregor and Co. to London in mid-February 1882, valued at £2,140.[8] Several months later the steamer *Southern Cross* shipped 10 tons of tin to Melbourne consigned to Alex. McGregor and Co. and valued at £1,068.[9] Continuing to relinquish his investment in local and intercolonial trade, however, in August 1882 Alexander sold the 113-ton schooner *Hally Bayley* to Thomas Kelly of Sydney.[10] The craft was subsequently placed in the Pacific Islands trade.[11] It was certainly a period of transition for Alexander McGregor, both personally and professionally. He had lost his wife, been elected to Parliament, lost and sold several vessels of his fleet, in the process minimising his involvement in intercolonial trade and the whaling industry, and increasingly invested in emerging though perhaps more profitable industries like mining and real estate.

[1] *Launceston Examiner*, 22 December 1881.
[2] *The Mercury*, 9 January, 21 March 1882.
[3] *The Mercury*, 7 April 1883.
[4] *The Mercury*, 29 December 1881, 5 January 1882.
[5] *The Mercury*, 29 April 1882.
[6] *The Hobart Herald*, 4 January 1882.
[7] *The Mercury*, 12 May 1882.
[8] *The Mercury*, 14 February 1882.
[9] National Archives of Australia, HOBART, Register of ships, Volume 9, 1865-1877, [pages 1-173, continues on film roll 2], Folio 72.
[10] *Launceston Examiner*, 28 August 1882.
[11] *The Mercury*, 1 July 1882.

One more area of interest for Alexander McGregor was the establishment of a direct steamship service between Hobart and London, of which he spent several months negotiating to be the local agent in mid-1883. Apparently receiving favourable expressions of interest from agents in London, it was proposed that first-class steamers be chartered by the Government of Tasmania to ply between the two locations, making their way through the newly-opened Suez Canal such that freight would arrive much earlier than the current steamers then sailing between Melbourne and London.[12] Hoping to lessen the time taken to send and receive shipments, removal of the Melbourne leg of the journey was seen as a necessary step to improve efficiency and also reduce costs. While it was obvious that the implementation of a direct steam line would result in reduced demand for Alexander McGregor's clipper barques then sailing between the two ports, he was a big proponent of the idea, at the time being Hobart's principal importer.[13]

With regards to land-based industries, another trade in Hobart then enjoying a period of renewed vigour was the building trade; Alexander McGregor doing his part to fuel its success with the construction of a new addition to 'Lenna'. With the work undertaken by Messrs Duncan and Crow, the contractors had commenced construction in October 1882 expecting the project to take six months to complete.[14] The need for additional space likely came with the continued residence of James McGregor and several of his children at 'Lenna'. However, in June 1883 James had sailed the whaler *Emily Downing* up the River Derwent where he subsequently disembarked due to ill health. Seeking medical advice and being told to remain on land, the vessel departed Hobart a few days later under the command of its chief officer, Jeremiah Scannon.[15] James McGregor died just over a month later, on 23 July 1883 at 'Lenna'.[16] The cause of death was '*malignant disease of stomach and liver*'.[17] The flags of the vessels in port were dropped to half-mast as a mark of respect.[18] James was 59 years of age and left the care of his three unmarried children, i.e., 23-year-old Elizabeth, 20-year-old Alexander James and 18-year-old Amy, to the guardianship of his brother Alexander.

Captain James McGregor (late 1870s).
Tasmanian Archives (NS6192/1/16).

[12] *The Mercury*, 11 June 1883.
[13] *The Mercury*, 11 June 1883.
[14] *The Mercury*, 5 February 1883.
[15] *The Mercury*, 21 June 1883.
[16] *The Mercury*, 24 July 1883.
[17] Tasmanian Archives (RGD35/1/10 no. 1020).
[18] *Daily Telegraph*, 24 July 1883.

Mariners, Marriages and Mansions

'Lenna', showing the second stage addition (c1884).
Tasmanian Archives (NS1013/1/366).

Up until this juncture in time, Alexander McGregor had been a cautious and generally inconspicuous member of the Legislative Council after first being elected in March 1880. However, after serving several years in the role, he was starting to break this mould. One issue of apparent concern to him was the development of additional railway lines, particularly in the north of Tasmania. Spurred by private investors, the Tasmanian Main Line Railway Company had established a railway between Hobart and Evandale in 1876.[1] However, because of a difference in gauge, a third rail was needed to complete the line through to Launceston. Meanwhile, a railway had been constructed from Deloraine to Devonport which first began operation in September 1885. With the need for a more systematic process of expansion in both the north and the south, as well as government oversight, a bill calling for the establishment of additional rail lines, including one between Hobart and New Norfolk in the Derwent Valley, had been entered into Parliament in October 1883 of which Alexander McGregor voted against; the bill was rejected by the Legislative Council by a majority of one.[2] Labelled an '*obstructionist*' by many of his constituents, the fact that Alexander was publicly not willing to provide any reasoning behind his no vote was seen as a significant black mark against his name and service to the Hobart community more generally.[3] In response to a deputation signed by 277 of his electors, Alexander had provided an obscure response as to why he had voted against expanding the colony's railways, casually stating that there was '*no urgent necessity for public works*'.[4] It was not long before there was further widespread indignation of Alexander's actions, or lack thereof, resulting in calls for his resignation.[5]

Alexander McGregor appears to have endured the public cries for his resignation by maintaining his silence. Described by this point in time as a figure that was neither '*agreeable*' nor '*amicable*', for reasons he would not state Alexander ignored the confrontation and also refused to meet with his constituents to discuss the matter.[6] The debate on the railway bill was subsequently delayed until the next session of Parliament some weeks away.[7] The contrast between Alexander's opposition to the further development of railway lines and his support for the establishment of a direct steam line between Tasmania and London did not go unnoticed.[8]

Another issue which Alexander McGregor was dealing with at the time involved his home 'Lenna'. With the construction of the new addition, the building was now partially obscuring the flagstaff located at the top of the hill near Runnymede and Cross streets. A new longer staff was erected in November 1883 and the yard raised such that signals could again be discernible from most parts of Hobart.[9]

'Lenna', prior to the second stage addition, showing the old flagstaff (c1880).
Tasmanian Archives (NS1013/1/494).

[1] https://en.wikipedia.org/wiki/Tasmanian_Government_Railways.
[2] *The Mercury*, 9, 10 October 1883.
[3] *The Mercury*, 8, 9 October 1883.
[4] *The Mercury*, 8, 9 October 1883.
[5] *The Mercury*, 15 October 1883.
[6] *The Mercury*, 15, 23 October 1883.
[7] *The Mercury*, 15, 23 October 1883.
[8] *The Tasmanian*, 12 January 1884.
[9] *The Mercury*, 1 November 1883.

After what had been a rather contentious period for Alexander McGregor he departed the colony for Melbourne, where he spent several days before returning on 30 November 1883 through the Port of Launceston as a passenger on board the steamer *Southern Cross*.[1] Whether visiting Victoria for business, pleasure or a combination of the two, upon disembarking in Tasmania's northern city, he ironically then caught the express train to Hobart, a fact that did not go unnoticed by the press.[2]

Alexander McGregor returned to Hobart and immediately became the subject of another issue that was widely publicised in the local papers. He appeared in court to argue his case after being sued by Captain James Riddle, Harbour Master, for breach of the Marine Board Act after failing to remove a range of anchors, cables, chains and other items from a parcel of Marine Board property located on the New Wharf after being given several notices to do so. Appearing in court on 20 December 1883 Alexander pleaded not guilty to the offence before leaving the room due to other business to attend to.[3] Defended by solicitor J. W. Gill, the case proceeded in his absence, the details of which appeared to be that Alexander had left the items in the same position on the New Wharf, some for up to 18 years, and though repeatedly asked to remove them over a period going back at least six years, had failed to do so. His apparent refusal to remove the items provoked the Marine Board to sue him in court. Some of the items, including six anchors, were large and heavy, thus proving a cumbersome nuisance, and had apparently been salvaged from the whaling barque *Flying Childers* which had been wrecked in June 1877.[4] Instead of admitting that he was in the wrong and undertaking remedial action, Alexander's solicitor argued that there was no proof that the Marine Board of Hobart existed as an organisation and that there was no evidence to suggest that the Marine Board owned the parcel of land in question.[5] These trivialities delayed the case even further, with parliamentary proceedings and the Government Gazette searched to confirm both the Marine Board's existence and its authority.[6] The pettiness of the case and its progression into bureaucratic absurdity did not bode well for Alexander. He lost the case.

Commonsense, however, continued not to prevail for Alexander McGregor. Instead of accepting the result of the case and having the items removed, he took the outcome personally and doubled down on his efforts to claim that he was being directly prejudiced against by the Marine Board and had not been treated in a just and equal manner. He also sought to alienate James Bayley from his business dealings owing to James' role as a member of the Marine Board.

There was some upswing though in Alexander McGregor's political favourability amongst his constituents. A few days after the Marine Board court case, at a sitting of the Legislative Council, he dutifully voted for the expansion of Tasmania's railway lines, having faced the wrath of his voters and acquiesced. Specifically, the bill approved the construction of rail lines between Bridgewater and Glenora, Launceston and Scottsdale and Conara Junction and St Marys.[7]

The year 1883 thus likely ended with rather subdued celebratory activities for Alexander, despite the annual fireworks display from the grounds of 'Lenna'.[8] He had persisted through a tumultuous period of his business and political affairs and, because of his stubbornness and

---

[1] *Daily Telegraph*, 1 December 1883.
[2] *The Tasmanian*, 8 December 1883.
[3] *The Tasmanian*, 20 December 1883.
[4] *The Tasmanian*, 20 December 1883.
[5] *The Tasmanian*, 20 December 1883.
[6] *The Tasmanian*, 29 December 1883.
[7] *The Mercury*, 19 December 1883.
[8] *Tasmanian News*, 1 January 1884.

outright gruff obstination, was seemingly willing to lose a true friend, an ally and a close relation in James Bayley. It was obviously not the first time that Alexander McGregor had faced the brunt of the law for his actions, nor would it be the last. Still, just how much was he willing to lose to stake his claim of righteousness? It was likely that his late wife Harriet was the calming mediator in previous circumstances whereby Alexander had become involved in a fracas, whether business or personal. With her death he had been navigating life's problems solo and the outcomes were becoming more and more noticeable.

The year 1884 began with the establishment of a business partnership between Alexander McGregor and Charles Piesse such that Alex. McGregor & Co. morphed into McGregor, Piesse and Co. Still operating out of premises at 1 Elizabeth Street in Hobart, the change was likely due to more of Alexander's time being spent undertaking activities associated with his role as a member of the Legislative Council. Still, he remained engaged in both aspects of his professional dealings, also looking for ways to coalesce the two areas to his own benefit. There also remained his other obligations, including his large investments in mining companies and the Cascade Brewery Company Limited, as well as his role as a director of the TSN Company.[9] He had a lot going on.

One of Alexander McGregor's key projects during this period remained his involvement in the establishment of a government contract, by way of a subsidy worth up to £18,000, for a direct Hobart to London 50-day steam service that would be carried out by a large shipping company, i.e., P&O or Orient, both then delivering passenger and mail services to Australia. Behind the scenes Alexander was manoeuvring for his business to be awarded the contract to oversee the service and act as the local agent. Clearly capable and having the experience and expertise to fulfil the role, the conflict of interest did not go unnoticed. In an editorial labelled '*Another good man gone wrong*', *The Mercury* chastised the seemingly apparent clause of the Constitution Act which forbid members of both houses of Parliament from entering into government contracts whereby they could personally profit.[10] This was definitely the case with Alexander; he was set to receive a handsome sum if his company was to become the principal agent for the steamer service.[11] Calls for his resignation from the Legislative Council only became more and more vocal and widespread the closer the contract came to being signed.[12] Several weeks later, however, it was announced that negotiations had fallen through. Moreover, Alexander wanted it made clear that he had withdrawn from any contract discussions and that his seat was no longer in dispute.[13] The biggest losers in the murky proceedings were the recipients of overseas mail, Tasmania's importers and exporters, particularly those that shipped perishable freight, and passengers looking to reduce the travel time between Tasmania and Europe. For the moment, nevertheless, despite his involvement in international and intercolonial trade, Alexander was willing to relinquish a faster and more efficient shipping line at the expense of his own political gain.

Coinciding with this challenging period in Alexander McGregor's business and political dealings, he was dissolving his commercial partnerships with James Bayley. Just prior to the death of James' brother Charles Bayley in 1875, and thereby Alexander's brother-in-law, the pair had become joint owners of several vessels, including the whaling barques *Asia*, *Derwent Hunter* and *Water Witch*. Still upset about the Marine Board of Hobart's court case and the assumed role

---

[9] *The Argus*, 11 February 1884; *The Mercury*, 27 February 1883; *The Age*, 20 April 1883; *Tasmanian News*, 12 February 1884.
[10] *The Mercury*, 3 April 1884.
[11] *Daily Telegraph*, 8 April 1884.
[12] *The Mercury*, 3 April 1884.
[13] *The Mercury*, 24 April 1884.

James Bayley had played in the proceedings as a warden of the Board, Alexander took steps to cut ties with James. In April 1884 it was announced that James had unwillingly sold his half-share in the three vessels to Alexander.[1] Reporting on the transaction the local press stated, '*The [sale] amount appears somewhat small, but Captain Bayley not feeling inclined to purchase the three whalers out right, the offer made by Mr. McGregor being to purchase all or none, he having previously refused to sell by auction, Captain Bayley decided to sell at the prices fixed by Mr. McGregor*'.[2] The article continued, '*The transfer of the other whaling vessels will be completed as they arrive in port. Information has also been received that it is the intention of Captain Bayley to complete the sale of the shipping interest he has held for a number of years in connection with Mr. McGregor, and that in addition to the whaling ships, sale will soon be made of the barque Helen, of which Mr. McGregor owns one-quarter, Captain Evans one-quarter, and Captain Bayley one-half; and of the Lufra, of which Mr. McGregor owns one-quarter, Captain Bayley one-eighth, the remainder being held by other owners in this port.*'[3]

While the details reported in the article above appear mostly impartial, Alexander McGregor took them as offensive and the following day published this note in The Mercury. '*In yesterday's shipping columns reference was made to the disposal of Captain Bayley's interest in certain vessels, and which we are requested by Mr. McGregor to supplement by the following: "The actions of the Marine Board toward Mr. McGregor for some time past having caused him much annoyance, he decided to effect the sale of all ships owned jointly with Captain Bayley, and requested Captain Bayley to make him an offer of purchase, which he declined to do. Captain Bayley then requested Mr. McGregor to fix prices he would accept or sell at. The prices named were made to induce Captain Bayley to buy, and after several delays, during which Captain Bayley asked others to join him in the purchase, he declined to buy, and agreed to sell. Mr. McGregor did not wish to effect sale by auction, as he had no desire to force Captain Bayley to the adoption of such a course, and hence his offer to sell or buy, it being open to either party to afterwards dispose in any way he thought fit*".'[4]

The two parties were by this point not talking to one another as evidenced by James Bayley's response which was published in The Mercury on 23 April 1884. Still, it would be some time before the transfer of ownership

> **MR. McGREGOR AND THE WHALE SHIPS.**
>
> Sir,—I was much surprised, in perusing your issue of this morning, to find that Mr. Alex. McGregor was so displeased with the independent course that I have taken, as a member of the Marine Board, in dealing witter matters in which he was concerned, that he has given you to understand it caused him to wish to dissolve the partnership hitherto existing between us in whaling and merchant ships, and also to end the friendship that has existed between us for some 42 years. Mr. McGregor endeavours to lead the mercantile public to believe that all that he did with reference to the ships was in a kindly spirit towards me. In this he is in error, seeing that he would not, for weeks prior to the sale, follow out in any way the course I deemed best, and when at last he was induced to name a price, at which he would either buy or sell, he gave me so short a time that I had not any opportunity to make much enquiry from others, having received his letter making the offer on Friday, with a request that my answer would be given by 10 a.m. on the Saturday.
>
> There was not any necessity for forcing me to a sale by auction, because it was my wish, as expressed to Mr. McGregor, that the vessels should be sold by auction, that being to my mind the most ready way of obtaining fair value for the ships.
>
> I regret that Mr. McGregor should have thought fit to introduce the Marine Board into our business relations, and that he should think it necessary to attempt to justify his doing it under the plea that the actions of the board for some time past have not met with his approval. Had it not been for Mr. McGregor's reference to the Marine Board, of which I am a member, I should not have troubled you with a letter.—Yours, etc.,
>
> JAMES BAYLEY.
>
> April 22.
>
> [We publish the above letter in justice to Mr. Bayley, but, as the matter is a private one, we cannot allow the correspondence to be continued.—Ed. *M*.]

The Mercury, 23 April 1884.

---
[1] The Mercury, 21 April 1884.
[2] The Mercury, 21 April 1884.
[3] The Mercury, 21 April 1884.
[4] The Mercury, 22 April 1884.

of the vessels was complete. For example, James Bayley did not sell his half-share in both the *Derwent Hunter* and *Helen* to Alexander McGregor until 7 April 1886.[5]

Just what Alexander McGregor did next seems far out of character and rather remarkable considering all that was going on in his life, and everything that had transpired for him in the first half of 1884. It is also worth stating plainly; he sailed to Melbourne and got married.

His new bride would become one of Hobart's fiercest suffragettes and advocates for women's rights, as well as a champion of numerous social and health-related causes impacting women and children. Yet all this was well into the future, for at the time of her marriage to 63-year-old Alexander McGregor, Margaret 'Maggie' Pigdon was only 25 years old.

Born in Long Horsley, Northumberland, England, in 1832, Maggie's father John had first arrived in Melbourne in 1851.[6] A carpenter and joiner by trade, he quickly capitalised on high demand for his work, at the time an artefact of the Victorian gold mining boom, within a few decades becoming one of Melbourne's more prominent builders and contractors.[7] He also successfully speculated on the development of land in and around North Melbourne and what would become its surrounding suburbs.[8] Some of John Pigdon's more notable projects included construction of the Wesleyan Church in Emerald Hill (1863); St Jude's Church in Lygon Street, Carlton (1866); the Royal Colosseum Hall at 283 Bourke Street, Melbourne (1868); the Wesleyan Church in Palmerstone Street, Carlton (1869); the Registrar-General's Office, 247-283 Queen Street, Melbourne (1876); the Customs House, Flinders Street, Melbourne, now the home of the Immigration Museum (1876); and the western facade of Victoria's Parliament House (1888).[9]

M'GREGOR—PIGDON.—On the 12th inst., at the residence of the bride's parents, by the Rev. C. Stuart Perry, the Hon. Alexander M'Gregor, M.L.C., Hobart, Tasmania, to Maggie, eldest daughter of John Pigdon, J.P., Coburg.

The Argus, 21 June 1884.

It was from humble beginnings, however, that the Pigdon family evolved. John Pigdon married Jane Clelland in 1857 and the couple initially made their home in a small brick cottage above a pub (the Lincoln Inn) in Cardigan Street, North Melbourne.[10] With the birth of their first child, a son named Thomas Miers Pigdon in 1858, the couple had moved to a six-roomed home in Faraday Street, Carlton, at its intersection with Rathdowne Street, where the family remained for two decades.[11] It was here that John and Jane Pigdon also expanded their family, welcoming their daughter Maggie on 17 December 1859. Another three sons and five daughters would be born between 1862 and 1877, though sadly one son and one daughter would not survive infancy.[12] The family then relocated to a larger home in the vicinity of Royal Park before moving to the expansive 'Moreland Hall' in Coburg.[13]

Coinciding with these professional and personal developments and his rising stature in the community, in July 1869 John Pigdon was elected to the Melbourne City Council representing the Smith Ward.[14] He would continue his service in local government for several decades until

---

[5] National Archives of Australia, HOBART, Register of ships, Volume 9, 1865-1877, [pages 1-173, continues on film roll 2], Folio 44; HOBART, Register of ships, Volume 8, 1865-1877, Folio 107.
[6] *The Argus*, 4 April 1851.
[7] *The Argus*, 25 February 1857.
[8] *The Age*, 24 November 1858, 28 September 1864.
[9] *The Age*, 12 August 1863, 9 June 1869, 2 October 1886; *The Argus*, 19 October 1866, 25 June 1868, 19 January 1876.
[10] *The Argus*, 14 September 1857.
[11] *The Argus*, 7 July 1858, 14 July 1859, 29 June 1864, 18 July 1866, 30 June 1868, 2 November 1869.
[12] McGregor family tree on Ancestry.com compiled by author.
[13] *The Argus*, 31 July 1879, 21 October 1882.
[14] *The Argus*, 30 July 1869.

his death in 1903.[1] In 1874 he was additionally elected a Magistrate and Justice of the Peace for Melbourne.[2] Notably, between November 1877 and October 1878, John Pigdon would serve as Mayor of Melbourne.[3] In addition, he was on the committee of the Melbourne Tramways Trust and was a founding member of the Builders and Contractors Association.[4]

It was in this context that Alexander McGregor first met Maggie Pigdon, assumed to be via a business or political connection formed with her father. Educated, fashionable and from a prominent Melbourne-based family that had enjoyed a similar successful progression from working-class roots, she was also well versed in upper-class society, including the ceremonial duties of a local politician's wife. For these reasons the pair's marriage would have been seen as a strategic alliance, though some may have questioned their 38-year age gap and if the partnership was based more on companionship as opposed to romance. Still, the pair seemed eager to start their married life together, boarding the steamer *Flinders* as saloon passengers for Launceston one day after they were married.[5]

For Maggie McGregor, her new life would have been something of a different, perhaps exciting, though definitely challenging adventure, seeing her living in a new house in a new colony and having to find herself and thrive in a new social hierarchy and structure. However, she appears to have been up to the task and, given her apparent strength of character, also seems to have been able to rein in Alexander McGregor's temper and public abruptness, complementing his personality with one significantly more diplomatic and personable. There were also instant companions once Maggie arrived in Hobart, with Alexander's nieces Elizabeth and Amy still living at 'Lenna', as well as his nephew Alexander James.

Settling in to 'Lenna', Maggie appears to have immediately taken on the role of lady of the house, advertising for the services of a cook and a laundress.[6] She likely also acted as matchmaker, with her older brother Thomas Miers Pigdon marrying 24-year-old Elizabeth McGregor at 'Lenna' on 2 October 1884, with Maggie's parents also travelling from Melbourne to Hobart to witness the ceremony.[7] The newlywed couple then moved to Melbourne to begin their married life. Maggie McGregor would not be without her family for long intervals, however, with many of her siblings spending large chunks of time at 'Lenna' over the coming years and decades; Maggie acting as their guardian.

Indicative of the positive effect of the marriage, Alexander and Maggie McGregor were soon noted in the press as attending the theatre in the Vice-Regal box, taking carriage rides through the Botanical Gardens and undertaking picnics.[8] There were also frequent trips to Melbourne to plan, anticipate and enjoy.

---

[1] *The Argus*, 10 October 1877, 7 November 1883, 27 October 1887; *The Age*, 2 November 1878, 26 October 1903.
[2] *The Age*, 21 September 1874.
[3] *The Argus*, 10 October 1877; *The Age*, 2 November 1878.
[4] *The Age*, 16 July 1869; *The Argus*, 31 May 1884.
[5] *Launceston Examiner*, 14 June 1884.
[6] *The Tasmanian*, 8 July 1884.
[7] *The Age*, 30 September 1884; *The Mercury*, 20 October 1884; *Tasmanian News*, 30 January 1886.
[8] *Tasmanian News*, 22 January, 19 February 1885.

The Last Surviving Sibling

James Bayley turned 62 years old in 1885. Though he no longer had over-arching stakes in commercial vessels, particularly since the very public rift between him and Alexander McGregor, James remained active as a director of the Derwent and Tamar Fire and Marine Assurance Company and as a warden of the Marine Board of Hobart.[9] The latter role involved him regularly visiting lighthouses and port facilities, as well as inspecting vessels. Other outlets for his time were his involvement with the Hobart Chamber of Commerce, the Road District of New Town and the New Town Reading Room and Library.[10]

At his estate of 'Runnymede' James continued to enjoy the quiet life of a gentleman farmer. The property was only a 10-minute carriage ride from Hobart and was thereby very quickly becoming part of the growing suburb of New Town. In addition to managing the estate's gardens and fields, James exhibited livestock at shows convened by the Southern Tasmanian Agricultural and Pastoral Association, canaries and other birds at shows held by the Tasmanian Poultry Society, and was also vice president of the Hobart Horticultural Society.[11]

Sport remained another area of interest for James, particularly cricket. He additionally maintained an interest in aquatic events and was vice president of the newly-formed New Town Regatta Association.[12] However, it is through James' involvement with cricket administration that his daughter Hally undoubtedly met her future husband, Henry Vincent Bayly. A prominent bowler, Henry played for and was a long-time member of the Wellington Cricket Club.[13]

Born at Dulcot, just outside of Richmond, Tasmania, in November 1850, Henry Bayly was the last child born to Benjamin Bayly and his wife Mary Ann Cameron (nee Wylly). A captain of the 21st Regiment of Foot, sadly Henry did not know his father, being born six months after Benjamin's death on 3 March 1850 at Maria Island where he had been visiting as part of his magisterial duties.[14] Despite the loss of its patriarch, the Bayly family managed to live comfortably with Henry and his siblings well educated.[15] Henry was also a keen sportsman, playing both cricket and football. However, he appears to have excelled at the former, in the 1870s being regularly named in representative teams for his bowling capabilities, playing against sides from Tasmania's north, as well as teams visiting from Victoria, New South Wales and England.[16]

[9] *Launceston Examiner*, 15 May, 3 November 1885; *The Mercury*, 16 May 1885, 13 December 1887, 10 December 1889.
[10] *The Mercury*, 9 July 1884, 9 December 1887, 15 April 1890.
[11] *The Mercury*, 22 October 1885, 18 August 1887; *Tasmanian News*, 13 January 1886.
[12] *Tasmanian News*, 19 January 1886.
[13] *The Mercury*, 12 September 1882.
[14] Tasmanian Archives (RGD33/1/29 no. 571); *The Colonial Record*, 6 May 1839; *The Courier*, 27 March 1850.
[15] Tasmanian Archives (RGD33/1/29 no. 571); *The Colonial Record*, 6 May 1839; *The Courier*, 27 March 1850.
[16] *Tasmanian News*, 7 January 1903.

James Bayley at 'Runnymede', New Town.
Tasmanian Archives (NS1619/1/102).

On a professional level Henry Bayly was an accountant for the Hobart Post Office, by the late 1870s working in the department that handled money orders.[1] In 1882 he was promoted to the position of clerk and cashier in charge of money orders, as well as the post office's savings bank.[2] However, it was through their overlapping sporting circles that Hally Bayley was first introduced to Henry. The couple were married at 'Runnymede' on 29 October 1885 in the presence of the bride's father James, as well as Frederick Salier.[3] Reporting on the nuptials the *Tasmanian News* relayed that '*nearly all the vessels in port, both large and small, were gaily bedecked with bunting in honor of the marriage of Mr H. V. Bayley [sic] to Miss Bayley, a daughter of Captain Bayley, who has been many years closely connected with the shipping interests of the colony and who had made himself deservedly popular in shipping circles*'.[4]

Marriage registration of Hally Bayley and Henry Vincent Bayly, 29 October 1885.
Tasmanian Archives (RGD37/1/44 no. 355).

While Hally and her husband Henry Bayly moved to a home named 'Aloha' in Park Street, New Town, James Bayley remained at 'Runnymede' where he lived with his wife Elizabeth and his ageing sister Mary Bull. With Hally in close proximity, it was likely a joyous occasion for James when he first became a grandfather. Hally Mary Butchard Bayly was born at Park Street on 28 July 1886 and baptised a month later.[5] Two more daughters would soon follow, with Mary Wylly Bayly born at the couple's Park Street home on 3 May 1888 and Emma Matty Bayly arriving two years later on 4 May 1890.[6] Unlike previous generations all three children survived infancy. Mortality, however, would not ignore the Bayley family completely with the death of Mary Bull at 'Runnymede' on 12 January 1892 from stomach cancer.[7] She was 83 years old and buried at the nearby Cornelian Bay Cemetery.

With the Bayley family enjoying the new additions to their brood, for reasons not known Alexander McGregor and his new wife Maggie were not in the same position: the couple did not have any children. Instead, Alexander remained relentlessly

Hally Bayley (c1880s).
LINC Tasmania eHeritage Database (2012).

---

[1] *The Mercury*, 1 January 1878.
[2] *The Mercury*, 30 September 1882.
[3] Tasmanian Archives (RGD37/1/4 no. 355).
[4] *Tasmanian News*, 3 November 1885.
[5] Tasmanian Archives (RGD33/1/14 no. 1129); *The Mercury*, 30 July 1886.
[6] Tasmanian Archives (RGD33/1/15 no. 1508, RGD33/1/17 no. 362); *The Mercury*, 8 May 1888, 6 May 1890.
[7] Tasmanian Archives (RGD35/1/13 no. 121, AF35/1/1, BU 8028); *Tasmanian News*, 13 January 1891.

Asia (left) and Harriet McGregor (right) at the Hobart Wharf, with 'Lenna' in the background (c1890s).
State Library of South Australia (PRG 1373/40/17).

involved in his commercial and political enterprises, including being re-elected to his seat in the Legislative Council in July 1886 as the only candidate.[1] On 31 December 1886, after three years in partnership, Alexander also dissolved his relationship with Charles Piesse whereby the pair had jointly carried on operations acting as merchants, shipping, commission and insurance agents.[2] Instead, Alexander reconstituted his old firm of Alex. McGregor & Co. He also became a large shareholder and director of the Perpetual Trustees and Executors Company, formed in 1887, and remained a director of the TSN Company and the Tasmanian Loan Guarantee and Finance Company Limited, as well as an agent for the New Zealand Fire and Marine Insurance Company.[3] Real estate investments continued to be part of his portfolio, including farming properties in Tasmania's midlands, as well as mining ventures.

Of his commercial fleet, by this point in time Alexander McGregor remained the sole owner of the barques *Harriet McGregor*, *Helen* and *Lufra*, all employed in international or intercolonial trade; he was also part-owner of the intercolonial trading barque *Loongana* with his brother John. Moreover, Alexander's barques *Asia* and *Water Witch* remained involved in the whaling industry, though their long-term survival was not guaranteed. In 1886 the *Derwent Hunter* was converted into a coal hulk suffering the same fate as the *Emily Downing*, until being sunk at the Domain shipyard in 1890 by Messrs Dalgleish and Taylor to be used as somewhat of a makeshift jetty.[4]

[1] *Tasmanian News*, 7 July 1886.
[2] *Tasmanian News*, 13 December 1886.
[3] *The Mercury*, 1 April 1887, 21 February, 9 July 1890; *Tasmanian News*, 17 August 1889.
[4] *The Mercury*, 11 December 1885, 7 July 1890.

Water Witch (left) and Derwent Hunter (right) at the Domain slipyard (c1897).
Tasmanian Archives (NS1013/1/73).

Both were broken up or deliberately scuttled a few decades later. The *Loongana* would be sold in April 1891 to a Sydney-based fruit trading company. However considering John McGregor had sued his brother Alexander in Vice-Admiralty Court in late 1889 for lack of earnings with regards to the vessel, the partnership between the two half-owners may have been strained for some time.[5] The *Helen* would be laid up in late 1891, though three years later was fitted out for whaling, joining the *Water Witch* as the last two vessels involved in this industry based out of the Port of Hobart, though their stints were only for a short period of time.[6] The *Harriet McGregor* would be sold in July 1895 to Aktieselskab Marcus Nissen of Copenhagen, Denmark.[7] Renamed *Waterqueen*, the vessel was placed in the London to Brazil trade until sinking following a collision with a seagoing steamer in the Elbe River, Germany, in October 1897 with the unfortunate loss of four crew members.[8] The barque *Asia* would be sold a few months later to New Zealand owners.[9]

The old whaling days of Hobart were by now very much in the past. From upwards of 30 whaling vessels operating out of the port in the 1850s and 1860s, the number had declined significantly to less than a handful, with the volume of whale oil these few ships procuring barely able to make a voyage financially viable, if at all. Competing pathways for secure working-class jobs had also lessened the interest of those men willing to risk their lives and spend months away at sea.

---

[5] *The Mercury*, 10 December 1889, 16 September 1890; *Tasmanian News*, 20 April 1891.
[6] *The Mercury*, 15 May 1894.
[7] *Tasmanian News*, 12 August 1895.
[8] *Tasmanian News*, 23 December 1897; https://vragwiki.dk/wiki/Waterqueen_1897_Elbmundingen_ved_Elbe_1.
[9] *The Mercury*, 11 August 1895.

Another factor impacting the shipping industry was trade unionism. Having recently been implemented by an act of Parliament, in the late 1880s the loading and unloading of several of Alexander McGregor's vessels within the Port of Hobart were impacted by strikes, leading to several situations where unionised labourers refused to work alongside non-union men.[1] With maritime trade, its employers and employees not only transitioning from the methods of the past, and also under significant strain, both Alexander McGregor and James Bayley continued to invest in alternative industries, including mining. They were two of many speculators looking to secure a share of this growing though labour and infrastructure-intensive market.

The ongoing affairs of the Marine Board of Hobart remained a continuing cause of concern for Alexander McGregor. Other parties had also been interested in the management of these boards across the colony, including in Launceston and Leven, such that the Marine Board Act of 1889 was passed by Parliament. The legislation defined the authority of the various marine boards then in operation as corporate bodies, as well as their responsibilities with regards to wharf management, pilotage and other marine-related matters such as lighthouses. For Alexander McGregor the restructuring of the Marine Board of Hobart gave him the opportunity to seek election as a warden. With the old board dismissed on 19 December 1889, Alexander was subsequently voted onto the board.[2] Of note, James Bayley did not seek re-election.

Meeting every fortnight, the proceedings of the newly restructured Marine Board of Hobart reveal that Alexander continued with his very vocal opinions on certain matters, often coming across as downright combative, particularly over his proposal to extend the New Wharf that would be of benefit to his existing business enterprises.[3] He was, however, not solely thinking of his own needs. With the further development of railways and infrastructure needed for mining, the Port of Hobart was quickly becoming a depot for the off-loading of cargoes from large overseas vessels. In time, the needs of steamships and other ships of increasing tonnage visiting the port would outgrow the existing wharves if nothing was done.[4] Whereas conflicts of interests between his legislative and business concerns appear to have faced allegations of misconduct in previous instances, his actions with the Hobart Marine Board were not deemed as such, nor was there any apparent conflict between his meetings with Treasury on behalf of the Marine Board to request funds for large-scale port improvements, despite the fact that he was a member of the Legislative Council. Further still, Alexander McGregor voted on legislative actions directly impacting the Marine Board, all with positive results, including provisions for wharf improvements.[5]

The late 1880s was the start of a period of much change, not only within Tasmania's industries and its import and export markets, but also its citizenry. With a population approaching 150,000 people, the colony was enjoying a significantly high rate of births, as well as a greatly reduced level of infant mortality. Net migration was also at a high owing to the increasing availability of jobs, particularly in the mining sector centred around Zeehan, Mt Lyell, Mt Bischoff and Beaconsfield.[6] Aided by the development of roads, bridges, railways and tramways, and improvements to communication, tin, gold, copper and silver mines were steadily increasing their outputs, just as the production of wool was in decline.

---

[1] *Daily Telegraph*, 14 December 1889.
[2] *The Mercury*, 21 December 1889.
[3] *Tasmanian News*, 14 June 1890.
[4] *The Mercury*, 9 August 1890.
[5] *The Tasmanian*, 27 June 1890.
[6] W. A. Townsley (1991). *Tasmania: From Colony to Statehood 1803-1945*.

Agriculture was also growing in production levels, helped by improvements in breeding stock, soil cultivation and the introduction of machinery. In Tasmania oats, potatoes and peas had overtaken wheat and barley as the primary commodities of the industry, particularly in the colony's north and north-west, whereas hops, apples and berry production had increased six-fold in the southern part of the colony, fuelling a rapid development in both the jam-making industry and fruit export markets.[7]

At the social level reform was slowly being introduced. The British Married Women's Property Act of 1882 had given married women in all of Australia's colonies equal property rights to those of their unmarried counterparts. Married women were now able to own property independent of their marital status, a welcome reprieve for those women inheriting property through their own lineage. Enactment of this legislation was part of a growing chorus of women's rights issues, including suffrage, education, health and equal wages for equal work. Temperance and other organisations were established to promote these ideas and help coalesce a more organised and systematic approach to usher in positive changes for women.

Likely receiving much encouragement from his wife Maggie, in July 1889 Alexander McGregor was one of the first members of Parliament to publicly state his support for universal suffrage, i.e., that all adult citizens over the age of 21 had the right to vote, irrespective of sex or landholding status.[8] It was a radical change proposing to allow previously disenfranchised groups to vote and one that had been germinating within the Tasmanian political sphere for several years, especially considering that at the time only adult male ratepayers whose properties were assessed at £5 or more were allowed to vote in Upper and Lower House elections.[9] There was a lot of backlash against expanding the voting pool, with change against the current restricted regime hard to germinate into popular opinion amongst politicians, particularly given the lack of turnover in parliamentary elections, with the old guard very much staying the course. One estimate of the impact that male suffrage would have on the Tasmanian voting pool estimated that it would double the number of eligible voting males from 16,000 to 34,000 irrespective of the right of women to vote.[10] However, it would not be until 1900 that universal male suffrage was approved in Tasmania, followed three years later by the adoption of voting rights for women.

The 1890s in general was a decade fraught with much change, not all of it welcoming. Not only was the shipping industry undergoing uncertainty, so was the global economy. The Panic of 1893 that began in the United States as a result of a stock market crash led to a 25 per cent rate of unemployment in that country and widespread social and political upheaval. Soon the aftermath shattered global economies. Making its way to Australia, the population experienced its first depression in 50 years. The property and mining boom of the previous decade, financed by a rapid increase in bank and building society lending, soon turned sour, resulting in the collapse of many institutions. In Tasmania the impact was felt profoundly and much earlier, even before the stock market crash of 1893.

The financial strain of over-lending had caused the Bank of Van Diemen's Land to collapse, suddenly closing its doors on 3 August 1891. Founded in 1823, the institution had traded for nearly 70 years before it became the first major bank to fail, ultimately heralding an Australian banking crisis; the result of the institution lending too heavily and beyond conservative lines to

---
[7] W. A. Townsley (1991). *Tasmania: From Colony to Statehood 1803-1945.*
[8] *The Mercury,* 9 July 1889.
[9] *Launceston Examiner,* 28 October 1881.
[10] *Daily Telegraph,* 10 July 1884.

Customers outside the Bank of Van Diemen's Land on the corner of Elizabeth and Collins streets, Hobart (3 August 1891).
Tasmanian Archives (PH30/1/9923).

those involved in the silver mining sector.[1] Unable to survive the number of defaulted loans when mineral prices suddenly declined, it was forced to shut its doors to patrons. Reporting on the situation the press intimated that the only evidence of its lack of financial fluidity was a sign on the door at the Hobart branch stating, '*Bank closed by order of the Board of Directors*'.[2] Up until this point in time the bank was considered a genuine investment by the general public, though *The Mercury* did report one day following the collapse that, '*Several of our leading merchants and financiers were more or less cognisant of the state of affairs, and saw the disaster approaching, although they admit it came sooner than they anticipated*'.[3]

The sudden closure of the Bank of Van Diemen's Land was disastrous for its thousands of customers, mostly based in and around Hobart and in Tasmania's growing mining centres. With over £800,000 in deposits gone, many people lost some or all of their savings, their homes that were under mortgage to the institution, and/or their businesses, being unable to make payroll; its demise impacting Tasmanians across all classes, rich and poor.[4] The collapse also had a

---

[1] *The Mercury*, 4 August 1891.
[2] *The Mercury*, 4 August 1891.
[3] *The Mercury*, 4 August 1891.
[4] *The Mercury*, 4 August 1891; Parliament of Tasmania (1893). *Statistics of Tasmania for 1891*.

cascading impact. Property prices fell as did prices for agricultural and other commodities. Public confidence hit an all-time low. Moreover, a run on additional banks throughout the Australian colonies occurred, including the Launceston branch of the British Bank of Australia; the frenzies being another precursor to further economic decline.[5] Many of these institutions suspended transactions or closed altogether, thus further hitting depositors hard. The fluidity of the economy was at a standstill. There was no trust only scepticism.

With the economic depression continuing in Australia and throughout the globe, there were many mining investors trying to find a quick financial fix out of this melancholy. Fortunately for Tasmania the mining industry remained somewhat sheltered from the worldwide panic, helping to soften the blow of further economic peril, particularly via Tasmania's exports of gold, silver and copper which were steadily increasing even though prices had declined.[6] However, given the overall state of the colonial economy, many families had little to no money to invest in these industries, let alone to put food on the table, particularly when a new Tasmanian government led by Premier Henry Dobson sought to reduce the number of public servants and halt public works projects in an attempt to return to fiscal responsibility. The boom times of the previous decades were well and truly over. With the annual interest payment on the money the Government of Tasmania had borrowed to build roads, bridges and railways increasing during this period from £75,000 to £275,000, it was quite a load for the population to handle, considering the workforce was only around 40,000 men.[7]

With little work available many found it hard to survive and crime increased. James Bayley felt the repercussions more personally when his home of 'Runnymede' was ransacked and a watch and chain, several pieces of jewellery and a revolver were stolen, though the items were later discovered and returned.[8] He and his family appear to have remained somewhat sheltered from the impact of the economic depression; James' assets seemingly diverse enough to counter any losses. His daughter Hally and her family were also managing well, though her husband Henry Bayly was forced to take two months' leave of absence from his role at the Hobart Post Office in July 1891 due to ill health.[9] The couple used the opportunity to travel to Melbourne, perhaps seeking medical opinion. Returning to work a few months later, Henry was promoted to the position of Postmaster with an annual salary of £400.[10]

In contrast to the Bayley family it is not known how much of an impact the closure of the Bank of Van Diemen's Land had on Alexander McGregor and his businesses, though given his status as both a prominent merchant and a politician at the time, one can assume that, unlike the general public, he had prior warning of the pending disaster. Two months after the collapse, however, he sold his Elizabeth Street offices. The property was purchased by the Commercial Bank at a price of £5,000.[11] The building would ultimately be knocked down to make way for construction of Hobart's General Post Office. Another real estate transaction involving Alexander was the building of a new house he had commissioned on property he owned in Macquarie Street next door to St John's Presbyterian Church, likely built as a rental.[12]

---

[5] *The Mercury*, 17 August 1891.
[6] W. A. Townsley (1991). *Tasmania: From Colony to Statehood 1803-1945*.
[7] *The Tasmanian Democrat*, 16 April 1892.
[8] *The Mercury*, 16 July 1887.
[9] *The Mercury*, 13 July 1891.
[10] *The Mercury*, 9 October 1891; Parliament of Tasmania (1893). *Statistics of Tasmania for 1892*.
[11] *Tasmanian News*, 6 October 1891.
[12] *Tasmanian News*, 19 March 1892.

With regards to his political career Alexander McGregor was up for re-election in April 1892. With the awful state of the economy by now affecting his constituents, the press labelled the opening as an opportunity to return a more progressive candidate to the Legislative Council, further opining that Alexander was '*too antiquated*' to advance the colony towards a new century.[1] His constituents appear to have been apathetic to politics, however, returning him to Parliament unopposed.[2] In thanking the voters Alexander stated that he was '*sorry to observe the present depression in business and mining matters*' and that he looked forward to the '*dark cloud*' soon passing. He also stated that he hoped the '*Government would exercise caution in dealing with the finances of the colony, considering the state of the money market*'.[3]

There was no choice but for the government to continue to exercise caution, particularly when it came to budgetary matters. The colony was very much in debt and struggling to pay its creditors. Large swaths of its population were also suffering; unemployment within the commercial, industrial and agricultural sectors on the rise.[4]

Deciding not to shelter herself from the plight of those in need, it was at this point in time that Alexander's wife Maggie became involved in various causes and charities. These included the Women's Sanitary Committee, which was established in September 1891 to advocate for practical solutions to improve drinking water and sewerage systems, primarily through lobbying for parliamentary and municipal change.[5] It was a benevolent pursuit. Deaths due to typhoid were on the rise owing to a local epidemic in Hobart that had occurred during the winter. Statistics reveal that 49 people died in Tasmania from typhoid in 1890, whereas 82 died from the illness the following year; in 1892 the number was reduced to 46.[6]

Chaired by Lady Hamilton, wife of then Governor Sir Robert Hamilton, with the Premier's wife Emily Dobson acting as honorary secretary, the committee offered Maggie McGregor a notable pathway with which to pursue her interest in charitable causes, as well as to make friendships. It was the start of a new frontier for Maggie, not only allowing her to spend time with like-minded women of the same social class but pursue her interests to gain and apply her skills and expertise in management and finances. She remained a member of the Women's Sanitary Committee for several years.[7]

In the winter of 1893 Maggie became honorary secretary of the Hobart Restaurant Committee, an organisation established to provide meals to the poor.[8] Chaired by Emily Dobson, over a period of several months the initiative served approximately 800 meals per week to impoverished people, including families, supported by donations of money and food.[9] A few months later Maggie was noted as a member of a committee raising funds for the construction of a convent.[10] In February 1894 she helped organise a garden party held at Government House to raise money for the Village Settlement Fund, an organisation established to assist families who had been heavily impacted by the ongoing depression. The premise of the charity was to raise funds to help relocate 28 able-bodied men, their wives and children to the township of Southport in Tasmania's far south where

[1] *The Tasmanian Democrat*, 16 April 1892.
[2] *Tasmanian News*, 28 April 1892.
[3] *Tasmanian News*, 3 May 1892.
[4] Parliament of Tasmania (1892). *Statistics of Tasmania for 1891*; Parliament of Tasmania (1893). *Statistics of Tasmania for 1892*.
[5] *The Mercury*, 23, 26 September, 24 October 1891.
[6] Parliament of Tasmania (1891). *Statistics of Tasmania for 1890*; Parliament of Tasmania (1892). *Statistics of Tasmania for 1891*; Parliament of Tasmania (1893). *Statistics of Tasmania for 1892*.
[7] *Tasmanian News*, 30 August 1892; *The Mercury*, 6 December 1892.
[8] *Tasmanian News*, 16 June 1893.
[9] *Tasmanian News*, 19 June, 1, 3 July 1893.
[10] *Tasmanian News*, 23 January 1894.

they would be given allotments of 25 acres to clear and farm, along with clothes, tools, rations, tents, seeds and other items.[11] After three years of occupancy it was expected that the settlers would start paying a rent for their property; after 15 years it was expected they would receive its title.[12]

As assistant secretary of the Southport Village Settlement Fund, a committee made up entirely of women, Maggie McGregor spent the next few years organising meetings, including at her home of 'Lenna', and assisting with the relocation efforts, notably travelling to the Huon region in October 1894 with an initial group of settlers.[13] The organisation was ultimately wound up in mid-1898, by which point only six families remained on their land; its administration having been transferred to the Government of Tasmania under oversight of the Minister for Land.[14] Concurrent with these roles and responsibilities, in early 1894 Maggie was elected to the Parish Council of St George's Anglican Church, Battery Point, helping to assist in administration of the church and its services.

As evidenced by the types of benevolent activities Maggie McGregor was involved with, there were many people experiencing the depths of poverty throughout Tasmania during the early to mid-1890s. Despite the doom and gloom, however, there were several large-scale diversions to this generational melancholy, one of them being the Tasmanian International Exhibition which first opened to the public on 15 November 1894, running for approximately six months during which time nearly 300,000 people are estimated to have visited the spectacle.[15] Held at Hobart's Domain in a purpose-built temporary building, the Exhibition was intended to showcase Tasmania's arts, manufacturers, industries and enterprises, along with those of other colonies. Funded by a company raised by shares and supplemented by government funds, the event took many years to organise and administer before its grand opening. Among the hundreds of organisers was Maggie McGregor who was a member of a sub-committee tasked with organising the Women's Section of the Exhibition.[16] Making use of the building itself, which included a concert hall, she also helped organise a variety fair and flower show at the venue in November 1893 to raise funds for the Village Settlement Fund, as well as a *Plain and Fancy Dress Bread and Butter Ball*, held under the patronage of Viscount Gormanston, Tasmania's then Governor, in August 1895 to raise funds for the Victoria Convalescent Home.[17] While photographs of these two events are yet to be found, images of season ticket holders for the Tasmanian International Exhibition thankfully remain in existence as part of the Tasmanian Archives collection. It is through this series that we are able to gain glimpses of Maggie McGregor and several members of the Bayly family, including Henry and Hally's three daughters Hally (Jr), Mary and Emma.

Sadly, one person missing from this collection of photographs is James Bayley. He died at 'Runnymede' on 16 September 1894 of liver cancer.[18] He was 71 years of age and was buried at Cornelian Bay Cemetery.[19] James left his entire estate, including 'Runnymede', various properties, his furniture, stock, money and other effects to his wife Elizabeth and his daughter Hally jointly in trust.[20] Probate was granted on 26 February 1895 valued at £5,515.[21]

[11] Parliament of Tasmania (1896). *Village Settlement: First Report of the Committee; The Mercury*, 19 July 1898.
[12] *The Mercury*, 6 November 1894.
[13] *The Mercury*, 31 October, 2 November 1894.
[14] *The Mercury*, 19 July 1898.
[15] *Launceston Examiner*, 16 November 1894.
[16] *The Mercury*, 11 July 1894.
[17] *Tasmanian News*, 31 July 1895.
[18] Tasmanian Archives (RGD35/1/14 no. 1335).
[19] Tasmanian Archives (AF35/1/2 BU 9983).
[20] Tasmanian Archives (AD960/1/20).
[21] *Daily Telegraph*, 26 February 1895.

Tasmanian Exhibition Building at Hobart's Domain (c1895).
Tasmanian Archives (NS1013/1/1119).

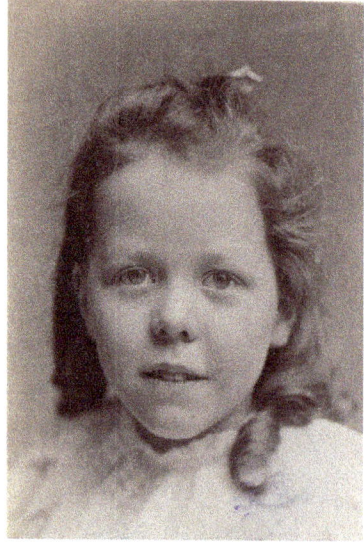

Hally Mary Butchard Bayly (1894).
Tasmanian Archives (NS738/1/391).

Mary Wylly Bayly (1894).
Tasmanian Archives (NS738/1/168).

Emma Matty Bayly (1894).
Tasmanian Archives (NS738/1/165).

Maggie McGregor (1894).
Tasmanian Archives (NS738/1/1820).

Captain James Bayley (c1880s).
Tasmanian Archives (NS1013/1/844).

James Bayley's death marked the end of a generation. He had been the last surviving sibling remaining in Tasmania, outliving his brother Charles Bayley by 20 years, his sister Harriet McGregor by 16 years, and his sister Mary Bull by three years. He was survived by his wife Elizabeth, his daughter Hally, his son-in-law Henry Bayly and three granddaughters. On 13 November 1894, just under two months following his death, Hally would give birth to a son, out of respect named James Bayley Bayly.[1] The baby was born at 'Runnymede'; Hally, Henry and their children moving into the residence following the death of her father.[2] The couple advertised the lease of their seven-roomed home named 'Aloha' in Park Street in February 1895.[3] Taking over administration of James Bayley's estate, Henry Bayly also advertised several of 'Runnymede's' paddocks for lease in January 1895.[4] Unlike James he did not have the time to spend on farming the property, particularly since he had been promoted to head of the newly amalgamated Post and Telegraph Department at the Hobart Post Office in July 1894.[5]

With regards to Alexander McGregor, it is unfortunately not known if he attended James Bayley's funeral. Nevertheless, it was early in 1895 that Alexander appears to have reduced his public duties. He is notably absent from key events and meetings that he would normally have attended, including those related to the Marine Board of Hobart, to which he had been appointed Master Warden for the year 1894.[6] He would resign from the Board in late 1895.[7]

Alexander was also looking to reduce his business concerns though his company still remained in operation. With regards to his political activities, newspaper reports from the time note him as the oldest member of the Legislative Council and that, owing to his advancing age, he was reducing his public and business activities, particularly those that required his personal attention.[8]

One part of Alexander's business that he was looking to offload was a tin mine located on a 280-acre site near Lottah in Tasmania's north-east.[9] Known as the Anchor Tin Mining Company, Alexander had owned half of the business since 1886, during which time it had been relatively successful at producing a yield. In 1893 he had purchased the second half of the company

Tasmanian News, 17 September 1894.

[1] Tasmanian Archives (RGD33/1/20 no. 609).
[2] *The Mercury*, 29 November 1894.
[3] *The Mercury*, 16 February 1895.
[4] *The Mercury*, 2 January 1895.
[5] *The Mercury*, 7 July 1894.
[6] *Tasmanian News*, 27 December 1893.
[7] *Tasmanian News*, 12 December 1895.
[8] *The Mercury*, 24 June 1895.
[9] *The Mercury*, 24 June 1895.

from his partners Francis Pike and James Robinson before setting out to sell the business as a whole.[1] However, instead of selling the company locally, Alexander sent two representatives, Marshall Heatley and Richard Mitchell, to England in late 1894 to arrange for its sale; the money to be used to offset a large overdraft and mortgage that Alexander had taken on.[2] Perhaps over-inflating the mine's potential and value, it was soon sold to a London-based syndicate headed by Robert Nicholson for £20,000 and shortly thereafter successfully floated on the London Stock Exchange; its new owners proposing to raise £150,000 in capital by way of £1 shares, with the intention of investing £50,000 in new plant and machinery.[3] It was more than just a modest profit that the new directors of the tin mine anticipated to generate; turning their initial investment of £20,000 into £100,000. The magnitude of the transaction did not go unnoticed, particularly by those in Tasmania that had previously invested in the mine in its early years.[4] Several law suits were enacted over the sale, all of which Alexander McGregor and his estate managed to win.[5]

With his health continuing to decline, on 1 September 1895 it was announced that a long-term employee was taking over the business of Alex. McGregor & Co effective immediately.[6] Very experienced, Samuel T. Kirby had worked for the organisation for 20 years and for the previous seven years was noted to have been in sole charge of its operations, including all of its branches related to shipping.[7] Alexander issued a public notice wishing his employee well in this new endeavour. Three months later, in December 1895, it was announced that Alexander was '*not likely to appear in public life again, his health, bodily and mentally having completely broken down*'.[8] Despite this statement he did not immediately resign from Parliament even though he could not attend any sessions.[9] Instead he was granted a leave of absence.[10]

In February 1896 it was announced that Alexander McGregor's health was improving, though there was no prospect of him appearing in public life again.[11] A month later he finally resigned from his seat in the Legislative Council.[12] With his health continuing to decline, his wife Maggie took over his financial and personal affairs, including being involved in a court case centered around commission owed to Marshall Heatley and Richard Mitchell for the sale of the Anchor Tin Mine in London; the McGregors again won the case.[13]

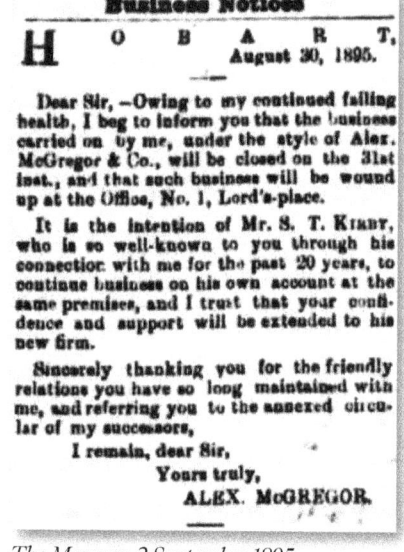

The Mercury, 2 September 1895.

---

[1] *Tasmanian News*, 16 July 1897.
[2] *Daily Telegraph*, 17 June 1896.
[3] *The Mercury*, 24 June 1895, 4 May 1896; *The North West Post*, 7 September 1895.
[4] *Launceston Examiner*, 23 September 1895.
[5] *Launceston Examiner*, 23 September 1895; *Tasmanian News*, 18 August 1897.
[6] *Daily Telegraph*, 2 September 1895.
[7] *Daily Telegraph*, 2 September 1895.
[8] *Daily Telegraph*, 23 December 1895.
[9] *Daily Telegraph*, 23 December 1895.
[10] *The Mercury*, 10 January 1896.
[11] *Daily Telegraph*, 22 February 1896.
[12] *The Clipper*, 28 March 1896; *Daily Telegraph*, 1 April 1896.
[13] *Daily Telegraph*, 17 June 1896.

Alexander McGregor died of '*senile dementia and hemiplegia*', i.e., paralysis likely caused by a stroke, on 4 August 1896 at his home of 'Lenna'.[14] He was 75 years of age. He was buried at Cornelian Bay Cemetery four days later in a vault with his first wife Harriet.[15]

Alexander was survived by his second wife Maggie, then aged 36 years. His will left his entire estate to her with the exception of a house located on the esplanade at the New Wharf which was given to Alexander's sister Elizabeth Mason.[16] Probate was granted on 21 December 1896 with his estate valued at £4,364.[17] Not included in this amount was £10,000 that Alexander had settled on Maggie McGregor at the time of their marriage.[18]

View of Hobart's New Wharf and 'Lenna' (c1890s).
Tasmanian Archives (NS1013/1/316).

Tasmanian News, 5 August 1896.

---

[14] Libraries Tasmania (RGD35/1/15 no. 834).
[15] Libraries Tasmania (AF35/1/2 p39).
[16] Libraries Tasmania (AD960/1/23/5017).
[17] *Daily Telegraph*, 22 December 1896.
[18] www.thelist.tas.gov.au (Historic Deed 08/1167); *Tasmanian News*, 16 July 1897.

Alexander McGregor (c1890s).
Tasmanian Archives (PH30/1/6937).

Women's Rights & Generational Patrimony

The deaths of James Bayley and Alexander McGregor in 1894 and 1896, respectively, heralded the end of a generation for the larger Bayley and McGregor families, as well as for the maritime, business, political and sporting interests of Hobart and greater Tasmania. Though it is not known if they ever renewed their friendship after their rift in the mid-1880s over the sale of the commercial vessels that they jointly owned, it is assumed that maturity eventually prevailed and they were able to make amends. While their legacies remained firm, the years following their combined deaths continued to be transitional in terms of political, economical and social issues.

Buoyed by the money and other assets bequeathed to them, James Bayley's daughter Hally Bayly and Alexander McGregor's widow Maggie ushered in a new wave of community outreach, volunteerism and service, quite disparate from the whaling ways and mercantile trade that had initially fuelled the family's riches. Both women had obviously been raised within family units steeped in industrious and honest though humble beginnings, and both women had embraced the need to actively and positively impact their communities. Causes of interest to them were women's rights, education and health.

Change was certainly on its way with the voices of the Australian public, including its women, finally being heard. A major shift affecting everyone in the colonies came on 1 January 1901 with Australia's six self-governing British colonies, Queensland, New South Wales, Victoria, Tasmania, South Australia and Western Australia, becoming united as the Commonwealth of Australia. It had been a rather slow and tedious process to reach this historical feat, encompassing multiple referendums, conventions and discussions held over several decades across all six colonies, and with England, before final agreement had been reached. The initially wary public had been increasingly swayed by Australian-born citizens becoming more and more active in their support for nationalism, a group of which both Hally and Maggie were part of. Eventually the parties had come to agreement as to what the Commonwealth of Australia would look like in terms of its constitution (executive, legislature and judiciary structure and power), finances and trade, the role of the states, and administration. It was a historical achievement.

With the Commonwealth of Australia now a reality and an interim government in place until national elections could be held, it was the start of a period of somewhat trepidation and uncertainty about how the new system of government would be implemented, including how customs, excise and other taxes would be allocated back to the six states. Up until this point in time the individual colonies, now states, had been responsible for their own income generation and spending. The new parliamentary system was also raising some concerns, as was the High Court. Overall, it was a period fraught with teething problems, some big and some small. Perhaps it is fortunate that Alexander McGregor was not around to witness the Federation of Australia as he may have been a reluctant bystander to all of the changes.

More changes soon followed, including enactment of the 1901 Midwifery Nurses Act in Tasmania, the first legislation of its type in Australia intended to raise the quality of midwifery, including through a registration, training and assessment process. In 1902 Tasmanian women were given the right to vote in federal elections and the right to sit in federal Parliament. At the state level Tasmanian women also became eligible to vote in House of Assembly elections the following year, while the franchise of those eligible to vote in Legislative Council elections was expanded to owners of freehold properties paying annual rates of £10 or leaseholds of £30, both men and women.

While the lead up to Federation and then its implementation across the Australian states and increased voting rights for women would have been seen as historical and ultimately life-changing events, daily life for Maggie McGregor and Hally Bayly carried on. With regards to Maggie more specifically, in the months immediately following her husband Alexander's death, she was not noted as doing any volunteer or charitable events, nor was she noted at being present at any society events. However, gradually she returned to her routine, participating in meetings with regards to the Southport Village Settlement project, as well as the privately-run Victoria Convalescent Home, to the board of which Maggie was appointed honorary secretary in August 1897.[1] She also rented out 'Lenna' for several weeks over the summer of 1896/97 to the Royal Navy with Rear-Admiral Cyprian Bridge taking up residence at the home coinciding with a visit from his squadron led by HMS *Orlando*.[2] A year later the residence would host Rear-Admiral Pearson and his family of HMS *Royal Arthur*.[3]

Taking command of her late husband's estate, in the years that followed Maggie began systematically selling off real estate that Alexander had previously owned, including the Lord Rodney Hotel in Salamanca Place

> Valuable City Properties, and the Domain Shipyard, on account of the late Mr. A. McGregor's Estate.
>
> ROBERTS & COMPANY LIMITED
>
> Are instructed to sell at the Mart, as above, at 12 o'clock,
>
> LOT 1.
> COMMODIOUS BRICK HOUSE, No. 106, Macquarie-street, adjoining St John's Presbyterian Church, and now occupied by Mrs. Seith as monthly tenant. It contains 9 good rooms, kitchen, and every convenience.
>
> LOT 2.
> Substantial Stone and Brick House, on the New Wharf, next the Government Stores, let to Mrs. Dwyer as weekly tenant. It contains 8 rooms, bath, kitchen, etc.
>
> LOT 3.
> Cut Stone Cottage, at angle of Hampden-road and De Witt-street, Battery Point, let to Mrs. Ansell as weekly tenant. It contains 4 large rooms, 2 attics, bath, kitchen, good cellars, and has a 2-stall stable, with side cart entrance.
>
> LOT 4.
> The Three Large Stone Stores at the end of the New Wharf, near Mr. Johnston's Cooperage.
>
> LOT 5.
> Large Allotment of Land, with house and stables, having frontages on Cross-street, 139ft.; Runneymede-street, 313ft.; and Moriarity-street, 188ft., opposite "Lenna."
>
> LOT 6.
> W.B. Cottage, No. 247, Upper Bathurst-street, containing 4 rooms, let on a weekly tenancy.
>
> LOT 7.
> The Shipyards, near Macquarie Point, in the Domain, let to Messrs. Dalgleish and Taylor as yearly tenants.
>
> Title Correct.
>
> Terms — 25 per cent cash deposit; balance on completion.
>
> Reference—Messrs. Dobson, Mitchell, and Allport, Solicitors, Stone-buildings.

The Mercury, 13 December 1899.

---

[1] *The Mercury*, 13 July, 28 August 1897.
[2] *The Mercury*, 14 November 1896.
[3] *The Mercury*, 16, 31 December 1898.

and the Domain shipyard.[4] The unexpired portion of the 99-year lease of the shipyard was purchased by the Government of Tasmania for £1,100.[5]

One property she did not sell was 'Lenna'. Though her younger siblings continued to periodically live with her over the coming years and decades, Maggie did not look to downsize into a smaller and more manageable residence. Instead she used 'Lenna' to host suppers, garden parties, meetings and other events, particularly those associated with her many charitable causes.

During the late 1890s and into the early 1900s, Maggie McGregor increased her involvement with efforts to support the Victoria Convalescent Home, which provided care to patients recovering from illnesses, mostly catering to poor and working-class children.[6] As a representative of this organisation, in May 1899 she attended the inaugural meeting of the Tasmanian National Council of Women. Intended for the '*promotion of unity and mutual understanding between all associations of women working for the common welfare of the community*', the outcome of the first meeting was the formation of the Council to which Maggie was elected honorary secretary.[7]

Maggie McGregor. Tasmanian Mail, 29 September 1900.

Under the umbrella of the Victoria Convalescent Home, in June 1899 Maggie McGregor and her fellow committee members successfully acquired a large house named 'Beltana' at Lindisfarne on the eastern shore of the River Derwent, helped by a substantial donation from the Guesdon Bequest.[8] Needing resources to equip and renovate the property into a medical facility fit for their needs, Maggie organised for the performers from the cast of the comic opera 'The Brigands of La Macha,' then in Hobart and playing at the Theatre Royal, to put on a charity performance to raise much-needed funds. As a thank you she invited the cast and many supporters and friends to a garden party at 'Lenna' during which she was noted as '*one of Hobart's most charming hostesses*'.[9]

The official opening of the Victoria Convalescent Home at 'Beltana', which featured 16 rooms, a private jetty accessible to river steamers, a dairy and sea water baths, was another opportunity for Maggie McGregor to showcase her organisational and social skills.[10] Attended by Hobart's upper echelon of socialites, dignitaries and politicians, as well as Maggie's father John Pigdon and two of her sisters, the event took place on 30 January 1900 with the '*Committee, of which Mrs. A. McGregor is the energetic Hon. Secretary, deserving of the thanks of the community for establishing so necessary an institution - which is kept in splendid order in such a healthy locality*'.[11]

Another member of the Victoria Convalescent Home's committee was Thomas Bennison. A well-respected accountant, alderman of the Hobart City Council and Justice of the Peace, he had additionally served as Hobart's coroner for many decades. It is thus not surprising to learn that Thomas and Maggie McGregor travelled in the same social, benevolent and business circles, including both being members of the Parish Council of St George's Anglican Church.[12]

---

[4] *Tasmanian News*, 2 February 1898, 31 July 1899.
[5] *Daily Telegraph*, 19 December 1899.
[6] *The Mercury*, 30 August 1898.
[7] *The Mercury*, 13 May 1899.
[8] *The Mercury*, 3 June 1899; *Tasmanian News*, 30 January 1900.
[9] *Tasmanian News*, 18 August 1899; *The Mercury*, 18 August 1899.
[10] *The Mercury*, 31 January 1900.
[11] *Tasmanian News*, 30 January 1900; *The Mercury*, 31 January 1900.
[12] *The Mercury*, 23 April 1894.

Tasmanian Mail, 23 September 1899.

Thomas was also widowed with an adult son. With many opportunities to interact and establish a relationship, on 27 December 1900 Thomas Bennison and Maggie McGregor were married at 'Lenna' in a '*semi-private character*'.[1] He was 58 years of age, she was 41.

Contrary to convention of the day, Maggie Bennison did not move into her new husband's home. Instead, Thomas moved into 'Lenna' with Maggie remaining active in charity work and womens causes, including holding meetings for the Victoria Convalescent Home and the Women's Suffrage Association at the residence.[2] The couple also used 'Lenna' to host public and private events, and continued to offer it to the government as a summer residence for visiting naval dignitaries.[3] In September of 1902 'Lenna' hosted the new rector of St George's Church, Reverend A. Brain and his family, who stayed until their official residence was ready.[4]

---

[1] *Tasmanian News*, 27 December 1900; *The Mercury*, 1 January 1901.
[2] *The Mercury*, 19 April 1901; *The Mercury*, 3 February 1904.
[3] *The Mercury*, 20 February 1901; *Daily Telegraph*, 27 November 1901.
[4] *Tasmanian News*, 2 September 1902.

Tasmanian Mail, 19 January 1901.

In late 1902 Thomas Bennison was elected Mayor of Hobart for the calendar years 1903 and 1904. As Mayoress, Maggie Bennison proposed to hold an 'at home' at 'Lenna' every fourth Tuesday of the month.[5] As the Mayoral residence 'Lenna' was also used by the couple as a platform to entertain and host social events. The press described Mayoress Bennison as a '*lady of infinite tact*', further stating that '*her mission seems to make everyone happy*'.[6] With Thomas Bennison's term as Mayor ending, the ladies of Hobart made a presentation to the Mayoress in gratitude stating that she had '*made herself very popular in the social world*'.[7] For reasons not known the Bennisons appear to have quietly separated soon thereafter with Maggie remaining at 'Lenna' and Thomas moving into a residence in nearby Battery Point.

By now the honorary treasurer of the Tasmanian branch of the Victoria League for Commonwealth Friendship, amongst many volunteer roles and responsibilities, in February 1905 Maggie Bennison travelled to Europe, departing Hobart in early April as a passenger on board the P.&O. liner *China*.[8] She returned to Tasmania in December 1905, soon thereafter being the special guest at a welcome home party hosted by Emily Dobson at her residence in Elboden Place.[9]

With social and political status and wealth Maggie Bennison continued to advocate for women's rights and those of the poor through various philanthropic activities and organisations, using 'Lenna' as a base with which to host meetings and events.[10] As a delegate to the Tasmanian branch of the National Council

Tasmanian Mail, 9 January 1904.

---

[5] *Tasmanian News*, 12 January 1903.
[6] *Daily Telegraph*, 3 June 1903.
[7] *Daily Telegraph*, 10 February 1904.
[8] *The Mercury*, 4 February, 3 April 1905.
[9] *Tasmanian News*, 22 December 1905.
[10] *The Mercury*, 25 July 1906.

Tasmanian Mail, 27 February 1913. Maggie Bennison is seated on the far left in the front row.

of Women, she also travelled to Geneva in Switzerland to attend the Congress of Women in 1908, along with fellow Hobartians Emily Dobson and Mrs Ashton Jones.[1]

Maggie Bennison made several more trips to Europe in the succeeding years.[2] She was also not without family with several nieces spending large swaths of time with her at 'Lenna'.[3] However, in the years leading up to World War I Maggie finally appears to have found the residence too big for her needs, particularly since she was travelling overseas regularly. 'Lenna' was advertised for sale by auction in February 1914 though, despite a large number of parties in attendance and very spirited bidding, it failed to reach the reserve and was passed in.[4] Six months later 'Lenna's' furniture and household effects were advertised for sale by auction.[5] On 1 September 1914 Maggie Bennison sold 'Lenna' to Alfred Henry Ashbolt for £5,000.[6]

The Mercury, 14 February 1914.

[1] *The Mercury*, 17 November 1908.
[2] *Critic*, 6 March, 1 May 1909.
[3] *Daily Post*, 23 April 1910.
[4] *The Mercury*, 14, 24 February 1914.
[5] *The Mercury*, 25 July 1914.
[6] www.thelist.tas.gov.au (Historic Deed 13/4257).

A well-known partner in Henry Jones and Co. Ltd., New Zealand-born Alfred Ashbolt had arrived in Hobart in the early 1890s, very quickly becoming one of Tasmania's leading businessmen and merchants.[7] After purchasing 'Lenna' he and his wife Alice moved into the residence where she sadly died four years later on 31 January 1918 aged 44.[8] Remarrying in December 1919, Alfred and his new bride Muriel then moved to London with Alfred serving as Agent-General for Tasmania for a number of years; 'Lenna' being leased to the Kremmer family during the interim.[9] The couple and their son then returned to Hobart, resuming their occupation of 'Lenna' where a daughter was born in April 1926.[10]

Knighted in 1925, Sir Alfred Ashbolt died at 'Lenna' on 24 January 1930 aged 59.[11] His widow and their two children remained living at the property until early 1945 whereby it was sold to Roy Gibson.[12] 'Lenna' was then converted into several residential flats until purchased by A. E. Boyes in June 1949 for subsequent conversion into a luxury hotel.[13] A new wing was added to the property in the 1970s when it was owned by Innkeepers Limited. Classified by the National Trust, 'Lenna' is now under the guardianship of Lloyd and Jan Clark and remains a standout tourist destination as one of Hobart's premier boutique hotels.

'Lenna' (2020s).
Lenna of Hobart Heritage Hotel.

The Mercury, 25 July 1914.

---

[7] https://adb.anu.edu.au/biography/ashbolt-sir-alfred-henry-5065.
[8] *Daily Post*, 1 February 1918.
[9] *The Mercury*, 12, 24 December 1919, 9 December 1924.
[10] *The Mercury*, 2 August 1921, 31 October 1922, 5 April 1926.
[11] *The Examiner*, 25 January 1930.
[12] *The Mercury*, 6 December 1944; www.thelist.tas.gov.au (Historic Deeds 22/4373, 24/4565).
[13] *The Mercury*, 14 August 1946; www.thelist.tas.gov.au (Historic Deed 24/4565).

Following the sale of 'Lenna' in September 1914 Maggie Bennison moved into several residences in Davey Street, Hobart, ultimately building a new home at 199 Davey Street which she named 'Wisconsin'.[1] With any international travel plans curtailed by World War I, she continued to be involved in the management and administration of various charities, including the Queen Alexandra Hospital which first opened in 1908, of which she was president, and the Tasmanian Association of the Victoria League for Commonwealth Friendship of which she was treasurer.[2] Owing to other commitments, however, in 1916 she resigned as honorary secretary of the Victoria Convalescent Home, though in the succeeding years she would become a member of the Child Welfare Association, the Sanatorium for Consumptives, the Tasmanian Bush Nursing Association and the Tasmanian Society for the Blind, Deaf and Dumb.[3]

In mid-1922 Maggie McGregor travelled to Europe with Emily Dobson to attend the International Conference of Women in The Hague.[4] She returned to Europe a year later to attend the wedding of Prince Albert, Duke of York (later King George VI), and Lady Elizabeth Bowes-Lyon in London in April 1923 where Maggie unfortunately suffered a heart attack.[5] Aided by a younger sister she returned to Hobart following many months spent convalescing, though the demise of her health meant that Maggie was forced to resign from many of her committee roles.[6]

Maggie Bennison died at her Davey Street home on 5 September 1924 at the age of 64.[7] Her body was conveyed to Melbourne where a funeral was held. She was buried at the Melbourne General Cemetery in the Pigdon family's vault.[8] Maggie was survived by many siblings, nieces and nephews whom she bequeathed the bulk of her estate to, valued at a substantial £69,000.[9] Her husband Thomas Bennison, whom Maggie had discretely separated from several decades prior, had died in Hobart on 15 August 1921 at the age of 79.[10]

Delegates to the National Council of Women Interstate Conference held in Hobart in January 1922. Maggie Bennison is standing in the back row, second from left
Tasmanian Mail, 26 January 1922.

[1] *The Mercury*, 10 January 1917, 9 December 1924.
[2] *The Mercury*, 8, 22 May 1915.
[3] *The Mercury*, 30 September 1916; *World*, 9 May 1919, 11, 18 August 1920, 17 August 1921.
[4] *The Mercury*, 21 February 1922, 24 June 1922.
[5] *Daily Telegraph*, 27 April 1923.
[6] *Critic*, 13 April 1923, 21 March 1924; *The Mercury*, 5 June 1923, 9 July 1924.
[7] *The Mercury*, 8 September 1924; *The Age*, 8 September 1924.
[8] Victoria, Australia, Cemetery Records and Headstone Transcriptions, 1844-1997.
[9] Tasmanian Archives (AD960/1/49 no. 15112); *The News*, 9 May 1925.
[10] *The Mercury*, 16 August 1921.

Returning to the other subject of this chapter, Hally Bayly, there is also much to relay. Following her father James Bayley's death in 1894, Hally's husband Henry Bayly had taken over management of James' estate including 'Runnymede', where the couple moved to with their young family. Sharing the home with Hally's step-mother Elizabeth Bayley, Hally and Henry welcomed three more children to their fold: Henry Vincent Bayly, born at 'Runnymede' on 19 September 1896; Elizabeth Matthews Bayly, born at 'Runnymede' on 7 September 1898; and Margaret O'Neil Bayly, born at 'Runnymede' on 15 February 1902.[11]

Professionally, during this period Henry Bayly continued to do well as secretary of the Post and Telegraph Department of the Tasmanian Post Office, though in January 1897 had been granted three months' absence due to ill health.[12] He used the time to travel to New Zealand on a recuperative holiday and to visit family.[13] Returning to work, Henry began overseeing the introduction and installation of telegraph lines throughout Tasmania, often accompanied by his wife Hally during his travel commitments.[14] The Federation of Australia had also ushered in a period of change for his organisation, the Post and Telegraph Department being transferred to the Commonwealth Government on 1 March 1901 as opposed to coming under the management of a new Government of Tasmania.[15] Coinciding with this transition Henry Bayly was promoted to Deputy Postmaster General for the state.[16] Sadly, his tenure only lasted two years. Henry died on 7 January 1903 at 'Runnymede' aged 52.[17] The cause of death was apoplexy, i.e., a stroke.[18] He was buried in the Bayley family vault at Cornelian Bay Cemetery.[19]

Henry Bayly was survived by his wife Hally, by now aged 41, their five daughters aged between 16 years and 11 months, and two sons aged eight and six. His estate was left solely to his wife with probate valuing it at a rather meagre sum of £67.[20] Hally was also left to administer the estate of her late father, which had likely supplemented the family's income considerably.

In a move reminiscent of her own childhood following her mother's death, Hally opted not to remain in Tasmania. Instead she made plans for her family to return to England and the Bayley family's roots of Ipswich in Suffolk. Needing money to finance the trip Hally advertised several properties for sale that were part of James Bayley's estate, including five residential allotments located in Bishop and Swanston streets, New Town, as well as a cottage and land situated at 44 Kelly Street, Battery Point, that had previously belonged to her uncle Charles Bayley.[21] She was also given a small gratuity of £329 from the government.[22]

Henry Vincent Bayly.
Tasmanian Mail, 17 January 1903.

---

[11] Tasmanian Archives (RGD33/1/21 no. 792, RGD33/1/22 no. 980, RGD33/4/5 no. 672).
[12] *The Mercury*, 8 January 1897.
[13] *Launceston Examiner*, 31 March 1897.
[14] *The North Western Advocate and Emu Bay Times*, 20 February 1900.
[15] *Tasmanian News*, 9 February 1901.
[16] *The Mercury*, 1 March 1901.
[17] *Tasmanian News*, 7 January 1903.
[18] *Tasmanian News*, 7 January 1903.
[19] *Tasmanian News*, 8 January 1903.
[20] Tasmanian Archives (AD960/1/24 no 6113); *Tasmanian News*, 16 February 1903.
[21] *The Mercury*, 11 February 1904; Hobart Gazette 1904.
[22] *Daily Telegraph*, 9 September 1905.

Hally's plans for her family took some time to finalise and it was not until late 1904 that she advertised 'Runnymede' for lease, with the Ashton Jones family of Bothwell moving in to the residence.[1] By this point in time Hally's elder daughters, Hally (Jr) and Emma, were in the final years of their schooling, both performing well as students of the Girls' High School at Westella in Elizabeth Street.[2]

Expecting to be in Europe for three years, the Bayly family departed Hobart for London on 7 March 1905 as passengers on board the 12,500-ton steamship *Suevic*.[3] The group was accompanied by Claire Watchorn, likely a friend of the elder girls, and Henry Graveley, the son of Hally's cousin Charles.[4] The largesse of the vessel and its accommodations likely struck Hally as she remembered sailing out of the River Derwent on much smaller and rudimentary barques during her youth.

Steamship Suevic.
Maritime Museum of Tasmania (POMC19e).

After three years and four months spent in Europe, Hally Bayly and her children departed Liverpool on 31 July 1908 as passengers on board the White Star liner *Runic* bound for Melbourne via Cape Town, Albany and Adelaide.[5] The group arrived back in Hobart in late September and returned to their home of 'Runnymede'. Two months later Hally arranged for the sale of several more allotments that had been part of her late father's estate, including two conjoined cottages at 37 and 39 South Street, Battery Point, and a vacant allotment of land on the same street, though lying closer to Hampden Road.[6]

With the younger Bayly children returning to school, Hally made time to continue her charity work, including her interests in the Ministering Children's League and the Homeopathic Hospital.[7] Her three eldest daughters, Hally (Jr), Mary and Emma, were gladly welcomed home, being guests of honour at a party hosted by Mrs Arthur Watchorn. An article in the *Daily Post* providing details of the event noted, '*the Misses Bayly, of Runnymede ... have recently returned from a three years'*

---

[1] *Tasmanian News*, 3 December 1904.
[2] *Tasmanian News*, 24 December 1904; *Examiner*, 2 January 1905.
[3] *Tasmanian News*, 3 December 1904.
[4] *Tasmanian News*, 3 December 1904.
[5] *Daily Post*, 1 August 1908; *The Argus*, 15 September 1908; UK and Ireland, Outward Passenger Lists, 1890-1960 for Jas B Bayley.
[6] *The Mercury*, 12 November 1908.
[7] *The Mercury*, 14 December 1908.

stay in England'.⁸ It further relayed, *'The three short-skirted, long-haired little girls who went to Europe three years ago have returned to Tasmania as grown-up young ladies "with their hair up," much to the surprise of their friends. Three years, when they come between the ages of fifteen and eighteen, can be very transforming. The Misses Bayly, who say they are delighted to be home again, are busy renewing old friendships and acquaintances'.*⁹

The time spent overseas had not only been physically transforming but also educational. Hally (Jr), Mary and Emma returned to Hobart as certified teachers after receiving their qualifications at the Ipswich High School in Suffolk.¹⁰ As the year 1909 began they gained positions as kindergarten teachers at the Girls' High School which had relocated to premises at 'Roydon' in Patrick Street.¹¹ The trio was also elected to the membership of the Field Naturalists' Club.¹²

Circles are believed to be Mary, Hally (Jr) and Emma Bayly attending a camp for members of the Field Naturalists' Club.
Tasmanian Mail, 9 April 1910.

The Bayly family additionally found time to entertain, in April 1909 holding a party at 'Runnymede' for 60 friends with two rooms set up for games and one for dancing.¹³ In January 1910 the Bayly's held a garden fete at 'Runnymede' to raise funds for the Homeopathic Hospital as part of Hally's role on the institution's Ladies' Aid Association. The event included stalls for the sale of cakes and sweets, raspberries and cream, and ice creams, as well as performing dogs, a music band and a lawn tennis tournament.¹⁴ Admission was by silver coin donation.¹⁵

---

⁸ *Daily Post*, 19 December 1908.
⁹ *Daily Post*, 19 December 1908.
¹⁰ *The Mercury*, 26 January 1909.
¹¹ *The Mercury*, 16 April 1909.
¹² *Daily Post*, 19 March 1909.
¹³ *Critic*, 24 April 1909.
¹⁴ *The Mercury*, 19 January 1909.
¹⁵ *The Mercury*, 19 January 1909.

Another death soon transformed the 'Runnymede' household, however. James Bayley's widow and Hally's step-mother Elizabeth died on 19 May at the residence.[1] She was 70 years of age and was buried at Cornelian Bay Cemetery in the family's vault.

With regards to the other members of Hally Bayly's family, her two sons Henry and James were both by now entering their teenage years. Enjoying nature and the outdoors, the pair joined the Field Naturalists' Club, along with their elder sisters, and attended school at Leslie House, playing both cricket and football for the institution.[2] Her younger two daughters, Elizabeth and Margaret, attended the Girls' High School.[3]

A further outlet for the family's time was sports, with Hally providing land along 'Runnymede's' foreshore for the establishment of the Buckingham rowing and swimming clubs.[4] Her elder daughters also assisted with the clubs, which not only focused on competitive sports but also learn to swim programs, first aid and resuscitation, particularly for school-aged children.[5] The family additionally sought to raise funds for these organisations, including holding garden fetes at 'Runnymede'.[6]

The years preceding World War I saw the establishment of several free kindergarten schools in Hobart to provide education to young children from the poorer classes. A much-needed cause of which the Bayly family was very passionate about, Hally not only donated money to the Free Kindergarten Association which was headed by Emily Dobson but also joined the organisation's committee.[7] Continuing her involvement with the Ministering Children's League, Hally organised for another garden fete at 'Runnymede' to benefit this organisation, held in November 1913.[8] A similar event was held in January 1914, this time to aid both the Ministering Children's League and the Free Kindergarten Association.[9] These events were generally well attended, with the mayor or another dignitary opening the fete, and many prominent ladies of Hobart society and their daughters manning stalls or helping to provide entertainment during the day. Bands were often in attendance, as were animals, along with car or boat rides or other amusements.

Maintaining the family's interest in aquatic sports, in early 1913 a regatta was staged at New Town with Hally Bayly allowing the foreshore area of 'Runnymede' to be used by spectators and stall holders during the day.[10] The event was held annually for a number of years with Hally's sons Henry and James competing in rowing events as they grew older.[11]

Overall, the Bayly household was a busy and lively group of young adults and teenagers with its matriarch Hally instilling in her offspring a strong sense of community mindfulness, activism and participation. Having made sure that all seven of her children were well educated, she had also put them in good stead for the future, particularly the older girls who were making their way as teachers, one of very few respectable careers offered to women at the time. As life is barely stagnant, however, there were changes brewing, both personally and throughout the globe.

The first major change affecting the Bayly family was the marriage of Hally's second eldest daughter Mary to Erskine Clarence Watchorn, a Hobart-based solicitor. The wedding took place

---

[1] *Tasmanian News*, 19 May, 13 August 1910.
[2] *The Mercury*, 27 May 1910, 16 August, 29 November 1913.
[3] *Examiner*, 7 January 1914.
[4] *The Mercury*, 28 October 1910.
[5] *Critic*, 29 October 1910.
[6] *The Mercury*, 4 February 1911.
[7] *Critic*, 29 October 1910; *The Mercury*, 4 May 1912.
[8] *The Mercury*, 3 November 1913.
[9] *The Mercury*, 11 December 1913, 16 February 1914.
[10] *Daily Post*, 8 March 1913.
[11] *The Mercury*, 16 March 1914.

Tasmanian Mail, 12 March 1914.

on 24 February 1914 at St John's Church in New Town, with the newlyweds settling into a home in Sandy Bay.[1] The couple's first child would be born in November of that same year, a daughter named Mary (Jr); the start of a new generation.[2]

While the Bayly family anticipated the arrival of Mary's first child, worldwide events were playing out that would have a profound impact on the household. World War I officially began on 4 August 1914 when Great Britain declared war on Germany. With Australia pledging full and complete support to its sovereign, the 'call to arms' soon came with troops and equipment immediately deployed to Europe. The need to support the cause saw Hally's eldest son James, a 20-year-old university student, enlist just three weeks later.[3] He joined the 9th Battery of the 3rd Field Artillery Brigade as a gunner and was shipped with his unit to Gallipoli, Turkey, providing much needed reinforcement to the allied contingent in the area.[4] After over a year of fighting, in December 1915 James was evacuated with his unit to Alexandria in Egypt.[5] Promoted to bombardier, in March 1916 he was trans-shipped to Marseille, France, becoming involved in the Somme offensive. In August of that same year James experienced myalgia and was admitted to hospital where he remained for several months after being diagnosed with heart problems and acute rheumatism.[6] Two months later he was relocated to England, spending time in a military hospital at the Shorncliffe Barracks in Kent.[7] James was finally deemed well enough to return to Australia in February 1917 where upon arrival he received a medical discharge.

Meanwhile, with reports of soldier deaths and serious injuries filtering back to Australia, the mood in Tasmania became duly sombre with frivolities and social engagements postponed unless they were benefitting the cause. The Bayly family sought to help, donating to and volunteering with the Red Cross, and using 'Runnymede' as a base to hold garden parties to raise funds for the troops.[8] By this point in time Australia had been at war for less than two years but already the casualties were high. Men were returning home with varying degrees of injuries, some permanent. Others had been killed. Their plight revealed the conflict's true cost.

While they awaited news regarding James and his health, more worry seeped into the Bayly household when in March 1916 Hally Bally's youngest son Henry enlisted. He was 19 years old and upon finishing school had been working as an orchardist.[9] He joined the 120th Howitzer Battery of the Australian Field Artillery as a gunner and was shipped with his unit to France via England in March of the following year.[10] Henry remained in France with periodic sabbaticals in England, including for a hernia, until he returned to Tasmania in early 1919 following cessation of the fighting on 11 November 1918.[11]

GARDEN PARTY AT RUNNYMEDE.

Owing to the "Crowning of the Queen" on Saturday, November 13, Mrs. H. V. Bayly has decided **to alter the date** of holding the garden party **to next Saturday, November 6,** from 3 to 5.30 p.m., when it is hoped a good number of people will take advantage of her kindness in throwing open her grounds, and thus augment the fund for providing comforts for our soldiers in the trenches. Particulars will be found in the advertisement in this issue.

Critic, 6 November 1915.

[1] *The Mercury*, 4 May 1914.
[2] *The Mercury*, 1 December 1914.
[3] National Archives of Australia (item 3062896).
[4] National Archives of Australia (item 3062896).
[5] National Archives of Australia (item 3062896).
[6] National Archives of Australia (item 3062896).
[7] National Archives of Australia (item 3062896).
[8] *The Mercury*, 7 August 1915, 13 December 1918; *Critic*, 6 November 1915; *World*, 4 March 1920.
[9] National Archives of Australia (item 3059653).
[10] National Archives of Australia (item 3059653).
[11] National Archives of Australia (item 3059653).

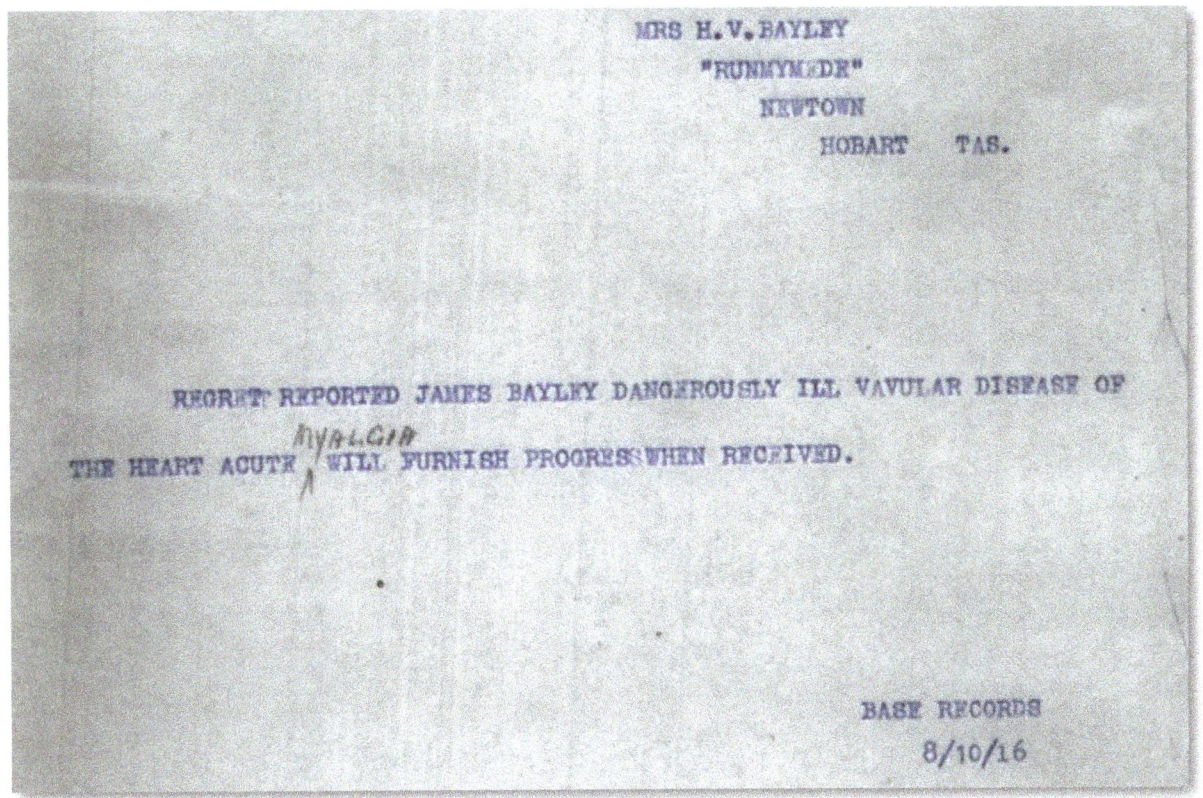

National Archives of Australia (item 3062896).

Hally Bayly's two sons were not her only offspring to volunteer for service. After successfully gaining accreditation as a nurse through the St John Ambulance Association in November 1915, Hally (Jr) travelled to England and joined the British Army Voluntary Aid Detachment.[12] Based at the Bethnal Green Hospital in London, Hally (Jr) spent three years as a nurse, returning to Tasmania in late 1919.[13] She was the last of Hally Bayly's three children that volunteered for service to return home from overseas.

The Great War had a lasting impact on Australia, the various members of the Bayly family doing their part to support and provide assistance to the conflict, whether by actively serving, helping to nurse wounded personnel, or raising funds to ensure servicemen received the care and rehabilitation they needed after they returned home. To this day it stands as the country's costliest conflict. The statistics are devastating. From a population of approximately five million people, nearly 420,000 enlisted of whom more than 60,000 were killed and 156,000 wounded, gassed, or taken prisoner. While there was much relief that the conflict had ended, a lengthy recovery process followed from multiple perspectives; globally, at the Commonwealth and state level,s from a business and organisational point of view, as well as personally, both physically and mentally.

Throughout the War Hally Bayly and her children had remained steadfast in their commitment to support those men and women serving overseas, in addition to Hally's continued patronage of the Free Kindergarten Association and other local charities.[14] Recognising the need to assist

---

[12] *The Mercury*, 6 November 1915.
[13] *Critic*, 29 November 1919.
[14] *The Mercury*, 8 April 1916, 13 December 1918; *Critic*, 30 June 1916.

those personnel returning home, she additionally became instrumental in the establishment of an A.I.F. Lounge in Collins Street, Hobart, joining the committee to ensure its operational success. The lounge was officially opened by the Governor and Lady Newdegate in September 1917.[1] Hally would remain involved with this organisation for a number of years; the welfare of returned servicemen being a cause of great concern for her.[2]

In addition Hally Bayly became a supporter of peace, particularly by prayer, in January 1918 helping to arrange a non-denominational service at the Hobart Town Hall.[3] Another organisation dear to her heart was the Purple Cross Service, recognising the contribution that horses were making to Australian military service. In January 1918, for example, she hosted a meeting of this organisation in the drawing room at 'Runnymede'.[4]

As expected, following the end of the conflict, it took some time for life to return to normal. As work, school, sport and pastimes slowly made a comeback, the return of the troops to Australia brought more worry owing to widespread concern regarding the Spanish Flu, at the time threatening the health of much of the world's population. The translocation of the virus to Tasmania was helped significantly by the return of the state's servicemen and women, with those arriving by ship into Hobart forced to quarantine on Bruny Island. It was another hurdle to overcome.

The return of military personnel brought further social and economic problems, with an increase in unemployment caused by contraction of the workforce during the conflict. There was also a significant lack of housing given the building industry had been considerably curtailed due to lack of workers and resources. With 'Runnymede' considered a substantial property comprising a vast number of acres that was by now situated in an increasingly residential area, Hally Bayly sought to subdivide a portion of the land to allow for the creation of additional housing stock. In January 1918 six building allotments situated along Bay Road were advertised for sale.[5] Perhaps also needing to supplement her family's income and lessen her own real estate commitments, a month later she advertised her family's previous home 'Aloha' for sale, situated on one acre of land on Park Street at its intersection with Bishop Street in New Town, receiving £1,800 for its purchase.[6]

The years immediately following the end of the Great War also coincided with Hally Bayly converting 'Runnymede' and some of its outer buildings into several self-contained flats, small cottages and single or two-roomed huts. Not needing so much space at the home now that several of her children had moved out, the self-contained residences were made available to rent, with the Bayly's preferencing returned servicemen and their families.[7] More building allotments that were part of the estate were advertised for sale in August 1922 on the provision that only brick houses be built.[8] The sale coincided with a general period of improvement across Hobart and its suburbs with streets widened; footpaths constructed; and sewerage, lighting, telephone wires and other infrastructure installed or upgraded. More formalised approaches to town planning were also being implemented with progress associations established to herald coordinated processes to the development and implementation of new construction, including the New Town Progress

---

[1] *The Mercury*, 15 September 1917.
[2] *The Mercury*, 30 May 1918.
[3] *The Mercury*, 9 January 1918.
[4] *The Mercury*, 15 January 1918.
[5] *The Mercury*, 23 January 1918.
[6] *The Mercury*, 20 March 1918; www.thelist.tas.gov.au (Historic Deed 14/2776).
[7] *The Mercury*, 16 August, 1 October 1918, 8 October, 8 December 1919.
[8] *The Mercury*, 19 August 1922.

Association and the Southern Tasmanian Town Planning and Progress Association, both of which Hally's son James became a member.[9] Following his return to Hobart from Europe during the latter stages of World War I, with his health permanently impacted by rheumatic fever, James had found employment in the architect's office of Messrs Hutchinson and Walter where he nurtured his interest in town planning and civic architecture.[10] In 1925 James travelled to England where he secured work with Lloyd George working on large-scale reconstruction projects.[11] On 16 October 1926 he married Helen Jane Gray Hooper in London. Sadly, the couple were expecting their first child when James Bayly died on 31 March 1928 in Bushey, Hertsfordshire, after a brief illness supposedly connected with his ongoing health issues.[12] His son (John) was born on 9 October in Bristol.[13]

More personal changes came for the Bayly family with Hally's youngest daughter Margaret receiving her diploma for kindergarten teaching and securing work at The Friends' School in nearby North Hobart.[14] Hally (Jr) and Emma had also resumed their teaching roles, both remaining living at 'Runnymede' where they grew flowers and vegetables for general sale to the public, including advertising that they were open on Christmas Day for those wanting flowers prior to visiting Cornelian Bay Cemetery, as well as exhibiting their produce in local horticultural shows.[15] Meanwhile Henry Bayly married. On 18 June 1924 at St Stephen's Anglican Church in Sandy Bay he married Gwendolyn Brownell.[16] The newlywed couple then moved to Campbell Town to take up farming at a property named 'Camelford', welcoming a daughter (Barbara) and a son (William) in the coming years.[17] Henry and Gwendolyn would also continue the Bayly's commitment to community service, becoming active participants in local sports, the Returned Sailors and Soldiers Imperial League of Australia and the Midland Agricultural Society.[18]

For Hally Bayly, the family's matriarch who was by now in her 60s, she continued to press for peace, the Great War obviously having a lasting impact on her mindset. By 1925 she was president of the Hobart branch of the Women's International League for Peace and Freedom. She would retain this role for many years, additionally using her platform to attend state-wide conferences on women's issues, including pre-natal care and the training of midwives.[19] Hally also served on the committee of the New Town Free Kindergarten Association, continuing to advocate for the free education of young children.[20]

Hally Bayly was notably absent from the annual meeting of the Women's International League for Peace and Freedom, held in Hobart in early December 1930 due to ill health.[21] She died at 'Runnymede' on 15 March 1931, aged 69.[22] Hally was buried at Cornelian Bay Cemetery in the Bayley family vault. She was survived by six of her seven children and numerous grandchildren. She left her estate to her living children and her son James' widow to be divided up equally between them.[23]

---

[9] *The Mercury*, 12 August 1925.
[10] *The Mercury*, 5 April 1928.
[11] *The Mercury*, 5 April 1928.
[12] *The Mercury*, 4 April 1928; London, England, Church of England Marriages and Banns, 1754-1940.
[13] *The Mercury*, 12 October 1928.
[14] *The Mercury*, 15 November 1923, 14 December 1925, 12 December 1927.
[15] *The Mercury*, 17 December 1926, 16 December 1927, 1 November 1928, 20 December 1930, 7 January 1932.
[16] *The Mercury*, 21 July 1924.
[17] *The Mercury*, 15 February, 7 July 1926; 14 March, 21 November 1928, 3 May 1929, 16 May 1930.
[18] *Examiner*, 3 March, 3 May 1928; *The Mercury*, 4 January 1929, 24 February 1931, 16 June 1936.
[19] *The Mercury*, 2 March 1925, 20 October 1927, 20 June 1928.
[20] *The News*, 18 June 1925; *The Mercury*, 5 November 1925, 17 June 1927.
[21] *The Mercury*, 9 December 1930.
[22] *The Mercury*, 16 March 1931.
[23] Tasmanian Archives (AD960/1/55 no. 18406).

The death of Hally Bayly (nee Bayley) marked the end of an era; the last connection between past and future generations of the Bayley family. She had known and been witness to the fierce hard work and determination that saw her uncle Charles Bayley, father James Bayley, and aunt Harriet McGregor advance themselves and their families in Tasmania, and she had spent time growing up surrounded by their kin in Suffolk and Essex, England. Hally had also experienced firsthand the evolution that their pursuit and perseverance had on the family, particularly the outcome of Charles and James Bayley's time spent at sea, allowing the lineage to transition through the social classes, though earnestly maintaining their unpretentious and unassuming ways. They had all lived lives worthy of this biography.

From humble roots the Bull siblings had transitioned into Bayleys, becoming upstanding, respectable and notable citizens of the Tasmanian community, far from their birth places in the small maritime communities along the English coast. They had shared professional success, love, wealth and friendship. Yet their lives were fraught with loss: their children, their spouses, their crew, each other. Of their offspring to survive to adulthood, there was only one: James' daughter Hally, born at sea during a whaling voyage in 1861.

Like the previous generation, Hally also lived a life of extremes, experiencing the loss of her mother at the age of five, as well as the deaths of her siblings, uncles, aunts, cousins, father, husband and son. Ultimately, however, she used her family's platform to guide a life of service, charity and benevolence. She produced seven children and, despite a history of maritime trades going back several generations, none of them took to the sea. By this time the stories of Hobart's mariners and their whaling ways were well into the past. Yet their profits had fuelled her future and endowed Hally's progeny on different pathways, their various professional, social, charitable and political causes coalescing into a positive impact and legacy in numerous ways.

The Bayley family's legacy also still exists in the walls, rooms, gardens and atmosphere of their homes, 'Lenna' and 'Runnymede'. Both of these residences are reminiscent of the family's plight and success and they resonate with their histories and personalities. 'Lenna' was built by Alexander McGregor to house his wife Harriet and their nieces and nephews and showcase his success, yet it became the home of his second wife Maggie, a woman staunchly advocating for women's rights and suffragettes. It is now a boutique hotel allowing guests to relive its history and experience its grandeur. Though less ostentatious 'Runnymede' is similarly available to the public, since 1965 owned by the Government of Tasmania and part of the National Trust (Tasmania). Both are well worth experiencing and visiting; anchors of the past that have moved with the tide into the future.

> **Death of Mrs. Bayly Last Week**
>
> Everybody knows that the "Voice" has no "Personal Column." But we cannot possibly allow the death of such a woman as the late Mrs. Harriet Louisa Bayly, which occurred at Runnymede, New Town, on Sunday last, to pass without a tribute of profound respect to her memory.
>
> **This deceased lady did noble work, and was the devoted President of the Hobart Branch of the Women's International League for Peace and Freedom from its inception up to the very day of her death.**
>
> She had a disposition that endeared her to all, abilities of a high order, and all those qualities of courage and capacity which mean so much in the sacred crusade for peace. She sought no publicity, but worked steadily, quietly and with tireless energy for one of the greatest ideals in the world to-day, and was an unfailing source of inspiration and strength to all associated with her. Flowers on her grave will fade and perish, and these few poor words in print will also pass, but what she did lives on and will not pass. It is interesting to note here that the Women's International League for Peace and Freedom is to-day one of the most widespread organisations in the world, with most important affiliations in all countries. The late Mrs. Bayly was 69 years of age when she died. She was the widow of the late Mr. H. A. Bayly and a daughter of the late Captain James Bayley.

Voice, 21 March 1931.

Hally (Jr) and Emma Bayly. The two sisters lived at 'Runnymede' until the 1960s.
Tasmanian Archives (NS1619/1/117).

Bayley Family Tree

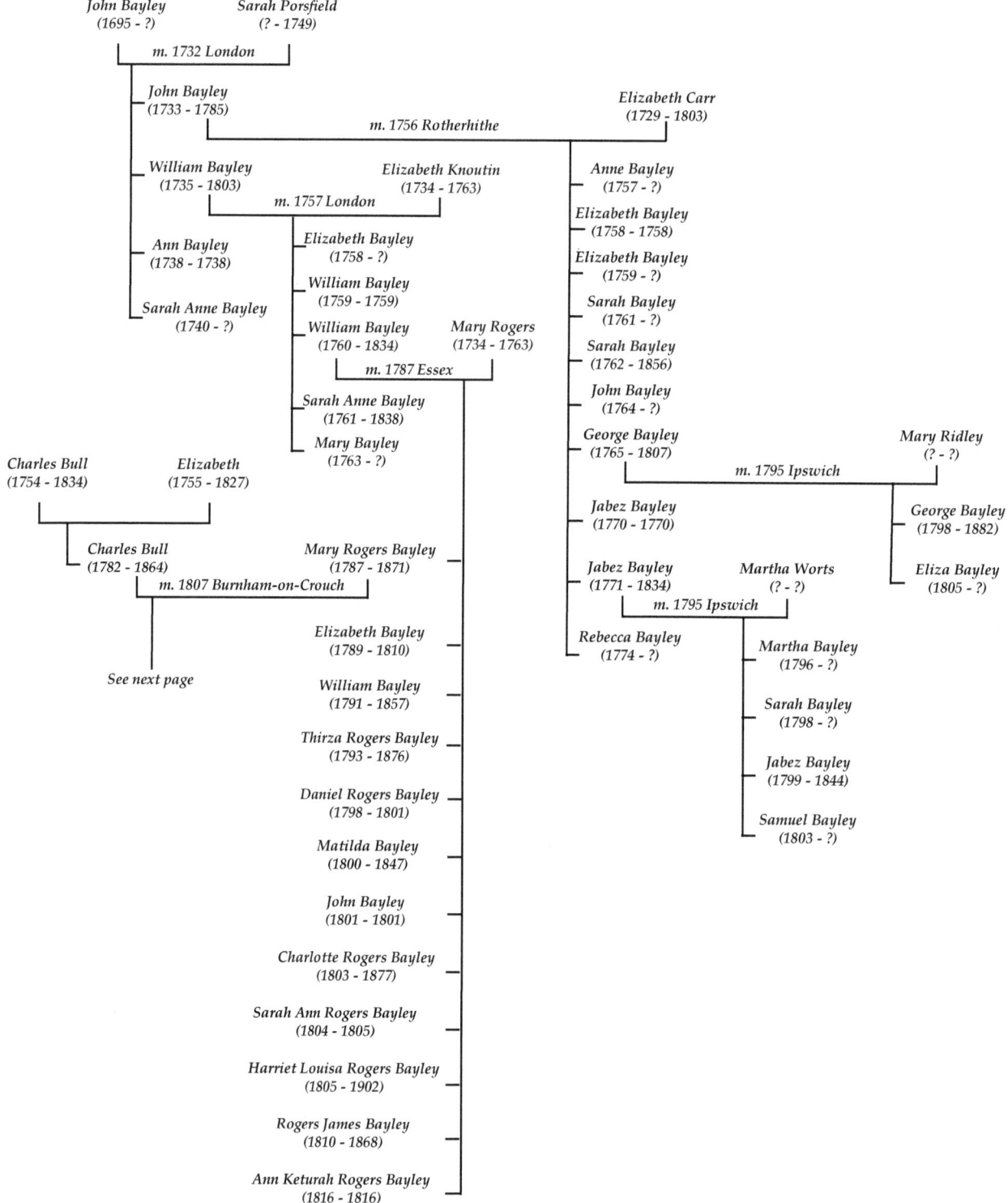

Bayley Family Tree

Children of Charles Bull and Mary Rogers Bayley

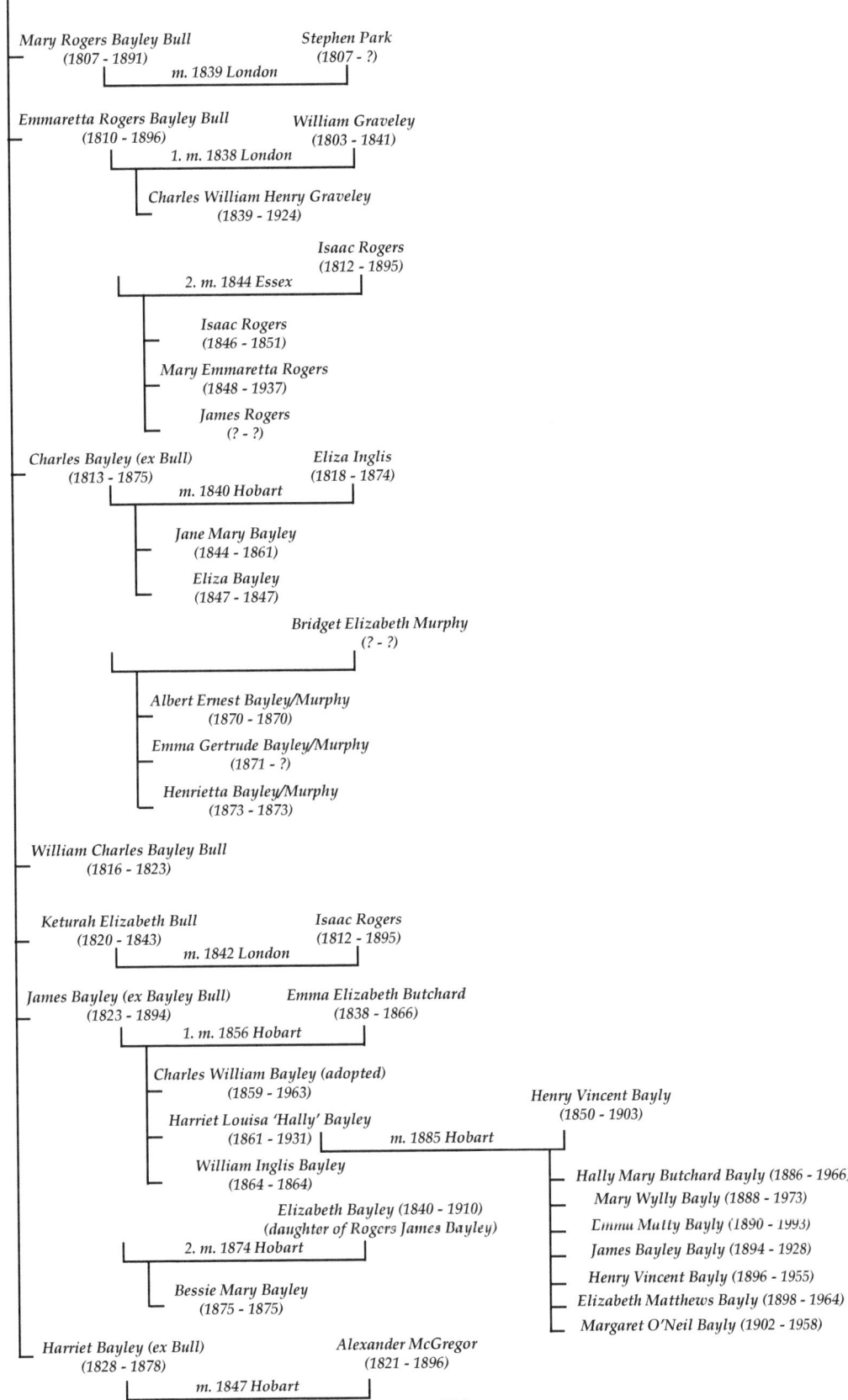

Partial map of England noting London, Rotherhithe, Burnham-on-Crouch, Maldon, Ipswich and Woodbridge (1842). Library of Congress (lccn.loc.gov/2021668664).

Appendix 1
The Bayleys of Surrey, Suffolk & Essex

This appendix summarises the ancestry of our three siblings, Charles, James and Harriet Bayley, and profiles the Bayley family's involvement in maritime trades over several centuries. The first predecessor we focus on is John Bayley who began his apprenticeship as a waterman employed on the River Thames, England, in October 1707. His master was William Lemmon of Rotherhithe, Surrey, a town located only a few miles south of London. In official records John Bayley's date of freedom, i.e., the date he was to complete his period of servitude, was listed as 11 January 1716.[1]

It is likely that John Bayley was born around 1695 in Rotherhithe or one of the neighbourhoods nearby. He would have commenced his waterman's apprenticeship at the age of 12 or 13 years with his parents or another relative paying a generous fee for the opportunity. As his master William Lemmon would not only have been tasked with providing training and mentorship to John Bayley, but also housing, food and clothing. However, perhaps because of illness, death, a disagreement or another change in circumstance, John Bayley's apprenticeship was transferred to Ursley Collward of Rotherhithe in August 1711.[2] John then spent another five years under his servitude, ultimately becoming a fully licensed waterman in late 1716.

For several centuries gaining employment as a waterman of Greater London was quite a respectable though rather low-paying profession. An Act of Parliament that gained Royal Assent from King Henry VIII in 1515 had first established a committee of overseers to regulate the industry. Several decades later the Company of Watermen and Lightermen of the River Thames was established to regulate those plying the trade between Windsor in Berkshire and Gravesend in Kent, a distance of around 60 miles.[3] With land-based transportation limited to horses and rudimentary roads, the movement of goods and passengers within the City of London and the surrounding metropolitan area, as well as to and from vessels moored along the river system, was considered an essential part of London's daily life. The profession played a founding and important role in the local economy; the watermen using their muscle and brawn to propel their wherries and skiffs up, down and across the Thames, thus becoming integral components of an aquatic-based commercial and passenger highway and in the process fuelling trade and movement.

Over the next few centuries the Company of Watermen and Lightermen, assisted by the passage of several more pieces of legislation, became largely responsible for regulating the watermen and bargemen, including with regard to the type and dimensions of boats employed, their maximum capacities for passengers and goods, and the fares charged per passenger and by

---

[1] Index of Thames Watermen & Lightermen 1688-2010.
[2] Index of Thames Watermen & Lightermen 1688-2010.
[3] I. E. Philp (1957). *The History of the Thames Watermen.*

weight and type of cargo. There were also provisions for safety and apprentices. With respect to the latter, all apprentices were to be examined at the end of their first two years with regard to their knowledge and fitness to navigate.[1] Upon receiving their licence, the watermen were proudly presented with a single-breasted red woollen coat, as well as a silver badge emblazoned with the Company's emblem and their licence number, to be placed on the sleeve of the coat. Thames watermen were noted for this distinctive uniform as well as a cap.

With vessels required to be marked and numbered, by the 1730s there were nearly 6,000 watermen plying their trade on the Thames with the number of barges used to carry cargo estimated at 750.[2] However, by this point in time, boat design and technological changes were impacting the industry. More purposeful and larger craft were introduced resulting in a steady decline in the number of men employed on the river. Horse-drawn coaches had also been introduced to the detriment of the smaller river craft, particularly for the movement of passengers. With this increase in land-based traffic, more streets and roads were built allowing for the development of substantial residential housing and commercial business districts further away from the river and the general outward trajectory of the City of London. This progress only exacerbated the threat to the livelihood of the watermen and bargemen, particularly since bridges were also beginning to be built across the River Thames making access to road and foot traffic much easier. Completion of the Westminster Bridge in 1749, for example, resulted in the watermen receiving compensation for a significant loss of income.[3] It was only the start of a pattern of bridge building that would see the two sides of the Thames connected at numerous locations. Increased bridging of the river system, combined with the introduction of wheeled transport and steam-propelled vessels, would slowly but ultimately ensure the watermen, bargemen and their oars were superseded.

River Thames waterman in uniform.
H. W. Petherick (1885). *Aunt Louisa's Welcome Gift.*

For John Bayley, however, most of these changes were well into the future and his position as a licensed waterman was secure for the most part, though it was still an occupation plagued with safety concerns. Incidents and accidents could occur at any time due to wayward loading and unloading procedures, bad weather, chaotic navigational practices and large amounts of traffic, as well as snags and submerged objects, disruptive passengers and, of course, the tide. Still, he persevered and in 1720 took on an apprentice by the name of James Bayley, a likely relative.[4]

Settling into the small though rather poor and marshy riverside community of Rotherhithe on London's outskirts, likely in a single-roomed dwelling, in April 1722 John Bayley married Martha

---

[1] I. E. Philp (1957). *The History of the Thames Watermen.*
[2] I. E. Philp (1957). *The History of the Thames Watermen.*
[3] I. E. Philp (1957). *The History of the Thames Watermen.*
[4] Index of Thames Watermen & Lightermen 1688-2010.

Jones.⁵ A son named John was born to the couple the following November.⁶ It is probable that more children were then born to John and Martha Bayley though no records have been found to date. Sadly, Martha died in late 1729 and was buried at St Mary's Church in Rotherhithe on 27 December of that year.⁷ The church had only been completed in 1716, replacing an earlier version dating back to medieval times that was located closer to the south bank of the River Thames and often subject to flooding.⁸

Following the death of his first wife, John Bayley remarried. On 9 April 1732 at St Botolph Bishopsgate Church in London he married Sarah Porsfield.⁹ A son named John was born to the couple just over a year later and baptised at St Mary's in Rotherhithe on 16 August 1733.¹⁰ Two years later another son, William, was born. He was baptised at St Mary's in Rotherhithe on 27 February 1735.¹¹ Two daughters were then born during the next few years: Ann who died within a month of her birth in late 1738 and Sarah Anne who was born in 1740.¹²

Growing up in the working-class area of Rotherhithe, the two brothers John and William Bayley would have become immersed in the local maritime community. They would have also been accustomed to the sight of large vessels moored in the river, loading for or returning from far off places including Europe, North and South America, Asia and the East Indies. Rotherhithe was additionally becoming a hub for shipyard services, including repair and refitting work. The nearby Howland Great Wet Dock for instance, notably the first commercial dock constructed in London, was operational by 1700 and capable of accommodating over 100 merchant ships. Covering a 10-acre site, the dock was intended to refit ships owned by the East India Company.

St Mary's Church, Rotherhithe, England (c1875).
Mary Evans/Peter & Dawn Cope Collection.

---

⁵ Parish Register Transcript for John Bayley and Martha Jones, Rotherhithe 14 April 1722.
⁶ Parish Register Transcript for John Bayley, Rotherhithe 22 November 1723.
⁷ Greater London Burial Index for Martha Baily, Rotherhithe, St Mary, 27 December 1729.
⁸ en.wikipedia.org/wiki/St_Mary%27s_Church,_Rotherhithe.
⁹ England, Select Marriages, 1538-1973 for John Baley and Sarah Porsfield, 9 April 1732.
¹⁰ Parish Register Transcript for John Bayley, Rotherhithe 16 September 1733.
¹¹ Parish Register Transcript for James Bayley, Rotherhithe 27 February 1735.
¹² Parish Register Transcript for Ann Bayley, Rotherhithe 25 October 1738, and Sarah Ann Bayley, Rotherhithe 26 December 1740; Greater London Burial Index for Ann Bayley, Rotherhithe 4 November 1738.

Nineteenth Century image of Howland Great Wet Dock in the Parish of Rotherhithe, England.
Wikimedia Commons.

John and William Bayley would have additionally witnessed the development of further docks and ship refit and repair sites on both sides of the Thames then under construction near their home. With increasing demand for coastal and international trade, more and more vessels were being built and entering service. Rotherhithe soon found itself amongst numerous locations along the River Thames where boat building facilities, shipyards and wharves became established; these construction projects ultimately linking the various towns and communities along the river to produce the greater metropolitan area of London.

By their teenage years, instead of following in their father's footsteps and becoming watermen, John and William Bayley secured apprenticeships with John Burr, a local boat builder.[1] Here the pair would have helped produce smaller vessels for use on board ships for customers including the Royal Navy and East India Company, as well as being involved in overhaul and repair work. Several years following the completion of their respective periods of servitude, John and William both married. On 19 December 1756 the former married Elizabeth Carr at St Mary's in Rotherhithe. Witnesses were John Bradley and Elizabeth's sister Mary Carr.[2] Less than a year later William married Elizabeth Knoutin at St Botolph Aldgate Church in London.[3]

The two couples settled in Rotherhithe in the vicinity of the Shepherd and Dog stairs which provided access to the River Thames for boarding or disembarking from river craft, including watermen's wherries and skiffs. Stairs were common along the river at the time, spaced out at regular intervals, depending on the size of the population that they served. Residential and commercial properties within individual parishes were thus defined by the name of the stairs to which they were closely located.

---

[1] National Archives UK (ADM 106/1185/321 and ADM 106/1226/309).
[2] London, England, Church of England Marriages and Banns, 1754-1940 for John Bayley.
[3] London, England, Church of England Marriages and Banns, 1754-1940 for William Bayley.

Appendix 1

With regards to John and William Bayley's personal lives, many children were born (and several sadly died) over the next decade. Specifically, children born to John and Elizabeth Bayley (nee Carr) were:

- Anne Bayley (1757)
- Elizabeth Bayley (1758-1758)
- Elizabeth Bayley (1759)
- Sarah Bayley (1761-1761)
- Sarah Bayley (1762-1856)
- John Bayley (1764)

The children of William and Elizabeth Bayley (nee Knoutin) were:

- Elizabeth Bayley (1758)
- William Bayley (1759-1759)
- William Bayley (1760-1834)
- Sarah Anne Bayley (1761-1838)
- Mary Bayley (1763-1803)

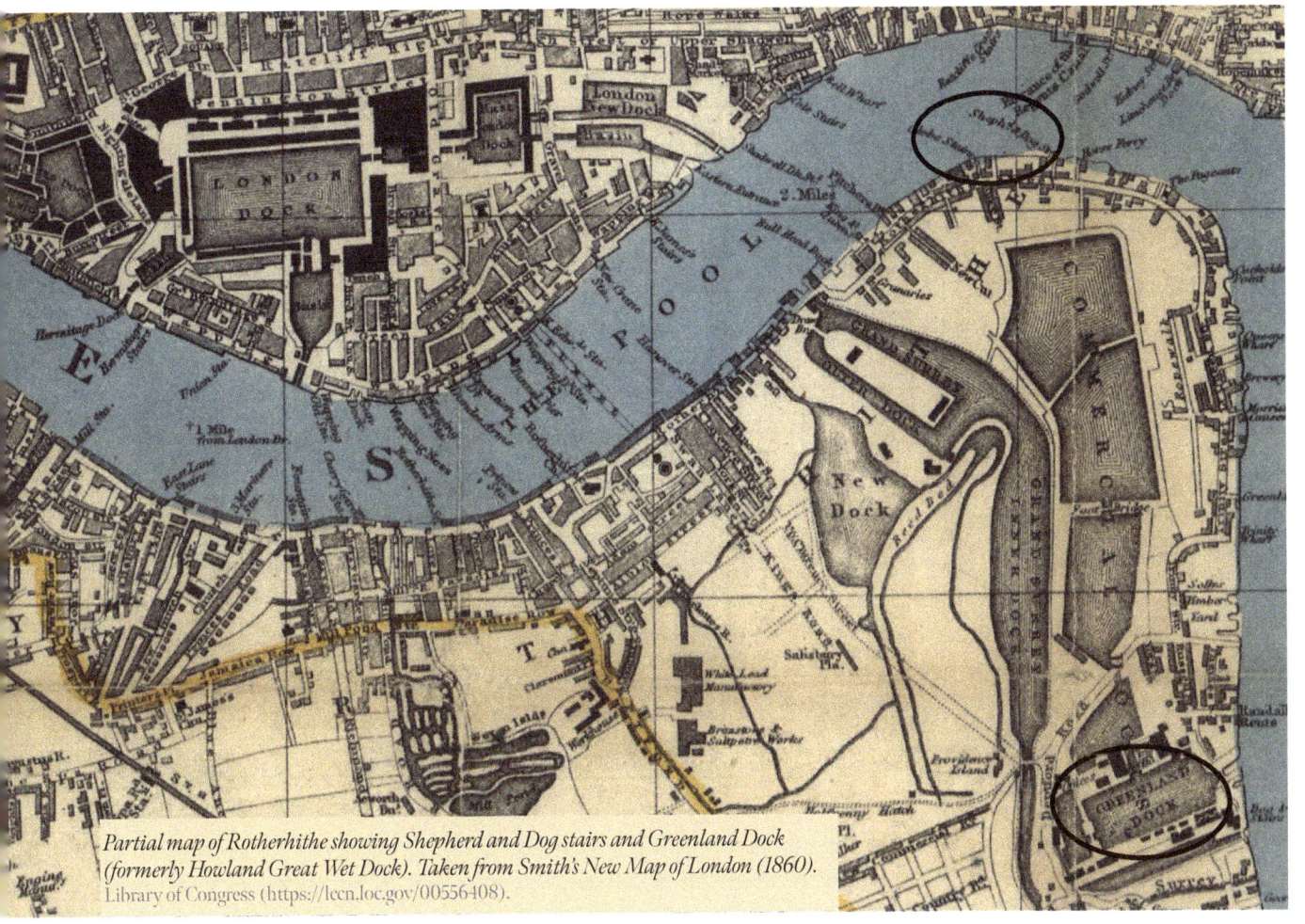

Partial map of Rotherhithe showing Shepherd and Dog stairs and Greenland Dock (formerly Howland Great Wet Dock). Taken from Smith's New Map of London (1860). Library of Congress (https://lccn.loc.gov/00556408).

In August 1763 William Bayley's wife Elizabeth died at the age of 29. She was buried at St Mary's Church on the 21st of that month.[1] Less than a year later William and John Bayley and their respective families relocated to Ipswich in Suffolk.

Situated on the River Orwell approximately 80 miles north-east of London, Ipswich was not only a thriving port town that offered the two brothers an opportunity for work but it was also a haven for like-minded religious non-conformists such as the Bayley family. John and William soon established a boat building business as sub-tenants of a yard owned by shipbuilder John Barnard.[2] Called the Nova Scotia Shipyard, the site was located on the west bank of the River Orwell less than a mile from the town centre.[3] It is highly likely that John and William found the opportunity via a newspaper advertisement published in March 1764.

> *To be* LETT *and Enter'd upon at* Michaelmas *next.*
> A Very convenient SHIP-YARD, at Nova-Scotia, within Half a Mile of Ipswich, in the County of Suffolk.
> For Particulars enquire at the Yard; or of Mr. John Barnard, Ship-Builder, at Ipswich.
> N. B. A Part of the Yard will be cleared, that any Person may lay in Timber by May next.

Ipswich Journal, 3 March 1764.

Operating solely as boat builders, the Bayley brothers began advertising their business, stating that they could build '*sailing boats, carvel or clenchwork; long boats, carvel or clenchwork; pinnaces, yawls, cutters, skiffs, Greenland Shallops, and pond boats of all sorts*'.[4] Over the next decade the boatyard prospered, the building of commercial and recreational vessels supplemented by repair work. By the mid-1770s the Bayleys were also undertaking contract work for the Royal Navy; the construction of flat-bottomed boats in high demand owing to the American War of Independence then underway.[5]

From a personal perspective, both John and William Bayley expanded their families during this period. John's wife Elizabeth gave birth to four more children, all of whom were baptised at the Tacket Street Congregational Chapel in Ipswich, a church established by a group of dissenters in the 1680s.

- George Bayley (1765-1807)
- Jabez Bayley (1770-1770)
- Jabez Bayley (1771-1834)
- Rebecca Bayley (1774)

William Bayley also remarried. On 7 February 1765 at St Botolph Bishopsgate Church in London he wed Mary Carr, the sister of his sister-in-law Elizabeth.[6] Returning to Ipswich, a daughter named Mary Anne was born to the couple in February 1767 and baptised at the Tacket Street Chapel on 2 March 1767.[7]

---

[1] London, England, Church of England Baptisms, Marriages and Burials, 1538-1812 for Elizabeth Bailey.
[2] J. Leather (1965). *The Shipbuilding Bayleys*.
[3] https://heritage.suffolk.gov.uk/Monument/MSF16909.
[4] J. Leather (1965). *The Shipbuilding Bayleys*.
[5] J. Leather (1965). *The Shipbuilding Bayleys*.
[6] London, England, Church of England Marriages and Banns, 1754-1940 for William Bayley.
[7] England & Wales, Non-Conformist and Non-Parochial Registers, 1567-1936 for Mary Anne Bayley.

Baptism record for Jabez Bayley, Tacket Street Congregational Church, Ipswich, England, 9 October 1771.
England & Wales, Non-Conformist and Non-Parochial Registers, 1567-1936 for Jabez Bailey (Bayley).

Marriage record for William Bayley and Mary Carr, St Botolph Bishopsgate Church, London, England, 7 February 1765.
London, England, Church of England Marriages and Banns, 1754-1940 for William Bayley.

With regard to the Bayley brothers' professional work, by the early 1780s demand for new vessels was waning. The American War of Independence had concluded in September 1783 with the British Army defeated, leading to reduced orders for new naval craft. John and William dissolved their partnership with the former remaining in Ipswich where he continued to operate a boatyard until his death from a riding accident in March 1785 whereupon it was managed by his widow Elizabeth and ultimately, in the decades to come, by two of his sons, George and Jabez.[8] In contrast, William and his family relocated to Burnham-on-Crouch in the county of Essex. Situated on the northern bank of the River Crouch, six miles from its opening with the sea and 50 miles south of Ipswich, the small coastal town was not only a fishing and ferry port but had also become synonymous for the cultivation and harvesting of native oysters.

Considered one of the finest species of oyster in England due to their flavour, those grown in the Burnham-on-Courch area were known to be small, ovate and deep-shelled.[9] Grown on artificial substrate known as beds along the estuary and its creeks since the early 1700s, the oysters were harvested at around five years of age by which point they were considered fully grown, though their shell was still easily plied open. With shoreline leased from Sir Henry Mildway, at

---
[8] J. Leather (1965). *The Shipbuilding Bayleys.*
[9] E. Forbes & S. Hanley (1853). *History of British Mollusca and their Shells.*

the time of William Bayley's relocation to the area the oyster industry was principally carried out by one company known as the Burnham Oyster Company. Established by five men in 1780 (John Auger, John Gibson, John Hawkins, Daniel Rogers and John Sweeting), the business monopolised the industry well into the next century, in the process providing much needed employment to the nearby town.[1] With the oyster fishery protected by legislation, stealing the molluscs and trespassing on the beds were both considered illegal, as was the unlawful dredging of oyster beds. To thwart any nefarious activity, the Burnham Oyster Company paid for a police inspector and two constables to service their grounds and the town in general, thus providing further protection and security for the local community.[2]

Maintaining oyster beds was an integral part of the oyster life cycle. Shallow-draft vessels were needed to not only reach the oyster leases but to also allow for the clearance of mud, the constant re-stocking of spawn, and the removal of predators, seaweed, barnacles, rubbish and other impediments.[3] Undoubtedly capitalising on a ready market of oystermen needing new vessels to reach their beds, as well as overhaul and repair of existing craft, William Bayley seems to have found enough work in the area to not only maintain a boatyard but also construct new boats and act as a conduit for the sale of used vessels.

While oysters were exported to Belgium, France and other locales in continental Europe, the close proximity of Burnham-on-Crouch to the River Thames meant that loads and loads of oysters were sent to London with William Bayley plausibly receiving numerous orders to build vessels to service both of these trades. With consumption greatest during the summer months, coinciding with the duration of the oyster season, the live molluscs were notably some of the freshest to arrive in London, owing to the short distance between the two locations as well as the processes employed to ensure they arrived in prime condition. In general, the bushels were packed tightly in crates and transported in the holds of various-sized craft. From the boats, they were offloaded to salesmen in London who kept them in spring water mixed with salt until a buyer could be sourced. Over the centuries, millions of bushels of oysters were transported by sea from Burnham-on-Crouch to the River Thames with consumers eager to eat the species common to this locality as opposed to those from other regions.[4]

With William Bayley, his wife Mary and their family settled in Burnham-on-Crouch, it was not long before his older children began to marry. His son William (Jr) married Mary Rogers on 26 July 1787 at the local church, St Mary the Virgin.[5] Mary had been born in 1770 and was notably the eldest surviving daughter of Daniel Rogers, one of the principal founders of the Burnham Oyster Company, and his first wife Elizabeth.[6] Though less than 10 years old at the time of William Bayley (Jr) and Mary Rogers' marriage, the oyster business would become extremely profitable over the coming decades, in the process making Daniel Rogers a wealthy man. This capital would ultimately filter down to his children and their spouses, during both Daniel's life time and following his death. The merging of the two families would have also been advantageous to the Bayley family's boatyard business of which William Bayley (Jr) was now part of. It was customary at the time for sons and heirs of boat and ship builders to learn the trade by 'Rule of Thumb' as opposed to receiving formal training in vessel design and measurement. It is in this context that

---

[1] H. Doubleday & W. Page (1965). *The Victoria History of the County of Essex - Volume 2*.
[2] H. Doubleday & W. Page (1965). *The Victoria History of the County of Essex - Volume 2*.
[3] E. Forbes & S. Hanley (1853). *History of British Mollusca and their Shells*.
[4] E. Forbes & S. Hanley (1853). *History of British Mollusca and their Shells*.
[5] Essex Marriages And Banns 1537-1935 for William Bayley.
[6] Essex Baptism Index 1538-1917 for Mary Rogers.

Marriage record for William Bayley (Jr) and Mary Rogers, St Mary the Virgin, Burnham-on-Crouch, England, 26 July 1787.
Essex Marriages And Banns 1537-1935 for William Bayley.

William Bayley (Jr) would have been apprenticed to his father with the goal of taking over the yard as part of its succession plan. However, while the boatyard appears to have been in operation until the late 1790s, William (Jr) was living in Maldon by this time, though returned in time to take over the business following the death of his father William in July 1803 from consumption, i.e., tuberculosis. William (Jr) then spent the next few years building and overhauling boats, primarily those associated with the local oyster industry.[7] However, financial duress caused him to declare bankruptcy in early 1809.[8] It was likely at this point in time that William Bayley (Jr) received £500 from his father-in-law Daniel Rogers, the large sum being used to support the couple's growing family and also maintain their boatyard business.[9] Some additional monies would have been due to William (Jr) and his wife Mary in 1813 following Daniel Rogers' death at the age of 73. Specifically his will stipulated that the bulk of his property, including his oyster leases and other assets, be divided up equally amongst his 10 surviving children.[10]

As stated, following their wedding William (Jr) and Mary Bayley (nee Rogers) initially settled in Burnham-on-Crouch close to both of their families. Between 1787 and 1791 at least three children were born to the couple:

- Mary Rogers Bayley (1787-1871)
- Elizabeth Bayley (1789-1810)
- William Bayley (Jr²) (1791-1857)

Perhaps because of better employment opportunities, or to establish his own boatyard, William (Jr), Mary and their children had then moved further north to Maldon. Situated 12 miles to the

---

[7] Essex Burial Index 1530-1994 for William Bailey.
[8] *Bury and Norwich Post*, 8 March 1809.
[9] Will of Daniel Rogers (1813). Essex Archives Online.
[10] Will of Daniel Rogers (1813). Essex Archives Online.

north-east of Burnham-on-Crouch at the head of the Blackwater Estuary, Maldon in the 1790s was a growing market and port town, increasingly the site of an upward trajectory of maritime traffic and a hub for boat and barge building. The location thus offered William Bayley (Jr) a more robust supply of customers for his boat building activities as opposed to primarily servicing those associated with the oyster industry of Burnham-on-Crouch. It was also in Maldon that five more children were born.

- Thirza Rogers Bayley (1793-1876)
- Daniel Rogers Bayley (1798-1801)
- Matilda Bayley (1800-1843)
- John Bayley (1801-1801)
- Charlotte Rogers Bayley (1803-1877)

As stated, for reasons unknown but perhaps because of a familiar clientele and his own father's declining health, at some point in time during the early 1800s William (Jr), Mary and their seven surviving children returned to Burnham-on-Crouch where another four children were born.

- Sarah Ann Rogers Bayley (1804-1805)
- Harriet Louisa Rogers Bayley (1805-1902)
- Rogers James Bayley (1810-1868)
- Ann Keturah Rogers Bayley (1816-1816)

While William Bayley (Jr) appears to have continued with the trade of boat building at Burnham-on-Crouch until his death in October 1834, it was his son William (Jr^2) that made the professional jump to shipbuilding.[1] It is William (Jr^2) and his older sibling Mary Rogers Bayley that we must now focus on, as well as their relative Jabez Bayley.

Undoubtedly learning the craft initially from his father and grandfather and being involved in the family's boatyard operations from an early age, as a teenager William Bayley (Jr^2) relocated to Ipswich, taking up an apprenticeship in shipbuilding with his father's first cousin Jabez Bayley (1771-1834). Jabez, together with his older brother George (1765-1807), had taken over their father John Bayley's boat building business after his death in 1785 which had from then on been run in conjunction with their mother Elizabeth. It was a pivotal time to be involved in the industry with one factor significantly driving the Ipswich shipbuilding industry being the Napoleonic Wars (1803-1815) then being waged between England and France. With national interests directed towards the conflict, Britain had mobilised its resources to expand its naval and military assets, in the process becoming a global industrial, economic and political powerhouse. Significantly, in terms of numbers, the Royal Navy's fleet had tripled in size during this period to nearly 1,000 vessels of various sizes and applications.[2]

Supplementary to the expansion of the Royal Navy, commercial shipbuilders in Great Britain were also constructing ships for the East India Company which carried an enormous amount of goods as part of its world trade monopoly. The Industrial Revolution (1760-1840), then also underway, had placed Britain on a global pedestal, with technological innovations associated with

---
[1] Essex, England, Church of England Deaths and Burials, 1813-1996 for William Bayley.
[2] N. Westphalen (2024). *Georgian Naval Warfare, Ships and Medicine 1714-1815.*

manufacturing, iron production, equipment and tool-making pioneering a new era, including for those industries associated with railways; shipping, including steamships; textile manufacturing; and communication. Capitalising on these new technologies Britain's businessmen became leaders in international commerce, banking, trade and shipping.

Seeing potential for success Jabez Bayley had leveraged England's high demand for new ships to his advantage. In May 1803, at the age of 31, the partnership between Jabez and his brother George Bayley was dissolved by mutual consent, with the operation going forward solely carried on by Jabez.[3] Up until this point in time the two brothers had been working out of the Nova Scotia Shipyard, adjacent to the River Orwell.[4] Within a few years Jabez would move his operation to new premises known as the Halifax Shipyard, a few hundred yards to the south.[5] Both sites are now part of the Port of Ipswich West Bank Terminal.

Though initially focusing his operations on small boat building, overhaul and repair work, Jabez Bayley very quickly diversified into ship construction, particularly of naval vessels. Between 1804 and 1814 he is known to have built at least 25 brigs, sloops or ships for the Royal Navy (summarised in Appendix 3), indicating that the yard was quite a large, extensive and productive operation and that its output included many significant ships such as HMS *Esk* (1813), HMS *Leven* (1813) and HMS *Dee* (1814) which were all Sixth-Rate Ships of the Line.[6]

HMS Sappho capturing the Danish brig Admiral Jawl in March 1808.
https://en.wikipedia.org/wiki/HMS_Sappho_(1806).

---

[3] *Ipswich Journal*, 7 May 1803; https://heritage.suffolk.gov.uk/Monument/MSF16909.
[4] *Ipswich Journal*, 7 May 1803; https://heritage.suffolk.gov.uk/Monument/MSF16909.
[5] *Ipswich Journal*, 30 November 1805; https://heritage.suffolk.gov.uk/Monument/MSF16908.
[6] https://en.wikipedia.org/wiki/Jabez_Bayley; https://en.wikipedia.org/wiki/HMS_Orestes_(1805), https://en.wikipedia.org/wiki/List_of_ship_launches_in_1807, https://en.wikipedia.org/wiki/List_of_ship_launches_in_1808, https://en.wikipedia.org/wiki/List_of_ship_launches_in_1809, https://en.wikipedia.org/wiki/List_of_ship_launches_in_1812, https://en.wikipedia.org/wiki/List_of_ship_launches_in_1813, https://en.wikipedia.org/wiki/List_of_ship_launches_in_1814.

With regards to the merchant craft built by Jabez Bayley at his Halifax Shipyard, one of the first was the schooner *Mainwaring* built to the order of the Hudson's Bay Company and launched in 1807.[1] A few years later he completed the 579-ton East Indiaman *Harleston,* launched in January 1811 to the order of Peter Everett Mestaers.[2] East Indiamen were merchant ships that operated under charter or licence to European trading companies, carrying both cargo and passengers.[3] The vessels were also armed for defence against pirates. The *Harleston*, in particular, was initially chartered by the British East India Company, sailing to Calcutta and Bengal from Portsmouth in June 1811.[4] It then remained in India, operating in domestic trade for many years.

The ship *Mary* was launched from Jabez Bayley's shipyard a few months following the launch of the *Harleston*, described as a '*fine West Indiaman of 360 tons*'.[5] This vessel later made five voyages to Australia carrying convicts.[6] Next off the stocks was the brig *Nautilus* also launched in 1811.[7] Three years later Jabez advertised for sale a new 56-ton sloop adapted for the domestic corn trade.[8] At least two more vessels were launched the following year: a brig named *Active* for the port of Southwold and a packet called *Castlereagh* for a Captain Macdonough of Harwich.[9] In June 1817 the brig *Traveller* was launched from Jabez Bayley's shipyard.[10]

In May 1816 Jabez Bayley laid the keel of his largest vessel to date; a craft that would ultimately prove to be his legacy as well as the precursor of his economic downfall.[11] Described as the largest and finest vessel ever built so far inland on the shore of the River Orwell, the commodious East Indiaman was built to the order of Captain Matthew Isacke of Greenwich over a 15-month period with the work furnishing employment, directly or indirectly, to hundreds and hundreds of tradesmen.[12] With an estimated 20,000 people present for the event, the 1,366-ton *Orwell* was launched on 28 August 1817.[13] The vessel went on to have a prosperous career over many decades, its annual survey in 1837 coincidentally undertaken by Jabez Bayley's nephew George Bayley (Jr) who was by now a London-based surveyor for the Registry of Shipping at Lloyd's.[14]

Nearly 16 months after the *Orwell*, Jabez Bayley completed the West Indiaman *Abberton*.[15] This craft was followed in the latter half of 1819 by the 230-ton *Transit* and the schooner *Paget*.[16] Sadly, this period also coincided with Jabez being on the brink of bankruptcy. Seeking to maintain financial fluidity he began advertising his assets for sale, including several shares in schooners commercially trading out of Ipswich that he had built, including the *Elizabeth of Ipswich, Sincerity of Ipswich* and *Charlotte of Ipswich*.[17] Also advertised were several newly-constructed vessels comprising a barge, sloop and schooner.[18] Four months later multiple commercial properties as well as nine dwelling houses were advertised for sale by private contract as part of his estate.[19]

[1] *Suffolk Chronicle*, 26 January 1811.
[2] *Suffolk Chronicle*, 26 January 1811.
[3] https://en.wikipedia.org/wiki/East_Indiaman.
[4] https://en.wikipedia.org/wiki/Harleston_(1811_ship).
[5] *Suffolk Chronicle*, 11 May 1811.
[6] https://en.wikipedia.org/wiki/Mary_(1811_Ipswich_ship).
[7] https://en.wikipedia.org/wiki/List_of_ship_launches_in_1811.
[8] https://en.wikipedia.org/wiki/List_of_ship_launches_in_1807.
[9] *Suffolk Chronicle*, 23 September 1815.
[10] https://en.wikipedia.org/wiki/List_of_ship_launches_in_1817.
[11] *Ipswich Journal*, 16 August 1817
[12] *Suffolk Chronicle*, 16 August 1817.
[13] *Suffolk Chronicle*, 30 August 1817.
[14] *Suffolk Chronicle*, 8 March 1834; Annual Survey Report for Orwell, 20 November 1837, Lloyd's Register Foundation.
[15] https://en.wikipedia.org/wiki/List_of_ship_launches_in_1818.
[16] https://en.wikipedia.org/wiki/List_of_ship_launches_in_1819; *Ipswich Journal*, 11 September 1819.
[17] *Suffolk Chronicle*, 20 May 1820.
[18] *Suffolk Chronicle*, 20 May 1820.
[19] *Suffolk Chronicle*, 20 September 1820.

Appendix 1

Portrait of the Orwell built at Jabez Bayley's Shipyard, Ipswich (August 1817).
The Trustees of the British Museum (1853,0112.2328).

Persevering, Jabez Bayley continued to negotiate and receive contracts for the construction of large vessels, though there was a marked decline in trade that was affecting the British economy in general. In September 1821 Jabez launched two ships for the British East India Company. These were the *Sir David Scott*, launched on 20 September, and the *William Fairlie*, launched a week later, both of 1,439 tons.[20] Only a month earlier the 74-ton schooner *Henry of Swansea* had been completed.[21] Despite these accomplishments Jabez Bayley continued to lack sufficient funds to thwart insolvency. He was forced to sub-lease the Halifax Shipyard property to his nephew, George Bayley (Jr), and in turn relocate to premises at St Clements, just across the River Orwell though slightly north of his existing yard.[22] Here he primarily built coastal schooners and smaller rowing boats and pleasure craft.[23] However, Jabez was unable to generate enough funds to maintain fiscal stability and in January 1825 was officially declared bankrupt.[24] Most of his remaining assets, including life insurance policies and stock in trade, were advertised for sale.[25] Reporting on the circumstances the local *Ipswich Journal* commented that he was reduced from a

---
[20] *Bury and Norwich Post*, 19 September, 3 October 1821.
[21] *Suffolk Chronicle*, 4 August 1821.
[22] *Bury and Norwich Post*, 12 September 1821.
[23] *Ipswich Journal*, 24 May, 16 August 1823.
[24] *Suffolk Chronicle*, 8 January 1825.
[25] *Ipswich Journal*, 12 February 1825; *Bury and Norwich Post*, 22 June 1825.

'state of usefulness and comfort to one of indigence and inactivity'.[1] The article continued, 'From his extensive engagements, and punctuality in business, the landed proprietor ever found a ready market for his timber, and several hundred industrious artisans an ample field for their exertions. Our regret that these sources of profit and employment have ceased is not lessened, when we reflect that from the talents and unwearied assiduity of Mr. Bayley, several of the finest and best built ships in the East India Company's and other services, first floated triumphantly upon the bosom of the Orwell. Mr. Bayley, on all grounds, seems entitled to public commiseration, and we understand his case has excited general sympathy. A subscription has been begun in his behalf, to be under the management of a Committee of Gentlemen, whose object it will be to appropriate the proceeds to his benefit, and enable him to resume his professional exertions.'[2]

With hundreds of pounds donated to aid in Jabez Bayley's cause, he continued to furnish vessels for the local merchant trades albeit at a significantly reduced output and level. He was, however, most appreciative of the help given to him and his family during this period, in May 1826 posting the following statement in the local press.

> **JABEZ BAYLEY** BEGS respectfully to express his sincere gratitude to his many Friends, whose benevolence has so seasonably met his necessities, that it inspires the best emotions of his heart towards the all gracious providence of God, and all those who have commiserated his case, which otherwise would have been deplorable; his property being wasted by circumstances over which he could exercise no control, and his spirits worn down by continual harassing to the lowest degree, till at length an epileptic fit laid him quite aside, under all which he must have sunk, but for the sympathy and aid of his beneficent friends, by whose liberal subscriptions he has been sustained, and furnished with the means of beginning business again, on a small scale, for the support of his family. He trusts all his Friends believe the principle of gratitude he possesses will ever produce the most fervent desire that the Great Governor of the Universe will render unto them an hundredfold for all their kindness.

Suffolk Chronicle, 20 May 1826.

In February 1826 Jabez Bayley leased his St Clement's yard to his relation and former employee William Bayley (Jr[2]), though the pair may have worked at the site together for some years as Jabez is known to have completed the schooner *Fortitude* there in July 1826 amongst other craft.[3] In January 1831 Jabez Bayley partnered with William Read to return to the Halifax Shipyard where they intended to conduct themselves as both ship and boat builders.[4] In having been the lessee of this particular site for the past 10 years George Bayley (Jr), i.e., Jabez's nephew, thanked his friends and the public for their patronage and support of his shipbuilding venture.[5] During this period George (Jr) had built several vessels including the 202-ton *Sir William Wallace* in 1824; the 112-ton schooner *Hope* launched in March 1825; the 104-ton schooner *Hero* completed in

---
[1] *Ipswich Journal*, 28 May 1825.
[2] *Ipswich Journal*, 28 May 1825.
[3] https://en.wikipedia.org/wiki/List_of_ship_launches_in_1826.
[4] *Suffolk Chronicle*, 1 January 1831.
[5] *Bury and Norwich Post*, 19 September 1821; *Suffolk Chronicle*, 1 January 1831.

July 1825; the *Ceres*, a steamship for a private owner completed in August 1825; and the paddle steamer *Ipswich* launched in November of that same year.[6] In April 1826 George (Jr) completed a cutter by the name of *Magnet*, with the *Orwell of London* launched a few months later.[7] The sloop *Clifton* was also launched from his yard that same year as was the 110-ton schooner *Fame* and the 202-ton smack *Earl of Wemyss*.[8]

In mid-1826 George Bayley (Jr) installed a Morton's Patent Slip at the Halifax Shipyard, supplementing his business activities with repair and overhaul work.[9] Following his relinquishment of the lease on his shipyard in January 1831 to his uncle Jabez, George (Jr) moved to Rotherhithe near London on the River Thames, i.e., the town where his grandfather John and great-uncle William had been born and undertaken their boat building apprenticeships, where he established himself as a shipbreaker. Unfortunately the operation failed to make a profit and he was forced to declare bankruptcy in February 1834.[10] A month later George (Jr) was appointed a surveyor of the Port of London for Lloyd's Shipping, a very prominent position which he maintained for several decades. He died in London in August 1882 at the age of 84 leaving a healthy estate to his family in the realm of £18,000.[11] In contrast his uncle Jabez Bayley had died on 23 September 1834 in Ipswich at the age of 63 near penniless.[12]

Turning our attention back to William Bayley (Jr^2), the son of William Bayley (Jr) and Mary (nee Rogers), as well as the first cousin-once-removed of Jabez Bayley and second cousin-once removed of George Bayley (Jr), it is important to recall that William (Jr^2) had moved to Ipswich from his family's home in Burnham-on-Crouch as a teenager, taking up an apprenticeship in shipbuilding with Jabez Bayley. His period of indenture had coincided with the Napoleonic Wars such that the shipyard was extremely busy constructing vessels for the Royal Navy.

The Napoleonic Wars ended, however, with the defeat of the French during the Battle of Waterloo in June 1815. The Second Treaty of Paris, signed on 20 November of that year, marked the official completion of the conflict. Possibly sensing a period of peace and stability, just over a month prior on 17 October 1815, William Bayley (Jr^2) married Mary Sage of nearby Freston, a town located four miles to the south of Ipswich.[13] He was 24 years of age while she was 21. The couple settled in Ipswich where William (Jr^2) continued to work for his relative Jabez Bayley, including participating with construction of the 1,366-ton *Orwell* launched on 28 August 1817.

Shortly following, with a growing family to support, combined with the realisation that his employee and mentor Jabez Bayley was facing financial difficulties, William Bayley (Jr^2) began building vessels of his own accord. In 1819, for example, he completed the schooner *Union*.[14] Two years later, coinciding with the removal of Jabez Bayely from the Halfax Shipyard site and its takeover by George Bayley (Jr), William Bayley (Jr^2) opted to take a risk and establish his own yard. While shipyards on the River Orwell were likely found unsuitable to his needs initially, Woodbridge offered just the location.

---

[6] *Suffolk Chronicle*, 17 July 1824, 5 March, 16 July 1825; https://en.wikipedia.org/wiki/List_of_ship_launches_in_1825.
[7] *Ipswich Journal*, 15 April, 8 July 1826; *Suffolk Chronicle*, 13 May 1826; https://en.wikipedia.org/wiki/List_of_ship_launches_in_1826.
[8] *Bury and Norwich Post*, 18 January 1826; *Suffolk Chronicle*, 13 May 1826; *Ipswich Journal*, 27 May 1826.
[9] *Ipswich Journal*, 12 August 1826.
[10] *Ipswich Journal*, 28 May 1825.
[11] England & Wales, National Probate Calendar (Index of Wills and Adminstrations), 1858-1882 for George Bayley.
[12] *Ipswich Journal*, 27 September 1834.
[13] Marriage Bond for William Bayley and Mary Sage, Suffolk Record Office.
[14] https://en.wikipedia.org/wiki/List_of_ship_launches_in_1819.

Part of the county of Suffolk, some 60 miles to the north-east of Burnham-on-Crouch and seven miles north-east of Ipswich, Woodbridge was another port town reliant on maritime trades to support the local economy. It was also home to rope and sailmakers thereby offering a more complete service to vessel builders, repairers and owners. However, it was still a rather small town with a population of around 3,000, slightly more than Burnham-on-Crouch though substantially less than that of Ipswich which was approaching 15,000 inhabitants. Woodbridge's close proximity to the latter nevertheless aided in the availability of materials, suppliers and business opportunities.

Post-1815, coinciding with the end of the Napoleonic Wars, combined with the abolition of the East India Company's monopoly on trade with India, as well as the abolishment of slavery, the bountiful years for commercial shipbuilders were over. It had been a long wave of prosperity for operators like Jabez Bayley, but the shipyards were now finding it harder to survive. For the various facets of the Bayley family still operating yards in Ipswich and Burnham-on-Crouch, those that survived this period were mostly small family-based businesses able to downsize in hard times. Given demand had been high, these smaller operators had spent little resources modernising their yards and introducing new technologies. Instead, they were often rudimentary worksites with accommodation for woodpiles, saw pits, provisions for blacksmiths, and storage sheds. Access to a waterway was of course essential, with a gently sloping beach preferred, as well as sufficient depth with which to launch a vessel at the right tide.

One of the primary resources needed for boat and ship building was timber, with English oak considered the species of choice by the Royal Navy as well as most merchant and commercial boat and ship owners. Its presence in the vast forests to the north of Ipswich and Woodbridge was considered pivotal to the development and continued longevity of boat and ship building operations within these two areas. By relocating to Woodbridge William Bayley (Jr^2) was capitalising not only on the availability of English oak for his commercial use, but also its cheaper cost to procure since it was grown nearby.

After establishing his shipyard at Woodbridge in the vicinity of the Lime Kiln Quay, William Bayley (Jr^2) soon got to work. He also sought help from relatives with his new venture. Of note, his brother-in-law Charles Bull relocated to the area from Burnham-on-Crouch with his family to work for William Bayley (Jr^2). Charles Bull, a mariner, had married Mary Rogers Bayley, the eldest sister of William Bayley (Jr^2), at Burham-on-Crouch in February 1807. Between this year and 1816 the couple had produced four children: Mary Rogers Bayley Bull (1807), Emmaretta Rogers Bayley Bull (1810), Charles Bayley Bull (1813) and William Charles Bayley Bull (1816).[1] With the Bull family's relocation to Woodbridge around 1820, another daughter, Keturah Elizabeth Bull, appears to have been born shortly thereafter.

While William Bayley (Jr^2)'s shipyard initially focused on repair and overhaul work, as well as the sale of large quantities of timber, including oak slabs, by 1823 it was producing vessels.[2] In August of that year the sloop *Mary* was completed for a private owner.[3] In April 1825 he completed the 81-ton schooner *Liverpool* as well as the sloop *Ranger* a few months later.[4] In May 1826 William Bayley (Jr^2) launched the merchant ship *Jane* from his Woodbridge-based yard.[5]

---

[1] Bull family tree on ancestry.com.au compiled by the author.
[2] *Suffolk Chronicle*, 10 March 1821; *Ipswich Journal*, 9 August 1823.
[3] https://en.wikipedia.org/wiki/List_of_ship_launches_in_1823.
[4] *Suffolk Chronicle*, 9 April 1825; https://en.wikipedia.org/wiki/List_of_ship_launches_in_1825.
[5] https://en.wikipedia.org/wiki/List_of_ship_launches_in_1826.

Appendix 1

In February 1826 William Bayley (Jr²) announced that he was relocating his shipyard from Woodbridge to Ipswich, establishing his operations in St Clements at the yard operated by his relation and mentor Jabez Bayley.[6] It would prove to be a pivotal decision for William (Jr²), heralding a successful career as a shipbuilder up until his death in 1857. However, for reasons not known, the Bull family did not make the move to the banks of the River Orwell, instead opting to return to Burnham-on-Crouch.

With regards to the output of William Bayley (Jr²), a few months after establishing his yard at Ipswich he launched the 150-ton brig *Hannah* to be based out of Harwich.[7] In May 1827 he completed the schooner *Flora* for John Roberts, that same month he announced that a Morton's Patent Slip had been installed on site.[8] In June 1827 he launched the schooner *Emily*, shortly followed by the smack *Charlotte*.[9] In April 1828 William Bayley (Jr²) completed the schooner *Thames* for John Roberts and Jeffrey Smith.[10]

The 1830s was another busy period for William Bayley (Jr²) whom by now was not only building vessels but also retaining full or part shares in several of them, soon becoming a shipowner with his own extensive fleet. Of the vessels that his yard is known to have built, in August 1831 the 200-ton schooner *Mona* was launched, built to the order of John Roberts of London.[11] The schooner *Superb* was then completed in April 1832 for John Christie and partners.[12] Next came the *Prima Donna*, a merchant vessel built to the order of H. S. Gibbs & Co. and launched in March 1833.[13] For John Christie and partners the schooner *Rapid* was launched in June 1833.[14] In July 1834 the schooner *Clementina* was completed, followed a few months later by the schooner *Enchantress*.[15]

In April 1836 the schooner *Letitia* was completed at the St Clement's yard of William Bayley (Jr²), followed a few months later by the sloop *Sophia*.[16] In January 1837 came the 70-ton sloop *Swallow* for a Mr Garrod, and the brigantine *Triumph* for a private owner.[17] That same year, now operating as William Bayley and Sons, the yard launched the *Tradesman*, a merchant vessel for a private owner, and the 90-ton schooner *Premier* intended for the Mediterranean trade.[18] Messrs Bayley then launched the brig *Queen Victoria* in February 1838, the brig *Courier* in April 1838, the schooner *Monarch* in July 1838, the schooner *Briton's Pride* in September 1838, the schooner *Rainbow* in November 1838, and the schooner *Queen* at some point during that same year.[19] In 1839 came at least six vessels, including the schooners *Jane*, *Quiz*, *Minerva*, *Eclipse* and *Azorian*.[20] With demand high, by this period in time William Bayley (Jr²) was also operating a secondary yard at Burnham-on-Crouch, employing his brother-in-law Charles Bull as a shipwright.[21]

The 1840s was a decade filled with the construction of new vessels for the Ipswich shipyard of William Bayley and Sons. In 1840 the schooners *Anglesey*, *Visitor* and *Parroquet* were completed,

---

[6] *Suffolk Chronicle*, 11 February 1826.
[7] *Ipswich Journal*, 8 July 1826.
[8] *Ipswich Journal*, 19 May 1827; https://en.wikipedia.org/wiki/List_of_ship_launches_in_1828.
[9] https://en.wikipedia.org/wiki/List_of_ship_launches_in_1827.
[10] https://en.wikipedia.org/wiki/List_of_ship_launches_in_1827.
[11] *Bury and Norwich Post*, 17 August 1831.
[12] https://en.wikipedia.org/wiki/List_of_ship_launches_in_1828.
[13] https://en.wikipedia.org/wiki/List_of_ship_launches_in_1833.
[14] https://en.wikipedia.org/wiki/List_of_ship_launches_in_1833.
[15] *Bury and Suffolk Herald*, 2 July 1834; *Suffolk Chronicle*, 11 October 1834.
[16] https://en.wikipedia.org/wiki/List_of_ship_launches_in_1836; *Suffolk Chronicle*, 1 October 1836.
[17] https://en.wikipedia.org/wiki/List_of_ship_launches_in_1837; *Chelmsford Chronicle*, 13 January 1837.
[18] https://en.wikipedia.org/wiki/List_of_ship_launches_in_1837; *Suffolk Chronicle*, 19 August 1837.
[19] https://en.wikipedia.org/wiki/List_of_ship_launches_in_1838; *Suffolk Chronicle*, 1 December 1838.
[20] https://en.wikipedia.org/wiki/List_of_ship_launches_in_1839; *Ipswich Journal*, 16 February, 28 September, 14 December 1839; *Suffolk Chronicle*, 4 May 1839.
[21] *Chelmsford Chronicle*, 24 May 1839; *Essex Standard*, 25 November 1842.

as well as the aptly-named brig *William Bayley,* with the schooners *Doctor, Rhoda* and *Invincible* launched the following year, in addition to a brig.[1] Mid-to-late 1841 additionally saw William Bayley (Jr[2]) compensated by the Ipswich Council for the forced removal of his shipyard operations, including a house, buildings, machinery and stock in trade, to a new shipyard built on reclaimed land a few hundred yards to the south of his old yard. Receiving £1,100 for the relocation, the former St Clement's site was turned into a wet dock.[2] With their shipyard's reestablishment then underway, 1842 saw William Bayley and Sons complete at least two more schooners: the *Laura Ann* and *Goddess*.[3] The former marked the 16th vessel constructed by William Bayley (Jr[2]) within a decade.[4]

Taking several years to fully complete their new shipyard, in July 1845 William Bayley and Sons launched the 220-ton barque *Ipswich,* the property of J. Le Sueur of Jersey and intended for the Brazil trade.[5] In the years that followed came the 184-ton brigantine schooner *John Cobhold* (1847), the 137-ton schooner *Mary Bayley* (1847), the 367-ton barque *British Tar* (1848), and the 329-ton West Indiaman *Mary Montague* (1849).[6]

By the 1850s the sons of William Bayley (Jr[2]), William Sage Bayley and James Rogers Bayley, had taken over their father's shipyard, continuing to build on his legacy for many decades. Regulatory changes and wage reform, however, resulted in a depressed shipbuilding industry with foreign competition also thwarting the new vessel market. Still, the two brothers persisted, building many larger vessels up until the late 1880s, as well as maintaining an interest in commercial craft that plied domestic and foreign trading routes.[7]

From watermen and boat builders to shipbuilders and shipowners, the Bayley family had certainly taken advantage of the maritime resources endemic to their communities and further afield, as well as local, national and international demands within these industries, making significant impacts over four generations. Some members had profited from these ventures while others had failed. Still, determination, tenacity and family support appear to have been key factors driving these men and their offspring to continue in these trades. Just where would the next generation lead us?

It is at this point in our story that we return to focus our attention on Charles Bull, his wife Mary Rogers Bull (nee Bayley) and their children. Of note, three of their offspring, Charles, Bayley and Harriet, would in time dispatch of the Bull surname instead opting to go by Bayley. By the late 1840s all three would also be settled in Van Diemen's Land, now referred to as Tasmania, successful and prominent members of a burgeoning maritime industry.

---

[1] https://en.wikipedia.org/wiki/List_of_ship_launches_in_1840; https://en.wikipedia.org/wiki/List_of_ship_launches_in_1841; *Suffolk Chronicle,* 29 February, 15 August, 17 October 1840, 23 January, 20 November 1841; *Bury and Suffolk Herald,* 29 April 1840; *Ipswich Journal,* 24 April, 1 May 1841.
[2] *Suffolk Chronicle,* 9 January 1841.
[3] https://en.wikipedia.org/wiki/List_of_ship_launches_in_1842.
[4] *Ipswich Journal,* 16 April 1842.
[5] *Suffolk Chronicle,* 12 July 1845.
[6] *Suffolk Chronicle,* 3 April, 14 August 1847; *Bury and Suffolk Herald,* 23 August 1848; *Ipswich Journal,* 8 September 1849.
[7] *Suffolk Chronicle,* 23 December 1871.

Appendix 2
The Bulls of Burnham-on-Crouch

As stated in the previous appendix Mary Rogers Bayley, born on 11 September 1787 in Burnham-on-Crouch, Essex, was the eldest daughter of William Bayley (Jr), a boat builder, and his wife Mary (nee Rogers). On 18 February 1807, at the age of 19, she married Charles Bull in the local parish church, St Mary the Virgin. Witnesses to the ceremony, performed by licence as opposed to banns, were Thomas Coker Rogers, the bride's uncle on her maternal side, and his soon-to-be wife Elizabeth Raven. Built in the eleventh century, the church of St Mary the Virgin was a place familiar to the Bayley family being the location of many baptisms, marriages and burials going back several decades.

Marriage record for Charles Bull and Mary Rogers Bayley, St Mary the Virgin, Burnham-on-Crouch, England, 18 February 1807.
Essex Archives Online.

Five years older than his bride, Charles Bull had been born in 1782 in Maldon, a port and market town situated 12 miles to the north-east of Burnham-on-Crouch, the eldest son of Charles Bull (Sr) and his wife Elizabeth. He was baptised at St Mary the Virgin Church in Maldon on 10 November 1782, likely only a few weeks of age at the time.[8]

---
[8] Essex Baptism Index 1538-1917 for Charles Ball.

Baptism record for Charles Bull, St Mary the Virgin, Maldon, England, 10 November 1782.
Essex Archives Online.

Charles Bull (Sr) was a mariner, in all probability employed on one of the many coastal trading vessels operating out of the port of Maldon. It is therefore not surprising that his son Charles followed him into the same profession. However, instead of remaining in Maldon, by his late teens Charles had relocated to Burnham-on-Crouch where he found work, possibly initially serving an apprenticeship on board a dredger involved in the oyster industry. Unfortunately records related to Charles' specific area of employment are lacking. Working-class families from that era generally left little in terms of a paperwork trail. It is only through baptism, marriage and death records of Charles and Mary Bull's children and a few newspaper advertisements that we can form a picture of the family unit in their early years, albeit rather piecemeal.

The first child born to Charles and Mary Bull was a daughter named Mary Rogers Bayley Bull. She was baptised on 27 September 1807 at the age of five weeks at St Mary the Virgin Church in Burnham-on-Crouch, indicating that Mary Bull was likely around three months pregnant at the time of their marriage.[1] Just under three years later, on 29 July 1810, Charles and Mary Bull's second child, a daughter named Emmaretta Rogers Bayley Bull was born. She was baptised at St Mary the Virgin Church just under a month following, on 26 August.[2]

[1] Essex Record Office Baptism for Mary Rogers Bailey Bull in 1807.
[2] Essex Record Office Baptism for Emmaritta Rogers Bayley Bull in 1810.

St Mary the Virgin Church, Burnham-on-Crouch, Essex, England.
https://stmarysburnham.co.uk/prayer-cycle/.

Two years later, in late November 1812, an interesting advertisement was published in newspapers across the Essex and Suffolk regions detailing the sale of cargo from the wrecked 351-ton ship *See Einhorn* that had become stranded off the coast of Essex, just south of Burnham-on-Crouch, on 27 October.[3] The vessel had been on a voyage from Archangel, Russia, to London at the time, carrying 130 tons of flax from Riga, 10 tons of hemp, 280 casks of soap tallow, two casks of hog's bristles and a quantity of red wood.[4]

Likely being in the right place at the right time Charles Bull near certainly came across the stranded vessel, risking his own safety to successfully aid those on board. It was an interesting point in time to be involved in ship salvage operations. The Napoleonic Wars were still ongoing in 1812, as was the War of 1812 between England and America. Piracy and privateering on the seas were rife, particularly between naval vessels; enemy property and assets being highly sought after and a strategic prize of war. It was also a time when contraband cargoes from France were making their way across the English Channel, the Napoleonic Wars having coincided with a ban on trade between the two countries. British consumers, however, were still eager for these goods with smuggling activities widespread and the Kent, Suffolk and Essex coasts a haven for those looking to offload goods in these less populated though accessible and navigable locations.

Ship salvaging, in contrast, was considered quite different to piracy, privateering and smuggling and had its own regulations. Salvors were rewarded for their efforts, with the prize given dependent on complicating factors, including the difficulty of the salvage, the length and risk involved in the operation, and the value of the cargo. There was also a legal stipulation that any cargo or item from a vessel that washed ashore could be claimed by a salvor who in turn would receive half of its value.

Ipswich Journal, 28 November 1812.

---

[3] *Bury and Norwich Post*, 2 December 1812.
[4] *Ipswich Journal*, 21 November 1812.

While it is not known to what extent Charles Bull was involved in the wreck and salvage of the stranded *See Einhorn*, it can be assumed that since his name is listed in the advertisement for the sale of its cargo that it was considerable and he was a primary party to the salvage operations. Given the cargo appears to have remained in good condition, it would also have been a profitable venture for Charles. Not only a good deed in the service of aiding mariners in need of rescue, his share of the funds realised from the sale of the cargo would have gone to support his expanding family. Though respectable the Bull family was ultimately working class, living on limited means and a meagre wage. The family's plight was also entirely reliant on Charles' work. Sickness and injury would have limited his ability to provide for his wife and children; any extra income would thus have been a welcome reprieve from the day-to-day slog of his labours, particularly since another baby was on the way. Though records of his birth and subsequent baptism have yet to be found, at some point during 1813 Mary Bull gave birth to the couple's third child and first-born son, Charles Bayley Bull. He too would follow in his father and grandfather's footsteps into the maritime industry.

In general, however, the situation of men working as mariners during this period was tentative. The plight of ordinary sailors perhaps no less highlighted by a petition made by Charles Bull (Sr) in 1817. By the end of the Napoleonic Wars Charles (Sr) was under financial distress and approaching 65 years of age. Living in the parish of All Saints with St Peter in Maldon, he and his wife Elizabeth had applied to Trinity House for relief.[1] Established in 1514 by Royal Charter, Trinity House was a corporation intended to not only build and maintain lighthouses and navigational buoys but also safeguard the welfare of mariners and other seafarers, including by providing monetary support and pensions to those in older age and/or unable to work due to injury or illness.

Though it is not known if the couple's petition was successful, Charles (Sr) was one of thousands of British mariners involved in coastal trade and advancing in age at a time when retirement years were generally not buffered by any personal savings. The men and their families mostly lived a precarious existence with their longevity often associated with hardship, particularly if ill-health meant that they were unable to continue working in the industry. Support often came from adult children, but if they too had large families to provide for and were also living by tight means, this help would have barely kept an elderly couple out of poverty. The availability of work for mariners was also at the mercy of changing trade patterns and demand. The years immediately following the end of the Napoleonic Wars, for example, were associated with low agricultural harvests which in turn resulted in a decline in coastal trade, particularly impacting the Essex and Suffolk corn trades. This may have been one of the reasons why Charles (Sr) sought aid from Trinity House.

Given Charles Bull (Sr) and his wife Elizabeth had several adult children living nearby, including their son Charles and his family in Burnham-on-Crouch, there were multiple pathways available to help maintain this couple in their twilight years, that is on the proviso that their children were in a position to provide that support. Their situation could also have been temporary; illness or injury forcing Charles (Sr) out of work for only a short period of time. Unfortunately records related to the movement of merchant vessels and their crew are lacking for this period. It was not until the 1830s that the British government began mandating the collection of information with regard to crew lists, agreements and vessel logs.

The movement of the Bull family is also hard to trace during this period due to the sparseness of records stemming from the small town of Burnham-on-Crouch in which they

---

[1] British Mariners, Trinity House Calendars 1787-1854 for Charles Bull.

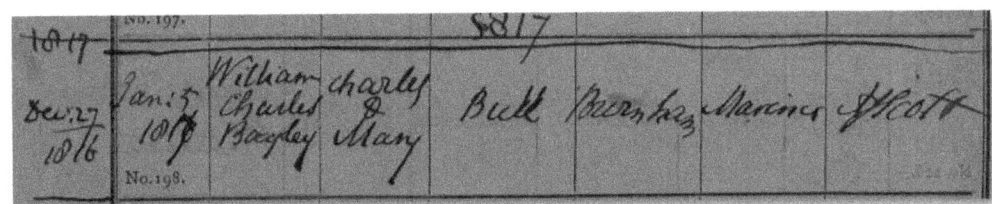

Baptism record for William Charles Bayley Bull, St Mary the Virgin, Burnham-on-Crouch, England, 5 January 1817.
Essex Archives Online.

lived, as well as their lack of interaction with the various institutions that existed at the time, including the local parish church. What we do know is that another son was born to Charles and Mary Bull on 27 December 1816. William Charles Bayley Bull was baptised 10 days later on 5 January 1817 at St Mary the Virgin Church in Burnham-on-Crouch.

While Charles Bull had been employed as a mariner up until this point in his married life, perhaps seeking to gain more secure and permanent employment in 1820 he and his wife Mary Bull and their four children relocated to Woodbridge in Suffolk. Situated 60 miles to the north of Burnham-on-Crouch, the family likely made the trip by sea given roads were underdeveloped in the region at the time and water transport was easier and more widely available. The location offered a reunion between various branches of the Bayley family, as well as the opportunity for Charles Bull to gain experience in the shipbuilding industry.

Here, working for his brother-in-law William Bayley (Jr[2]) at a newly-established yard in Woodbridge in the vicinity of the Lime Kiln Quay, the operation initially focused on repair and overhaul work, as well as the sale of large quantities of timber, including oak slabs. It was a period of change for the Bull family, both professionally and personally. Again, though records are lacking, at some point during 1820 Charles and Mary Bull welcomed another child, with the birth of the their third daughter Keturah Elizabeth Bull.

The shipyard was also soon prospering with the launch of new vessels. However, the Bull family endured devastating heartbreak when their youngest son William died in late August 1823 at the age of six years. He was buried at the Cuttings Lane Independent Chapel in Woodbridge on 28 August.

Burial record for William Charles Bayley Bull, Cuttings Lane Independent Chapel, Woodbridge, England, 28 August 1823.
England & Wales, Non-Conformist and Non-Parochial Registers, 1567-1936.

On 14 September 1823, i.e., less than three weeks following the death of their son William, Charles and Mary Bull welcomed another child, a son they named Bayley Bull.[2] Again, there are no birth or baptism records for the child, possibly because of a lack of records for the independent church where they worshiped.

---

[2] Britain, Merchant Seamen, 1835-1857 for Bayley Bull.

While Charles Bull continued to work for his brother-in-law during the intervening years, in February 1826 William Bayley (Jr²) began the process of relocating his shipyard from Woodbridge to Ipswich.[1] For reasons unknown, but possibly due to family or personal circumstances, the Bull family decided not to make the move further east, instead opting to return to Burnham-on-Crouch. The family by now comprised Charles (43 years of age), Mary (38 years of age) and their five children: Mary (18), Emmaretta (15), Charles (13), Keturah (6) and Bayley (2). The unit soon re-established themselves in Burnham-on-Crouch with Charles resuming work as a mariner. With their older children entering their formative teenage years, as was the custom at the time for working-class families it was essential for them to gain employment with the over-arching goals of both learning a trade and helping to support their family. Education had been a priority for the family, however, with all of Charles and Mary Bull's children able to read and write, obvious skills that put them in good stead for the future. There was also another expansion of the family with the birth of the couple's last child, a daughter named Harriet, born some time in 1828.

With regards to their older children, while Mary and Emmaretta very likely found work in service Charles entered the maritime industry, again following in the pathway set by his father and grandfather. However, he would soon travel to waters far beyond the coastal regions of Essex and Suffolk, in the process making a name for himself in an emerging industry that would become the foundation of the Port of Hobart Town in Van Diemen's Land: the whaling industry.

The 1830s and 1840s would prove to be pivotal decades for all members of the Bull family. From a professional standpoint its patriarch Charles Bull maintained his role as a mariner, as well as becoming an itinerant shipbuilder. Owing to high demand, his brother-in-law William Bayley (Jr²) had established a satellite shipyard at Burnham-on-Crouch in the early 1830s where several vessels were launched, including the schooner *Speedwell* completed in May 1839 to the order of Samuel Richmond and intended for coastal and foreign trades.[2] Employing his brother Rogers James Bayley as foreman and Charles Bull as a shipwright, the yard remained in operation for several years.[3] It was ultimately advertised for sale in November 1842, complete with 100 oak trees, 300 oak and elm tops and various other plant and equipment.[4]

Essex Standard, 29 November 1842.

---

[1] *Suffolk Chronicle*, 11 February 1826.
[2] *Essex Herald*, 10 November 1835; *Chelmsford Chronicle*, 24 May 1839.
[3] *Chelmsford Chronicle*, 24 May 1839, 15 January 1841; *Essex Standard*, 25 November 1842.
[4] *Essex Standard*, 25 November 1842.

By the mid-1830s records regarding the movement of merchant mariners were fortunately being collected and it is through this dataset that we are able to trace Charles Bull and his youngest son Bayley, albeit the dates are rather patchy. Of note, Charles Bull is listed as working on board the vessel *Iris* in late 1835 and early 1836.[5] The data provided on his record is quite interesting though takes some time to interpret.

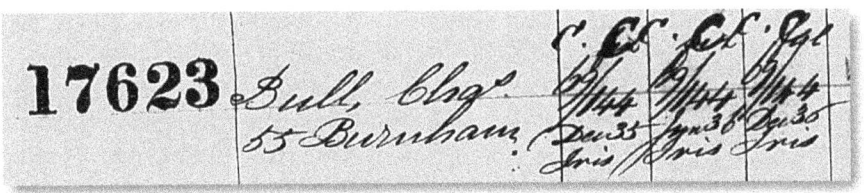

Charles Bull's listing in the Register of Merchant Seamen, 1835-36.
Britain, Merchant Seamen, 1835-1857.

From the record above we are able to glean the following information. First, Charles Bull's unique registration number was 17623. He was 55 years of age at the time of registration and he was from Burnham, i.e., Burnham-on-Crouch. The next three columns are coded but reveal that he was the captain of a coastal trading craft named *Iris* and that between December 1835 and December 1836 he rotated between two ports, with the number 69 referring to Maldon. Unfortunately the port designated number 144 is not currently known, though it is assumed to be one of the smaller coastal ports located nearby, possibly Burnham-on-Crouch.

Further down the same register is the listing for Charles Bull's youngest son Bayley, then aged 13 years though claiming he was actually 19 years of age in 1836. Similar to his father's record, at the time the dataset was collected he was involved in the coastal trade, working as a seaman on board the trading craft *Friends* which was plying between the two ports of Maldon (designated number 69) and Southwold on the Suffolk coast (designated number 91).

Bayley Bull's listing in the Register of Merchant Seamen, 1835-36.
Britain, Merchant Seamen, 1835-1857.

There is no record for Charles Bull's oldest son Charles Bayley Bull on the Register of Merchant Seamen for this period. Unfortunately his movements during the mid-1830s are difficult to trace, though he undoubtedly spent part of his teenage years involved in the coastal trade plying out of Burnham-on-Crouch or Maldon. He then made his way to London where he found work on board a larger foreign-trading vessel, making several voyages to Australia where by the late 1830s he was based in Van Diemen's Land. We have discussed his history in more detail in the preceding chapters. For Charles and Mary Bull's three eldest daughters, however, they were also making their way to new towns and communities and forming new relationships.

---
[5] Britain, Merchant Seamen, 1835-1857 for Charles Bull.

On 29 July 1838 at All Saints Church in Poplar, a neighbourhood of London on the north side of the River Thames opposite Greenwich, Emmaretta Rogers Bayley Bull married William Graveley. While Emmaretta was by now 28 years of age, her new husband was a 35-year-old widower employed as a baker and confectioner. He was also the father of four children by his first marriage to Sarah (nee Going), whose mother had coincidentally married Daniel Rogers (Jr), the son of the Daniel Rogers of Burnham Oyster Company fame, and thus a distant relation of the Bull family. This was very likely how the connection was made. Following the ceremony Emmaretta joined her new husband and his family, moving in to their home at 20 High Street in Poplar.[1] A son, Charles William Henry Graveley, was born to the couple a year after their marriage and was baptised at All Saints Church in Poplar on 13 October 1839.[2]

Two months following the birth of Charles and Mary Bull's first grandchild, their eldest daughter married. On 19 December 1839 at St Nicholas Church in Deptford near London, Mary Rogers Bayley Bull married Stephen Park by banns. She was 32 years of age and listed her residence as Mitre Place, Limehouse, which was a neighbourhood on the north bank of the River Thames. A few miles to the west of Poplar, it was known for its infrastructure associated with the maritime industry. In contrast Stephen Park was a porter at the Greyhound Inn in Greenwich, on the opposite side of the River Thames. Witnesses to the marriage were John Synes and Elizabeth Taylor. For reasons not known, however, the marriage was not a success and Mary would eventually move back to Burnham-on-Crouch, several decades later living with her parents, likely as their chief carer in old age. She later moved to Hobart, Tasmania.

Marriage record for Mary Rogers Bayley Bull and Stephen Park, St Nicholas Church, Deptford, London, 19 December 1839.
London, England, Church of England Marriages and Banns, 1754-1938.

The 1840s was a decade filled with notable events for the Bull family, some celebratory while others were absolutely devastating. The 1841 Census for England lists Charles Bull, his wife Mary Bull and their two youngest children, Bayley and Harriet, as living in Burnham-on-Crouch where Charles was employed as an oyster dredger.[3] Though Bayley had been working in the coastal trade for several years and was by now 17 years of age, there is no occupation listed for him in the document. By this point in time Charles and Mary Bull's oldest son Charles was residing in Australia and their three eldest daughters were based in London, two of them married, though Mary Rogers Bayley Bull (now Park) is not listed as living with her husband Stephen in Greenwich and has yet to be located in the census in general.[4]

---
[1] 1839 Pigot's Directory for William Graveley.
[2] London, England, Church of England Births and Baptisms, 1813-1924 for Charles William Henry Graveley.
[3] 1841 Census for Charles Bull.
[4] 1841 Census for Stephen Park.

Just over a month after the census was taken, the first of its kind in Britain, Emmaretta's husband William Graveley died. He was buried at All Saints Church in Poplar on 18 July 1841.[5] Emmaretta was left with one child and several step-children in her charge, though she was no doubt helped by relations with monetary support and care.

Another family wedding connecting the Bull and Rogers families of Burnham-on-Crouch took place on 5 June 1842 when Charles and Mary Bull's third daughter, Keturah Elizabeth Bull, married Isaac Rogers at St Alfege Church in Greenwich.[6] Employed as a sail maker at the time of the wedding and living in Bell Street, Greenwich, 29-year-old Isaac was the son of Daniel Rogers (Jr), i.e., Mary Bull's brother making Isaac her first cousin. Witnesses to the event were Keturah's sisters Mary and Emmaretta.

Marriage record for Keturah Elizabeth Bull and Isaac Rogers, St Alphege Church, Greenwich, London, 5 June 1842.
London, England, Church of England Marriages and Banns, 1754-1938.

Sadly, less than a year following her marriage to Isaac Rogers, Keturah died. She was 23 years of age and was buried somewhere in Poplar.[7] A year later, on 5 May 1844 at All Saints Church in West Ham, Essex, her sister Emmaretta, by now also a widow, married Isaac Rogers, resulting in another merging of the two families.[8] A son named Isaac and a daughter named Mary Emmaretta would be born in Poplar to the couple in the succeeding years.[9]

With all of these events taking place within a matter of a few years, there were likely many letters being carried across the oceans between Van Diemen's Land and England relaying the news. The letters sent by Charles Bayley Bull (now referred to as Charles Bayley) had their own information to relay however, including how his escapades in the whaling industry were faring and, of course, that of his own marriage. A long way from the small and humble working-class town of Burnham-on-Crouch in Essex, Charles Bayley was certainly making a name for himself, as has been detailed herein.

---

[5] London, England, Church of England Deaths and Burials, 1813-2003 for Charles Graveley.
[6] London, England, Church of England Marriages and Banns, 1754-1940 for Keturah Elizabeth Bull.
[7] England & Wales, Civil Registration Death Index, 1837-1915 for Keturah Elizabeth Rogers.
[8] Essex, England, Church of England Marriages, 1754-1937 for Emmaretta Roger Bayley Graveley.
[9] 1851 England Census for Emmaretta Rogers.

Appendix 3
Royal Navy Vessels built by Jabez Bayley

Year	Name	Tons	Type	Guns
1804	Daring	177	Gunboat Brig	12
1805	Hearty	180	Gunboat Brig	12/14
1805	Imogen	282	Brig	16
1805	Orestes	282	Brig	16
1805	Julia	282	Brig	16
1806	Favourite	343	Sloop (Ship)	16
1806	Peacock	382	Sloop (Brig)	18
1806	Sappho	382	Sloop (Brig)	18
1806	Barracouta	382	Sloop (Brig)	18
1807	Jasper	235	Sloop (Brig)	10
1808	Onyx	235	Sloop (Brig)	10
1808	Hope	235	Sloop (Brig)	10
1808	Drake	235	Sloop (Brig)	10
1808	Rosario	235	Sloop (Brig)	10
1808	Beaver	235	Sloop (Brig)	10
1809	Nimrod	382	Sloop (Brig)	18
1812	Espeigle	382	Sloop (Brig)	18
1812	Jaseur	382	Sloop (Brig)	18
1813	Fly	382	Sloop (Brig)	18
1813	Harlequin	382	Sloop (Brig)	18
1813	Harrier	382	Sloop (Brig)	18
1813	Esk	455	Sloop (Ship)	20
1813	Leven	455	Sloop (Ship)	20
1814	Dee	444	Sloop (Ship)	26/28
1814	Diligence	314	Transport	None

Appendix 4
Whaling Voyages of Charles and James Bayley out of Hobart Town

Vessel	Name and Role	Departure Date	Return Date	Location	Cargo and Value
Wallaby	Charles Bayley, Chief Officer & Captain	6 April 1839	19 August 1839	Southern coast of mainland Australia	Whale oil and bone
Wallaby	Charles Bayley, Captain	4 September 1839	28 October 1839	Coastal waters of Van Diemen's Land	Whale oil and bone
Wallaby	Charles Bayley, Captain	12 December 1839	5 March 1840	Intercolonial trade between Hobart Town, Melbourne and Launceston	Livestock, cargo and passengers
Wallaby	Charles Bayley, Captain & Chief Officer	7 April 1840	23 October 1840	Southern coast of mainland Australia	Whale oil and bone
Wallaby	Charles Bayley, Captain	31 December 1840	2 November 1842	Bass Strait, Pacific Ocean, equator, Coral Sea, Tasman Sea, south seas whaling grounds, Chatham Islands	80 tuns sperm whale oil, 50 tuns black whale oil, whale bone. £4,200
Fortitude	Charles Bayley, Captain	13 January 1843	15 October 1843	South seas whaling grounds	25 tuns of sperm whale oil, 212 tuns of black whale oil, 7 tons whale bone. £11,000
Fortitude	Charles Bayley, Captain James Bayley, Mate	10 November 1843	15 April 1844	South seas whaling grounds	37 tuns of sperm whale oil, 50 tuns of black whale oil, 2 tons of whale bone, 50 pounds of ambergris. £5,300
Fortitude	Charles Bayley, Captain James Bayley, Mate	8 May 1844	22 February 1845	South seas whaling grounds	20 tuns of sperm whale oil, 130 tuns of black whale oil, 6 tons of whale bone. £6,500
Fortitude	Charles Bayley, Captain James Bayley, Mate	2 May 1845	15 March 1846	South seas whaling grounds, east coast of mainland Australia	60 tuns of sperm whale oil, 60 tuns of black whale oil, 2 tons of whale bone. £7,500
Fortitude	Charles Bayley, Captain	20 April 1846	17 October 1846	South seas whaling grounds, east coast of Van Diemen's Land	8 tuns of sperm whale oil, 134 tuns of black whale oil, 5 tons of whale bone. £6,000
Fortitude	Charles Bayley, Captain	5 November 1846	1 July 1847	South seas whaling grounds	12 tuns of sperm whale oil. £1,000
Fortitude	Charles Bayley, Captain	17 November 1847	28 December 1848	East coast of Van Diemen's Land, south seas whaling grounds, southern coast of mainland Australia	60 tuns of sperm whale oil, 1 tun of black whale oil. £5,200

Vessel	Name and Role	Departure Date	Return Date	Location	Cargo and Value
Pacific	James Bayley, Mate	25 February 1847	12 November 1847	South seas whaling grounds	65 tuns of sperm whale oil, 34 tuns of black whale oil, 1½ tons of whale bone. £5,500
Pacific	James Bayley, Mate	6 December 1847	29 July 1866	South seas whaling grounds	25 tuns of sperm whale oil, £2,500
Runnymede	Charles Bayley, Captain	Early June 1849	6 March 1850	South seas whaling grounds	70 tuns of sperm whale oil. £5,600
Runnymede	Charles Bayley, Captain	17 April 1850	15 June 1851	South seas whaling grounds, southern coast of mainland Australia	60 tuns of sperm whale oil, 50 tuns of black whale oil, 1½ tons of whalebone. £5,400
Runnymede	Charles Bayley, Captain	21 July 1851	20 December 1851	Southern coast of mainland Australia	62 tuns of sperm whale oil. £4,100
Flying Childers	James Bayley, Captain	19 July 1851	25 November 1851	Southern coast of mainland Australia	42 tuns of sperm whale oil. £2,700
Flying Childers	James Bayley, Captain	27 December 1851	18 January 1853	South seas whaling grounds	60 tuns sperm whale oil. £4,020
Runnymede	Charles Bayley, Captain	18 January 1852	31 December 1852	South seas whaling grounds	40 tuns sperm whale oil, 30 tuns black whale oil. £3,800
Runnymede	Charles Bayley, Captain	14 February 1853	24 December 1853	South seas whaling grounds	119 tuns sperm whale oil. £7,970
Runnymede	Charles Bayley, Captain	11 February 1854	25 November 1854	South seas whaling grounds, Bass Strait and Great Australian Bight	100 tuns sperm whale oil. £10,000
Runnymede	James Bayley, Captain	16 January 1855	14 February 1856	South seas whaling grounds	70 tuns of sperm whale oil, £5,700
Runnymede	Charles Bayley, Captain	4 April 1856	22 December 1856	South seas whaling grounds, Bass Strait and Lord Howe Island	77 tuns of sperm whale oil, £7,084
Runnymede	Charles Bayley, Captain	10 February 1857	7 March 1858	South seas whaling grounds	63 tuns of sperm whale oil, £4,800
Runnymede	Charles Bayley, Captain	8 April 1858	8 March 1859	South seas whaling grounds	65 tuns of sperm whale oil, £4,745
Runnymede	Charles Bayley, Captain	8 April 1859	1 August 1860	South seas whaling grounds	74 tuns sperm whale, 2 tuns black whale oil. £6,000
Runnymede	James Bayley, Captain	12 September 1860	22 November 1861	South seas whaling grounds	78 tuns of sperm whale oil, £6,084
Runnymede	James Bayley, Captain	7 January 1862	18 June 1863	South seas whaling grounds	72 tuns of sperm whale oil, £5,904
Runnymede	James Bayley, Captain	2 October 1863	21 January 1865	South seas whaling grounds, east coast of Tasmanian and mainland Australia	80 tuns of sperm whale oil, £5,040
Runnymede	James Bayley, Captain	21 February 1865	2 December 1865	South seas whaling grounds, east coast of Tasmanian and mainland Australia including Kangaroo Island	65 tuns of sperm whale oil, £6,500

Index

A.I.F. Lounge 170
Abberton 188
Active 188
Adelaide Packet 60
Ahiou 32
Allport, Mr 57, 160
'Aloha' 139, 151, 170
Anchor Tin Mining Company 151, 152
Andromache 64
Anglesey 198
Angus, James 32
Anstey, George 74
Ashbolt, Alfred Henry (Sir) 160, 161
Ashbolt, Alice 161
Ashbolt, Muriel 161
Ashton Jones family 164
Ashton Jones, Mrs 160
Asia 96, 97, 100, 105, 110, 133, 134, 140, 141
Auckland Libraries 84
Auger, John 184
Aurora Australis 65, 67
Australian Field Artillery Brigade 168
Australian National Maritime Museum 13, 14, 18
Azorian 198

Bailey, Captain see Bayley, Charles
Bailey, R. 28
Baily, Miss 30
Bank of Van Diemen's Land 143-145
Barnard, John 182
Barret, William 16
Bayley family 62, 63, 69, 76, 77, 81, 89, 139, 145, 163, 171, 173-175, 177-194, 195
Bayley, Albert Ernest see Murphy, Albert Ernest
Bayley, Ann (b. 1738) 174, 179
Bayley, Ann Keturah Rogers 174, 186
Bayley, Anne (b. 1757) 174, 181
Bayley, Bessie Mary 107, 175
Bayley, Charles (ex Charles Bayley Bull) 1, 3, 4, 6-10, 12-17, 19, 23-31, 33, 35, 37-48, 50-51, 60-65, 67-69, 71, 72, 74-76, 80-82, 84, 86, 88, 90, 92-96, 99, 100, 102-107, 112, 123, 133, 151, 163, 172, 174, 177, 192, 194, 198, 200, 201, 203, 205, 206

Bayley, Charles William 73, 75, 76, 175
Bayley, Charlotte Rogers 174, 186
Bayley, Daniel Rogers 174, 186
Bayley, Eliza (b. 1805) 174
Bayley, Eliza (Jr) 35, 37, 39, 40, 175
Bayley, Eliza (nee Randolph, nee Inglis) 9-13, 17, 19, 24-27, 31, 35, 37, 39, 43, 44, 47, 51, 61, 62, 68, 69, 71-73, 75, 76, 80, 95, 103, 104, 175
Bayley, Elizabeth (b. 1758, #1) 174, 181
Bayley, Elizabeth (b. 1758, #2) 174, 181
Bayley, Elizabeth (b. 1759) 174, 181
Bayley, Elizabeth (b. 1789) 174, 185
Bayley, Elizabeth (nee Bayley) 103, 104, 107, 108, 139, 147, 151, 163, 166, 175
Bayley, Elizabeth (nee Carr) 174, 180-183
Bayley, Elizabeth (nee Knoutin) 174, 180-182, 186
Bayley, Emma Elizabeth (nee Butchard) 63, 65, 67, 68, 71-73, 76, 80, 82-84, 104, 175
Bayley, Emma Gertrude see Murphy, Emma Gertrude
Bayley, George (b. 1765) 174, 182, 183, 186, 187
Bayley, George (Jr, b. 1798) 61, 174, 188-191
Bayley, Gwendolyn (nee Brownell) 171
Bayley, Hally see Bayly, Harriet Louisa 'Hally' (nee Bayley)
Bayley, Harriet Louisa 'Hally' see Bayly, Harriet Louisa 'Hally' (nee Bayley)
Bayley, Harriet Louisa Rogers 174, 186
Bayley, Harriet see McGregor, Harriet (nee Bull ex Bayley)
Bayley, Henrietta see Murphy, Henrietta
Bayley, Jabez (b. 1770) 174, 182
Bayley, Jabez (b. 1771) 174, 182, 183, 186-193, 204
Bayley, Jabez (Jr, b. 1799) 174
Bayley, James (ex Bayley Bull) 1, 24-29, 31, 35, 39, 40, 42-44, 47-51, 60, 62-65, 67, 68, 71-73, 75, 76, 80-84, 86, 92-95, 103-105, 107-110, 112, 123, 124, 126-128, 132-135, 137-139, 142, 145, 147, 150, 151, 155, 163, 166, 172, 175, 177, 199, 205, 206
Bayley, James 178
Bayley, James Rogers 61, 194
Bayley, Jane Mary 27, 31, 43, 45, 51, 61, 62, 68, 69, 71, 73, 104
Bayley, John (b. 1695) 174, 177-179
Bayley, John (b. 1723) 179
Bayley, John (b. 1733) 174, 179-183, 186, 191

Bayley, John (b. 1764) 174
Bayley, John (b. 1801) 174, 186
Bayley, Martha (b. 1796) 174
Bayley, Martha (nee Jones) 178, 179
Bayley, Martha (nee Worts) 174
Bayley, Mary (b. 1763) 174, 181
Bayley, Mary (nee Carr) 180, 182-184, 186
Bayley, Mary (nee Ridley) 174
Bayley, Mary (nee Rogers) 174, 184, 185, 191, 195
Bayley, Mary (nee Sage) 191
Bayley, Mary Anne 182
Bayley, Mary (nee Sage) 191
Bayley, Mary Rogers see Bull, Mary Rogers (nee Bayley)
Bayley, Matilda 174, 186
Bayley, Rebecca 174, 182
Bayley, Rogers James 104, 174, 175, 186, 200
Bayley, Samuel (b. 1803) 174
Bayley, Sarah (b. 1761) 174, 181
Bayley, Sarah (b. 1762) 174, 181
Bayley, Sarah (b. 1798) 174
Bayley, Sarah (nee Porsfield) 174, 179
Bayley, Sarah Ann Rogers 174, 186
Bayley, Sarah Anne (b. 1740) 174, 179
Bayley, Sarah Anne (b. 1761) 174, 181
Bayley, Thirza Rogers 174, 186
Bayley, William (b. 1735) 174, 179-185, 191
Bayley, William (b. 1759) 174, 181
Bayley, William (Jr2, b. 1791) 19, 104, 174, 185, 186, 190-194, 199, 200
Bayley, William and Sons 193, 194
Bayley, William Inglis 80, 104
Bayley, William Jr, b. 1760) 174, 181, 184, 185, 186, 190, 195
Bayley, William Sage 61, 194
Bayly family 137, 145, 147, 164-171
Bayly, Barbara 171
Bayly, Benjamin 137
Bayly, Captain see Bayley, Charles (ex Charles Bayley Bull)
Bayly, Elizabeth Matthews 163, 166, 167, 175
Bayly, Emma Matty 139, 147, 148, 164, 165, 167, 171, 173, 175
Bayly, Hally Mary Butchard 139, 147, 148, 164, 165, 169, 171, 173, 175
Bayly, Harriet Louisa 'Hally' (nee Bayley) 71-73, 76, 80, 82, 83, 86, 92, 93-95, 103, 104, 107, 114, 127, 137, 139, 145, 147, 151, 155, 156, 163, 164, 166-173, 175
Bayly, Helen Jane Gray (nee Hooper) 171
Bayly, Henry Vincent 137, 139, 145, 147, 151, 163, 175
Bayly, Henry Vincent (Jr) 163, 166-168, 171, 175
Bayly, James Bayley 151, 166-169, 171, 175
Bayly, John (b. 1928) 171
Bayly, Margaret O'Neil 163, 166, 167, 171, 175
Bayly, Mary Ann Cameron (nee Wylly) 137
Bayly, Mary Wylly see Watchorn, Mary Wylly (nee Bayly)
Bayly, William 171
Beaton, James 14, 16

Belbin and Co., Messrs 127
Belbin, William 75
Bella Mary 82, 86, 100, 103, 105, 110, 125, 127
'Beltana' 157
Bennison, Margaret 'Maggie' (nee McGregor, nee Pigdon) 135, 136, 139, 143, 146, 147, 149, 152, 153, 155-160, 162, 172
Bennison, Thomas 157-159, 162
Bethnal Green Hospital 169
Bilton, George 52
Bird-in-Hand Hotel 92
'Bishopstowe' 77
Blue Bell 65
Bombay 52
Bowes-Lyon, Elizabeth (Lady) 162
Boyes, A. E. 161
Brain, A. (Reverend) 158
Bridge, Cyprian (Rear-Admiral) 156
British Army Voluntary Aid Detachment 169
British Bank of Australia 145
British East India Company 179, 180, 186, 188-190, 192
British Tar 194
Briton's Pride 193
Brown, Thomas 16, 19
Browne, Thomas Gore (Sir, Governor) 87
Brownell, Gwendolyn see Bayley, Gwendolyn (nee Brownell)
Buchanan, A. 38
Buckingham Rowing Club 166
Buckingham Swimming Club 166
Builders and Contractors Association (Victoria) 136
Bull family 192, 193, 195-203
Bull, Bayley see Bayley, James (ex Bayley Bull)
Bull, Charles 19, 25, 29, 31, 61, 62, 65, 81, 174, 175, 192-203
Bull, Charles (Sr) 174, 195, 196, 198
Bull, Charles Bayley see Bayley, Charles (ex Charles Bayley Bull)
Bull, Elizabeth 174, 195, 198
Bull, Emmaretta Rogers Bayley see Rogers, Emmaretta Rogers Bayley (nee Bull, nee Graveley)
Bull, Emmaretta see Rogers, Emmaretta (nee Bull)
Bull, Harriet see McGregor, Harriet (nee Bull ex Bayley)
Bull, John 84
Bull, Keturah Elizabeth see Rogers, Keturah Elizabeth (nee Bull)
Bull, Mary Bayley (nee Rogers) 25, 29, 31, 61, 62, 65, 92, 103, 174, 175, 185, 186, 192, 194-196, 198, 199-203
Bull, Mary Rogers Bayley (b. 1807, m. Stephen Park) 25, 29, 61, 92, 110, 139, 151, 175, 192, 196, 200-203
Bull, William Charles Bayley 175, 192, 199
Burgess, W. 126
Burnham Oyster Company 184, 202
Burr, John 180
Burton, Thomas 15
Bush, Robert 47
Bush. R. 47
Butchard, David 64

Index

Butchard, Elizabeth (nee Judy) 64
Butchard, Emma Elizabeth see Bayley, Emma Elizabeth (nee Butchard)
Butchard, Thomas David 64, 80
Butler, James 15, 16

'Camelford' 171
Camilla 72, 73, 75, 82, 86, 105, 110, 125, 127
Campbell, James 33
Canton 49
Carns, Robert 20
Carr, Elizabeth see Bayley, Elizabeth (nee Carr)
Cascade Brewery Company Limited 133
Castlereagh 188
Ceres 191
Chamberlain, Captain (Jr) 75
Chamberlain, Captain (Sr) 75
Champion, William 38
Chappell, Captain 68
Charlotte 193
Charlotte of Ipswich 188
Chieftan 128
Child Welfare Association 162
China 159
Christie, John 193
Circassian 38
City of Hobart 68
Clark and Son, Messrs 86
Clark, Jan 161
Clark, Lloyd 161
Clarke, Alexander 96
Clelland, Jane see Pigdon, Jane (nee Clelland)
Clementina 193
Clinch, John 72
Collicott, J. T. 21
Collward, Ursley 177
Colvin, Charles 92, 94
Commonwealth Government of Australia 163
Company of Watermen and Lightermen of the River Thames 177
Copping, Richard 100, 110, 127
Copping, Susannah 100
Cornelian Bay Cemetery 77-79, 104, 105, 107, 121, 139, 147, 153, 163, 166, 171
'Cottage Green' 19-22
Courier 193
Cracknell, James 15
Cressy 1, 25, 26
Crosby, Charles 99
Crowther, Dr 92
Crowther, E. L. 126
Crowther, W. L. 113
Crowther, William (Dr) 94
Customs House 135

Dalgleish, Mr 140
Dart 47, 60
Davis, Thomas 124
Day family 64
Day, William (Reverend) 64
Denison, William (Sir, Lieutenant-Governor) 54
Derwent and Tamar Fire and Marine Assurance Company 81, 102, 105, 137
Derwent Hunter 68, 69, 71, 72, 74, 75, 82, 86, 102, 105, 110, 127, 133, 135, 140, 141
Derwent Ship Building Company 52
Diana 52
Dobson, Emily 146, 159, 160, 162, 166
Dobson, Henry (Premier) 145
Doctor 194
Dog and Partridge Hotel 93
Domain Shipyard 52, 54-57, 60, 62, 82, 89-91, 93, 84, 97, 101, 106, 118, 126, 140, 157
Doubleday, H. 134
Douglas, Samuel 9
Dowdell, Charles 75, 99
Down, George 15
Drake, Elizabeth see McGregor, Elizabeth (nee Drake)
Drummore 37
Dry, Richard (Sir) 94
Duncan and Crow, Messrs 129

Eardley-Wilmot, John (Jr) 25
Eardley-Wilmot, John (Sir, Lieutenant-Governor) 25
Earl of Wemyss 191
Eclipse 193
Elizabeth Jane 64
Elizabeth of Ipswich 188
Emily 193
Emily Downing 82, 86, 110, 112, 123, 124, 128, 129, 140
Enchantress 193
Evans, Bill 81
Evans, Captain 134
Evans, Mary 179

Factor 33
Fair Tasmanian 38
Fame 191
Fanny 4
Featherstone, Inkerman 100
Field Naturalists' Club 165, 166
Fife, Robert 16
Flinders 136
Flora 193
Flying Childers 43, 44, 48, 50, 51, 62, 63, 71, 82, 86, 102, 110, 116, 132, 206
Flying Cloud 60
Forbes, E. 183, 184
Fortitude (barque) 1, 3, 24, 26-33, 35, 37, 39-43, 45, 47, 48, 50, 51, 55, 61, 75, 105, 151, 205
Fortitude (schooner) 190

Franklin, John (Sir, Lieutenant-Governor) 30
Free Kindergarten Association 166, 169
Friends 201
Frosham, Thomas 126

Gardiner, Robert 29
Garrett, Alfred 24
Garrod, Mr 193
General Hospital 93
General Wool 49
George, Lloyd 171
Gibbs, H. S. & Co. 193
Gibson, John 184
Gibson, Roy 161
Gill, J. W. 132
Giriclan, Captain 12
Girls' High School 164-166
Gleeson, John 126
Goddess 194
Golden Fleece Inn 38
Goldsmith family 52, 55
Goldsmith, Edward 52-57, 60, 83
Goldsmith, Edward (Jr) 56
Goldsmith, Elizabeth 52, 53, 56
Goldsmith, Richard 52, 55, 56
Gormanston, Viscount (Governor) 147
Government of Tasmania 77, 113, 116, 117, 129, 145-147, 157, 158, 163, 172
Government of the United Kingdom 10, 11, 116, 198
Government of Van Diemen's Land 4, 8, 22, 54-56
Grant, James 21
Graveley, Charles William Henry 94, 164, 175, 202
Graveley, Emmaretta Rogers Bayley see Emmaretta Rogers Bayley (nee Bull, nee Graveley)
Graveley, Emmaretta see Rogers, Emmaretta (nee Bull)
Graveley, Henry 164
Graveley, Sarah (nee Going) 202
Graveley, William 175, 202, 203
Gregory, James 113-115
Grey, Robert 15, 16
Greyhound Inn 202
Guesdon Bequest 157

Haig, Andrew 21, 52
Halifax Shipyard 187-191
Hally Bayley 91-93, 110, 125, 128
Hamilton, Lady 146
Hamilton, Mr 21
Hamilton, Robert (Sir, Governor) 146
Hanley, S. 183, 184
Hannah 193
Harleston 188
Harp 60
Harriet McGregor 96-101, 103, 104, 110, 112, 125, 140, 141
Harrison, G. P. 89, 92
Harrowby 92

Hawkins, John 184
Heather Bell 63
Heatley, Marshall 152
Helen 86, 97, 105, 110, 125, 134, 135, 140, 141
Henry of Swansea 189
Hero 190
Hill, H. F. 84, 89, 93
HMS *Barracouta* 204
HMS *Beaver* 204
HMS *Daring* 204
HMS *Dee* 187, 204
HMS *Diligence* 204
HMS *Drake* 204
HMS *Esk* 187, 204
HMS *Espeigle* 204
HMS *Favourite* 204
HMS *Fly* 204
HMS *Galatea* 87, 89
HMS *Harlequin* 204
HMS *Harrier* 204
HMS *Hearty* 204
HMS *Imogen* 204
HMS *Jaseur* 204
HMS *Jasper* 204
HMS *Julia* 204
HMS *Leven* 204
HMS *Nimrod* 204
HMS *Onyx* 204
HMS *Orestes* 204
HMS *Orlando* 156
HMS *Peacock* 204
HMS *Rosario* 204
HMS *Royal Arthur* 156
HMS *Sappho* 187, 204
HMSS *Orpheus* 76
Hobart Chamber of Commerce 128, 137
Hobart City Council 110, 157
Hobart General Post Office 125, 145
Hobart Horticultural Society 137
Hobart Post Office 139, 145, 151
Hobart Restaurant Committee 146
Hobart Town Bathers' Association 54
Hobart Town City Council 90
Hobart Town Cottage Garden Society 107
Hobart Town Hall 87, 170
Hobart Town Municipal Council 64
Hobart Town Public Cemetery (Cornelian Bay) 107
Hobart Town Savings Bank 113
Hogg, David 23
Hohman, E. 6
Homeopathic Hospital 164, 165
Hooper, Helen Jane Gray see Bayly, Helen Jane Gray (nee Hooper)
Hope 190
Horne, Harriet 96
Horne, Jean (nee McGregor) 37, 38, 74, 96

Index

Horne, Thomas Addison 96
Hudson's Bay Company 188
Hudspeth, W. H. 19
Hurburgh, H. B. 4
Hutchinson and Walter, Messrs 171

Immigration Museum 135
India 86
Indian Queen 56
Inglis family 10
Inglis, Eliza see Bayley, Eliza (nee Randolph, nee Inglis)
Inglis, James 10, 11, 104
Inglis, Jean 10, 11, 31, 69, 104
Inglis, William 10, 11, 27, 31, 35, 37, 69, 104
Innkeepers Limited 161
International Conference of Women 162
Invincible 194
Ipswich 194
Ipswich Council 194
Ipswich High School 165
Iris 201
Isacke, Matthew 188
Isle of France 110, 116
Isles of the South 67

James 52
Jane (schooner) 193
Jane (ship) 192
John Cobhold 194
Jones, Edward 15
Jones, Henry & Co. Ltd. 161
Jones, Martha see Bayley, Martha (nee Jones)
Jones, William Townsend 20

Kangaroo 56, 57
Kelly, James 19, 21
Kelly, Thomas 128
'Kelly Cottage' 28
Kennedy, S. 96
Kennerley Boys Home 102
King Billy see Lanne, William
King George VI (HRH) 162
King Henry VIII (HRH) 177
King William IV (HRH) 59
Kirby, Samuel T. 152
Knight, W. 74
Knight, William 19
Knopwood, Robert (Reverend) 19, 20, 23
Knoutin, Elizabeth see Bayley, Elizabeth (nee Knoutin)
Knox, Johnny 17

Ladies' Aid Association 165
Lady Franklin 123
Lady of the Lake 4
Lane, William see Lanne, William
Lang 4, 5

Lanne, William 93-95
Lathropp, Captain 32
Laura Ann 194
Le Breton, Guiaud 32
Le Sueur, J. 194
Leather, J. 182, 183
Lebrant, William 116
Legislative Council of Tasmania 123, 125, 126, 131-133, 140, 142, 146, 151, 152, 156
Lemmon, William 177
'Lenna' 1, 114, 115, 117-119, 127-132, 136, 140, 147, 153, 156-162, 172
Lenna of Hobart Heritage Hotel 66, 161
Leslie House 166
Letitia 193
Library of Congress 176, 181
LINC Tasmania 62, 69, 75, 80, 84, 104, 139
Lincoln Inn 135
Liverpool 192
Lloyd's of London 61, 86, 98, 99, 101, 124, 188, 191
London Stock Exchange 152
Loongana 120, 124, 125, 140, 141
Lord Rodney Hotel 82, 156
Lord William Bentinck 96
Lord, John 126
Lucas, Edward 75, 116
Lucas, John 68
Lucas, Thomas 23
Lufra 110, 113, 125, 128, 134, 140

Macdonald, John 38
Macdonough, Captain 188
Macdowell, T. 57
MacMillan, Donald 48, 99
Magnet 191
Mainwaring 188
Marine Board of Hobart 98, 128, 132, 133, 134, 137, 142, 151
Marine Board of Launceston 142
Marine Board of Leven 142
Maritime Museum of Tasmania 8, 33, 73, 74, 91, 97, 100, 120, 164
Marriett, Henry 32
Mary (ship) 188
Mary (sloop) 192
Mary Bayley 194
Mary Montague 194
Mason, Alfred 74
Mason, Elizabeth (nee McGregor) 38, 74, 153
Mason, Janet 74
Matthews, James 118, 119
Matthews, Janet Smith (nee McGregor) 112, 114, 118, 119
Mayer, Auguste Etienne Francois 32
McArthur, John 75, 93, 94
McGregor family 37, 38
McGregor, Agnes 37

McGregor, Alex & Co. 125, 133, 140, 152
McGregor, Alexander 1, 35-38, 40, 41, 43-49, 51, 56-58, 60, 62-68, 72-76, 81-96, 98-100, 102, 103, 107, 110-129, 131-137, 139-143, 145, 146, 151-156, 172, 175
McGregor, Alexander James 112, 114, 129, 136
McGregor, Amy 112, 114, 129, 136
McGregor, Elizabeth (born 1859) see Pigdon, Elizabeth (nee McGregor)
McGregor, Elizabeth (nee Drake) 63, 71, 112
McGregor, Elizabeth see Mason, Elizabeth (nee McGregor)
McGregor, Harriet (nee Bull ex Bayley) 1, 25, 29-31, 35-38, 40, 43, 45, 51, 58, 63-68, 73-75, 81, 84-86, 92-97, 103, 110, 112-114, 118, 121, 123, 127, 128, 133, 151, 153, 172, 175, 177, 200, 202
McGregor, James 37, 38
McGregor, James (Jr) 37, 44, 51, 63, 67, 71, 74, 112, 116, 118, 128, 129
McGregor, Janet (nee Smith) 37, 38, 74
McGregor, Janet Smith see Matthews, Janet Smith (nee McGregor)
McGregor, Jean see Horne, Jean (nee McGregor)
McGregor, John Gibson 37, 38, 47, 65, 67, 68, 74, 89, 90, 96, 98, 99, 116, 121, 124, 140, 141
McGregor, Margaret 'Maggie' see Bennison, Margaret 'Maggie' (nee McGregor, nee Pigdon)
McGregor, Piesse and Co. 133
McGregor, Thomas Joseph 37
McGuinnis, Duncan 55, 56
McLachlan, Charles 23
McMillan, D. 99
McNaugton, Mr 57
Meaburn, John 52
Melbourne City Council 135
Melbourne General Cemetery 162
Melbourne Tramways Trust 136
Mercia 61, 62
Messiter, E. 110
Mestaers, Peter Everett 188
Midland Agricultural Society 171
Mildway, Henry (Sir) 183
Minerva 193
Ministering Children's League 164, 166
Mitchell, Richard 152
Mona 193
Monarch 193
Montezuma 47
Moore, William 116
'Moreland Hall' 135
Morland, Thomas 94
Morrison, Askin 24, 39, 41-43, 45, 46, 49, 51, 52, 55-57, 60, 63, 67, 83
Mouheneener band of the South East Nation of Tasmanian Aborigines 19
Mulgrave Battery 20-23
Mulgrave, Earl of 20
Murphy, Albert Ernest 95, 96, 175

Murphy, Bridget Elizabeth 95, 102, 103, 105, 175
Murphy, Emma Gertrude 102, 105, 175
Murphy, Henrietta 103, 104, 175

National Archives of Australia 63, 67, 68, 72, 82, 96, 116, 127, 128, 135, 168, 169
National Archives UK 180
National Council of Women 157, 159, 162
National Library of Australia 2, 32
National Trust (Tasmania) 77, 161, 172
Nautilus 188
New Town Cricket Association 107
New Town Football Association 107
New Town Free Kindergarten Association 171
New Town Progress Association 170
New Town Public School 102
New Town Reading Room and Library 137
New Town Regatta Association 137
New Zealand Fire and Marine Insurance Company 125, 140
Newdgate, Governor 170
Newdgate, Lady 170
Nicholson, Robert 152
Nissen, Aktieselskab Marcus 141
Nixon, Francis Russell (Bishop) 77, 105
North America 68
Norval 52
Nova Scotia Shipyard 182, 187

O'May, H. 7, 8
Oldham, Mr 92
Orient 133
Orwell 188-191
Orwell of London 191

P&O 133
Pacific 1, 29, 31, 35, 39, 206
Page, W. 184
Paget 188
Parish Council of St George's Anglican Church 147, 157
Park, Stephen 29, 110, 175, 202
Parliament of Tasmania 117, 126, 128, 131, 142-147, 152
Parraquet 193
Parsons, R. 24
Pearson, Rear-Admiral 156
Perpetual Trustees and Executors Company 140
Petrel 82, 84, 86, 89, 90
Philp, I. E. 177, 178
Piesse, Charles 133, 140
Pigdon family 135, 157, 162
Pigdon, Elizabeth (nee McGregor) 112, 114, 129, 136
Pigdon, Jane (nee Clelland) 135
Pigdon, John 135, 136, 157
Pigdon, Margaret see Bennison, Margaret 'Maggie' (nee McGregor, nee Pigdon)
Pigdon, Thomas Miers 135, 136
Pike, Francis 152

Pitcairn, Dorothea 77
Pitcairn, Robert 77
Pitcairns, Mr 57
Porsfield, Sarah see Bayley, Sarah (nee Porsfield)
Port Arthur Penal Settlement 4, 123
Port of Ipswich West Bank Terminal 187
Premier 193
Prima Donna 193
Prince Albert, Duke of York (HRH) 162
Prince Alfred, Duke of Edinburgh (HRH) 87-89
Prince of Orange 16
Prince of Wales Hotel 23
Prince of Wales' Battery 110, 113, 116, 117
Prince Regent 82
Propsting, Superintendent 105
Purple Cross Service 170

Queen (schooner, Hobart) 52
Queen (schooner, UK) 193
Queen Alexandra Hospital 162
Queen Victoria 193
Queen Victoria (HRH) 59, 60
Quiz 193

Rachel 99
Rainbow 193
Randolph, Eliza see Bayley, Eliza (nee Inglis, nee Randolph)
Randolph, William 10, 12
Rapid 193
Rattler 53, 54
Raven, Elizabeth 195
Read, William 190
Red Cross 168
Registrar-General's Office (Melbourne) 135
Reid, G. F. 21
Returned Sailors and Soldiers Imperial League of Australia 171
Rhoda 194
Richards, R. 17, 24, 28, 30, 31, 33, 39, 40, 42, 63, 65
Richmond, Samuel 200
Ridley, Mary see Bayley, Mary (nee Ridley)
Riley, William 17
Risby, Alderman 99
Risby, Joseph E. 104
Road District of New Town 137
Roberts, John 193
Robinson, Edward 17
Robinson, James 152
Rogers, Daniel 184, 185, 202
Rogers, Daniel (Jr) 202, 203
Rogers, Emmaretta Rogers Bayley (nee Bull, nee Graveley) 25, 29, 61, 94, 175, 192, 196, 200, 202, 203
Rogers, George 32
Rogers, Isaac (b. 1812) 61, 175, 203
Rogers, Isaac (b. 1846) 175
Rogers, James 175

Rogers, Keturah Elizabeth (nee Bull) 25, 175, 192, 199, 200, 203
Rogers, Mary Emmaretta 175
Rogers, Mary see Bayley, Mary (nee Rogers)
Rogers, Thomas Coker 195
Ross, John 56
Rowntree, A. 20
Rowntree, Edward Casson 113, 114
Roxburgh Castle 48
Royal Botanical Gardens 136
Royal College of Surgeons 94
Royal Colosseum Hall 135
Royal Navy 156, 180, 182, 186, 187, 191, 192, 204
Royal Society of Tasmania 94
'Roydon' 165
Runic 164
'Runnymede' 1, 77-81, 86, 95, 96, 103-105, 107-110, 124, 127, 137-139, 145, 147, 151, 163-166, 168-173
Runnymede (barque) 1, 41-45, 47, 48, 50, 62-65, 67, 68, 71, 72, 75, 76, 80-86, 89, 92-94, 97, 102, 103, 105, 124, 126, 128, 206
Runnymede (whaleboat) 94

Sage, Mary see Bayley, Mary (nee Sage)
Sailors' Home 103
Salier, Frederick 127, 139
Salier, George 126
Sanatorium for Consumptives 162
Sanderson, Robert 15, 41, 42
Scannon, Jeremiah 129
Scotia 10, 12
Scott, Mr 13
Seal, Charles 31
See Einhorn 197, 198
Shorncliffe Barracks 168
Sincerity of Ipswich 188
Sir David Scott 189
Sir William Wallace 190
Smith, Janet see McGregor, Janet (nee Smith)
Smith, Jeffrey 193
Sophia 193
Sorell, William (Lieutenant-Governor) 20, 23, 38
Southern Cross 92, 93, 128, 132
Southern Tasmanian Agricultural and Pastoral Association 137
Southern Tasmanian Cricket Association 94, 102, 107
Southern Tasmanian Town Planning and Progress Association 171
Southport Village Settlement Fund 146, 147, 156
Spartan 64
Speedwell 200
St John Ambulance Association 169
Stacey, John 32
Stanfield, Daniel 104
Startup, Robert 17
State Library of South Australia 44, 140

State Library of Tasmania 113
State Library of Victoria 98, 101, 124
Stirlingshire 10
Stone Bros. 127
Struggles, Henry 67
Suevic 164
Superb 193
Surf 64
Surprise 75, 94
Swallow 198
Sweeting, John 184
Synes, John 202

Tamar 94
Tasmania 68, 86
Tasmanian Aboriginal Centre 94
Tasmanian Archives i, ii, iv, 4, 5, 8-11, 17, 19, 21-25, 27-31, 35-45, 47, 51, 53, 55-58, 61-63, 67, 69-71, 74, 76-80, 82, 84, 85, 87, 88, 93, 95, 96, 102, 103-108, 111-115, 117-119, 121, 122, 126, 127, 129-131, 137-139, 141, 144, 147-151, 153, 154, 162, 163, 171, 173
Tasmanian Bush Nursing Association 162
Tasmanian Hockey Centre 77
Tasmanian International Exhibition 147, 148
Tasmanian Loan Guarantee and Finance Company Limited 140
Tasmanian Main Line Railway Company 131
Tasmanian Mineral Exploration Company 102
Tasmanian Museum and Art Gallery 53, 54
Tasmanian National Council of Women 157
Tasmanian Post Office 163
Tasmanian Poultry Society 107, 137
Tasmanian Railway and Progress Association 90
Tasmanian Society for the Blind, Deaf and Dumb 162
Tasmanian Steam Navigation (TSN) Company 83, 86, 90, 102, 105, 107, 133, 140
Taylor, Elizabeth 202
Taylor, James 14
Taylor, Mr 140
Telegraph Office 125
Thames 193
The Friends School 171
The Trustees of the British Museum 189
Tonkin, H. B. 98
Townsley, W. A. 142, 143, 145
Tradesman 193
Traveller 188
Travis, J. B. 126
Trinity House 198
Triumph 193

Union 191

Victoria Convalescent Home 147, 156-158, 162
Victoria League for Commonwealth Friendship 159, 162
Visitor 198

Wagoola 101
Wagstaff, Richard 14-16
Wallaby 1, 3, 4, 6, 9, 12-18, 23, 29, 33, 41, 75, 105, 205
Watchorn, Arthur (Mrs) 164
Watchorn, Clarie 164
Watchorn, Erskine Clarence 166, 167
Watchorn, J. 126
Watchorn, Mary (Jr) 167
Watchorn, Mary Wylly (nee Bayly) 139, 147, 148, 165-168, 175
Water Witch 112, 133, 140, 141
Waterloo 52
Waterqueen 141
Watson, George 4, 24
Watson, John 38, 41-43, 46, 99
Wave 52
Wellington Cricket Club 102, 107, 187
'Westella' 164
Westphalen, N. 186
White, Brydge 48, 50, 72, 75
Wild Wave 97
Wilkinson, Richard 14, 15
William Fairlie 189
Williams, John 14
Williams, Thomas 15
Williamson, William 52
Wilson, G. S. 75
Wilson, George 83
Wilson, James Milne (Sir) 125
Wilson, Thomas Reed 49, 64
Windward 86
'Wisconsin' 160
Wishart, Henry 3, 4, 6, 24
Women's International League for Peace and Freedom 171
Women's Sanitary Committee 146
Women's Suffrage Association 158
Worts, Martha see Bayley, Martha (nee Worts)
Wylly, Mary Ann Cameron see Bayly, Mary Ann Cameron (nee Wylly)

Yarra Yarra 48
Young Eagle 32
Young, Mr 13, 16
Young, Russell 126
Young, William 24

www.ingramcontent.com/pod-product-compliance
Lightning Source LLC
Chambersburg PA
CBHW061110070526
44583CB00027B/3248